D1738445

PRISON SEX

PRISON SEX

PRACTICE AND POLICY

EDITED BY
CHRISTOPHER HENSLEY

LYNNE
RIENNER
PUBLISHERS

BOULDER
LONDON

Published in the United States of America in 2002 by
Lynne Rienner Publishers, Inc.
1800 30th Street, Boulder, Colorado 80301
www.rienner.com

and in the United Kingdom by
Lynne Rienner Publishers, Inc.
3 Henrietta Street, Covent Garden, London WC2E 8LU

Library of Congress Cataloging-in-Publication Data
Prison sex : practice and policy / edited by Christopher Hensley.
     p. cm.
    Includes bibliographical references and index.
    ISBN 1-58826-063-1 (hardcover : alk. paper)—ISBN 1-58826-087-9 (pbk. : alk.
paper)
    1. Prisoners—United States—Sexual behavior.　I. Hensley, Christopher, 1972– .
HV8836.P78　　2002
365'.6—dc21

                                                           2001058463

British Cataloguing in Publication Data
A Cataloguing in Publication record for this book
is available from the British Library.

Printed and bound in the United States of America

The paper used in this publication meets the requirements
of the American National Standard for Permanence of
Paper for Printed Library Materials Z39.48-1984.

5　4　3　2　1

To my mother, Virginia Payne;
to my grandmother, Hazel Norton; and
to the countless scores of men and women who are sexually
assaulted or contract HIV/AIDS while incarcerated

CONTENTS

vii

ACKNOWLEDGMENTS

Several people helped to make this project a reality. First, I would like to thank the contributors, who devoted much time, effort, and attention to their chapters. Thanks also to my family and friends for their continued faith in my professional endeavors. Bridget Julian, acquisitions editor at Lynne Rienner Publishers, gave this often stigmatized topic an opportunity to be read by the decisionmakers who create and enforce correctional policy. Finally, the reviewers, Suzanne E. Tallichet and Chau-Pu Chiang, looked beyond what has been described as titillating subject matter to provide constructive criticism.

—*Christopher Hensley*

1

INTRODUCTION:
LIFE AND SEX IN PRISON

Christopher Hensley

In 1934, Joseph Fishman, a former inspector for U.S. federal prisons, wrote, "We are living in a frank and realistic age, yet the subject of sex in prison—so provocative, so vital, so timely . . . is shrouded in dread silence" (5). Almost seventy years later, this statement still holds true. The subject of sex in prison has been largely ignored by social scientists and society alike. Although research on sex in prison began in the early 1900s, relatively few studies have focused on the pains of imprisonment. According to Sykes (1958), these pains include the deprivation of liberty, goods and services, autonomy, security, and heterosexual relationships.

The most obvious deprivation imposed on prison inmates is their loss of liberty (Sykes, 1958). People who are incarcerated are required to live in a world where their movements are restricted and their behavior contained. The rules and regulations imposed on inmates are typically aimed at strict traffic control. Inmates are told when to awaken, when to work, when to eat, and when to sleep. They are also typically cut off from family and friends (with the exception of letters, phone calls, and the occasional visit). As Sykes (1958) noted, "The prisoner's loss of liberty is a double one—first, by confinement to the institution and second, by confinement within the institution" (65).

Another pain of imprisonment imposed on inmates is the deprivation of goods and services. Prisons have been defined as microcosms of society. However, if this is the case, why are inmates not allowed to have the same material possessions as they would outside of the correctional facility? In some U.S. prisons, for example, inmates are required to watch television within a community setting rather than in their own

1

individual cells. Inmates are not allowed to choose what meals they can eat, what programs they can watch, and in some instances what material they can read. Services provided by medical personnel are also often insufficient or lacking. Therefore, as Sykes (1958) argued, "The average inmate finds himself in a harshly Spartan environment which he defines as painfully depriving" (68).

Prisons are often used to strip inmates of their individuality or autonomy. In some prisons, for example, inmates are required to cover identifying tattoos, wear state-issued clothing, and receive periodic haircuts. In addition, inmates are typically known by number rather than name. These rules and regulations are used to dehumanize the individual and "reduce the prisoner to the weak, helpless, dependent status of childhood" (Sykes, 1958: 75).

Inmates are also typically thrown into "prolonged intimacy[ies]" with other inmates who in many cases have long histories of violent behavior, most likely decreasing the amount of security perceived by each inmate within the facility (Sykes, 1958: 77). Newly arriving inmates into the correctional system are often tested by other inmates to see how far the new inmates will go to protect themselves or their possessions. If the inmate fails, they may become a target of future violence, including sexual assaults. If, however, the inmate succeeds, they may once again be tested by other inmates who seek to increase their own status by defeating someone with a reputation for resilience. Thus, according to Sykes (1958), "Both success and failure in defending one's self against the aggressions of fellow captives may serve to provoke fresh attacks and no man stands assured of the future" (78).

Finally, most inmates are deprived of heterosexual relationships while they are incarcerated. This deprivation forces prisoners to turn to alternative methods of achieving sexual gratification including masturbation, consensual same-sex sexual activity, and coerced same-sex sexual activity. The lack of heterosexual intercourse is disconcerting for inmates and continues to weigh heavily on their minds throughout the length of their sentence. This, in turn, creates a high level of stress, which often compels them toward having same-sex sexual relationships while they are incarcerated.

Very few studies prior to the 1980s specifically examined the pains of imprisonment felt by inmates, especially the deprivation of heterosexual relationships. Since 1980, three books have been published on the topic of sex in prison. Lockwood's *Prison Sexual Violence* (1980a) focused primarily on sexual violence in correctional facilities, and Bowker's *Prison Victimization* (1980) concentrated on psychological, economic, social, and physical violence in prisons. Wooden and Parker's (1982) book, *Men Behind Bars: Sexual Exploitations in Prison*, is the only comprehensive survey of sexual behavior in U.S. prisons, though the study focused on only one California correctional institution. Since the publication of Wooden and Parker's book, society's perceptions and attitudes toward inmates have hardened, turning to a "lock 'em up and throw away the key" attitude. In response to this public pressure, several state departments of corrections have dropped their conjugal visitation programs despite studies showing that these programs increase family stability and reduce violent behavior and same-sex sexual activity in prisons.

Since the 1970s, the United States has experienced the greatest increase in the number of new prisons. This increase is due in part to several factors, including citizens' greater fear of crime, an increase in media coverage and attention, "get tough" legislation, increased length and severity of new sentencing laws and guidelines, and the war on drugs. These factors have sent the number of inmates incarcerated in local, state, and federal correctional facilities soaring and causing overcrowding at these facilities.

The rising number of inmates incarcerated in U.S. correctional facilities has changed the inmate prison culture, and correctional administrators now have additional challenges that they must face. For example, one such challenge is the phenomenon known as prisonization. Clemmer (1940) described this process as "the taking on in greater or lesser degree of the folkways, mores, customs, and general culture of the penitentiary" (8). In other words, inmates' influence on one another within the prison either breeds or deepens criminal behavior that is already present. Inmates begin to learn the criminal ideology of the correctional facility. They develop new habits of dressing, sleeping, and eating. They develop a new language and become dependent upon others for food, work assignments, and protection. At the same time, prison wardens must also deal with fairly new correctional issues including "street smart" prison gangs, overcrowding, and HIV/AIDS within their institutions. The next three sections of this chapter will focus on each of these problems and their relationship to prison sex.

PRISON GANGS

At midyear 2000, more than 1.93 million people were incarcerated in U.S. state and federal prisons and jails (U.S. Department of Justice,

2001a). These inmates are younger, less respectful of authority, and more violent. Some of them are recruited to join prison gangs or come in as members. Toller and Tsagaris (1996) defined gangs as "a group, large or small, that has a name, common symbols, a territory, a meeting place or pattern and an organization toward criminality" (110). Because prison gangs are often a continuance of street gangs, many gangs inside correctional facilities have ties to gang members outside the prison walls. Following incarceration, numerous gang leaders still maintain complete control over their street gang members and simultaneously form prison gangs (Toller and Tsagaris, 1996).

Traditional prison gangs originated in state and federal correctional institutions in the 1960s and 1970s (Fleisher, 1989). Today, prison gangs are often referred to as "inmate disruptive groups" or "security threat groups" by prison officials. These groups are typically based on race, ethnicity, geography, ideology, or a combination of these factors (Fleisher and Rison, 1999; Toller and Tsagaris, 1996). Traditional prison gangs are generally highly structured and well organized, with a distinguished hierarchy. The leader of the gang is strong and forceful, often resorting to violence to achieve their desired goal (Cooksey, 1999).

Research has revealed that throughout the United States, prison gangs account for the majority of prison violence, in particular, homicides and assaults (Camp and Camp, 1988; Cooksey, 1999), often prompted by members' failure to repay their debts. Gangs are primarily interested in organizing the distribution of illegal drugs and alcohol and orchestrating protection for their members (Cooksey, 1999; Fong, Vogel, and Buentello, 1992). Therefore, when a service is rendered, whether it be chemical or protective, the inmate who accepts the service is often required to pay the other inmate either through monetary or physical payment. An inmate can repay their loan through sexual favors or other nonsexual physical requests. If an inmate is unable or refuses to repay the favor or loan, members of the loaning group (often a gang) will physically attack and/or sexually assault the inmate (Hassine, 1999). As Hassine (1999), himself an inmate, wrote:

> Gang bangers often rely on rape in prison to generate fear and to maintain power over the general population. While street gangs use gunplay and murder to gain power, prison gangs use the threat of rape to dominate inmates and to ensure the repayment of even small debts. Some prison gangs require new inmates to commit rape as a gang initiation ritual. The act of raping another inmate is viewed as a way for gang members to demonstrate courage, strength, and cunning. (138)

OVERCROWDING IN THE U.S. PENAL SYSTEM

Another major problem occurring within the current criminal justice system is the overcrowded conditions in prisons, jails, and juvenile correctional facilities. Reasons for this phenomenon have been attributed to the change of not only society's mores and laws but policies within the correctional system. Determinant sentences, "three strike" laws, get tough on crime attitudes, and the war on drugs initiatives have all substantially contributed to the staggering numbers of individuals being incarcerated. Considering all these factors, it is not surprising that the current incarcerated population is literally bursting at the seams within correctional facilities across the country.

Even though prisons are being both built and renovated constantly across the United States to accommodate the increasing number of offenders, there is simply not enough space to efficiently house inmates. Double-celling is currently the norm of today's institutions, and prison officials often make use of any available space to house inmates. Makeshift dormitories in day room areas and basement/attic spaces, tents, trailers, warehouses, and converted hospital facilities are all being incorporated to facilitate space for the inmates. This results in numerous problems for both inmates and correctional administrators (Allen, 1995).

One of the major problems confronting inmates and the correctional staff due to overcrowding is violence. According to the U.S. Department of Justice (1997), in 1995 correctional authorities had recorded more than 14,000 assaults by inmates on prison staff (an increase of 32 percent since 1990) and another 26,000 assaults on inmates by other inmates (an increase of 20 percent since 1990). In turn, prison violence often leads to social instability, a lack of programs, and tension among the inmates. The lack of space per inmate and the density of the inmate population has been shown to have a positive relationship with inmate misconduct (Adams, 1992; Bottoms, 1999; McCorkle, 1993b; McCorkle, Miethe, and Terance, 1995). Prisons containing more inmates than their regulated capacity have more violent incidents than those operating at or under capacity (Toch, 1985). Homicide, assault on other inmates or staff, and confrontations between inmates or between inmates and staff increase as the prison population density increases.

Another consequence of overcrowding may be coerced sex (Toch, 1985). For example, a study of a rural Midwestern state prison (Struckman-Johnson et al., 1996) found that 20 percent of the 516 inmates who responded to a questionnaire had been pressured or forced to have sexual contact against their will. A section of the survey afforded inmates an opportunity to discuss preventative ideas. Due to the overcrowding in the facilities, both the idea of single cells for inmates and an increase in the number of staff for better supervision of inmates were listed as methods that could reduce sexual coercion. Based on these results, coerced sexual activity may be a repercussion of overcrowding within correctional facilities.

Another consequence of overcrowding is the medical problems that arise when people are forcibly clustered together in close proximity. The major health problem that occurs in forced overcrowded situations is the spreading of communicable diseases including colds, hepatitis, tuberculosis, and sexually transmitted diseases (Flanagan, 1997). In addition, due to intravenous drug use by inmates—as well as consensual or coerced sexual activity—the number of HIV/AIDS cases have shown a steady rate of increase within the correctional facilities (U.S. Department of Justice, 2001b).

HIV/AIDS IN CORRECTIONAL FACILITIES

HIV/AIDS among prison inmates has been a growing concern since the mid-1980s for a variety of reasons, including increasing rates of incarceration and high-risk inmates (Blumberg and Laster, 1999). High-risk behaviors for HIV transmission in prison include sex, drug use, sharing of needles, and tattooing. Hammett, Harmon, and Maruschak (1999) reported that as of 1996, the overall rate of confirmed AIDS cases among state and federal prison inmates was approximately six times higher than in the U.S. population. In 1996, 24,881 inmates in state and federal prisons were known to be infected with HIV (Hammett, Harmon, and Maruschak, 1999). Approximately 20 percent of these inmates had progressed to full-blown AIDS (Blumberg and Laster, 1999).

Because of the difference in testing policies throughout the United States, it is likely that not all HIV-infected inmates were reported. In 1996, sixteen states reported that they tested all inmates incoming or in custody. Three states tested a random sample of inmates, twenty-seven states tested high-risk groups (upon incident or indication of need), and five states tested solely upon inmate request. Many correctional administrators and officers have called for mandatory HIV testing of all inmates in their institutions (Hammett, Harmon, and Maruschak, 1999). However, mandatory testing of inmates has remained controversial.

Proponents of mandatory HIV testing have suggested three reasons why all inmates should be tested. First, mass screening is the best way for correctional administrators to target education and prevention programs. Second, this policy would allow staff to provide appropriate supervision to reduce the risk of transmission to other inmates. Finally, the staff would ensure that infected inmates receive the appropriate medical treatment (Blumberg and Laster, 1999).

Preventative measures, such as condom and bleach availability, have been proposed and adopted in some prison systems. Currently, six correctional systems (including two state correctional systems and four city correctional systems) in the United States make condoms available to inmates: Vermont, Mississippi, Philadelphia, Washington, D.C., New York City, and San Francisco (Blumberg and Laster, 1999). In addition, a 1997 survey found that only 20 percent of correctional systems made bleach available to inmates for any purpose (Hammett, Harmon, and Maruschak, 1999).

Critics of mandatory HIV testing assert that the financial burden placed on prisons would be too great (Blumberg and Laster, 1999). Other opponents contend that segregating known HIV-infected inmates will give prisoners a false sense of safety, because all HIV-infected inmates may not be identified through testing (Blumberg and Laster, 1999). Civil libertarians assert that segregating known HIV-infected inmates will perpetuate the myth that HIV can be transmitted through casual contact. They also express concern regarding the substandard living conditions in which HIV-segregated inmates are forced to reside (Blumberg and Laster, 1999). HIV-segregated inmates are sometimes denied opportunities to participate in work and educational programs that may earn them early release. Moreover, because only sixteen states currently engage in the mandatory testing of inmates for HIV, persons who would voluntarily consent to be tested would be deterred if they knew they would be placed in segregation. Currently, only two state correctional systems (Alabama and Mississippi) continue to isolate known HIV-infected inmates (Blumberg and Laster, 1999).

Along with the transmission of HIV to other inmates is the concern among correctional officers over *their* increased risk of infection. Some officers have asserted their "right to know," claiming that the knowledge will help them take extra precautions with HIV-infected individuals. However, many inmates do not test positive during the acute stage of infection. Therefore, critics of mandatory testing argue that correctional officers will have a false sense of security if they believe they know all HIV-infected inmates. Critics also contend that correctional officers would not be able to remember all HIV-identified inmates in correctional systems where a large number of inmates are infected (Hammett, Harmon, and Maruschak, 1999).

The alternative to identifying all known HIV-infected inmates relies on the wisdom of universal precautions. This principle was first initiated by the Centers for Disease Control in the mid-1980s. The idea of taking universal precautions means that one should treat all individuals as if they were HIV-infected. One should avoid unprotected contact with infectious bodily fluids, such as blood and semen. Universal precautions are not necessary for contact with tears or saliva unless there are visible signs of blood. Many correctional institutions have implemented universal precautions among all staff dealing with inmates, and officers should receive appropriate education and training regarding HIV transmission. Thus, comprehensive and intensive educational and prevention programs aimed at high-risk behavior identification remain the best response to the issue of HIV transmission in correctional facilities (Hammett, Harmon, and Maruschak, 1999).

STUDYING PRISON SEX

Researchers who delve into the topic of prison sex are often looked upon with skepticism by society, correctional administrators, and their colleagues (Tewksbury and West, 2000). "Research on sex in prisons is controversial, often neglected, and fairly scarce in the field of criminal justice, because sex in prison is not a 'clean,' 'easy,' or 'safe' topic . . . such an approach, however, is misinformed and potentially perilous for the continued theoretical and substantive development of the discipline" (Tewksbury and West, 2000: 368). It must be noted, though, that prison sex researchers have made valuable advances to the study of inmate culture and life. They have attempted to shape policy efforts aimed at reducing prison violence involving sex, advocated condom distribution within correctional facilities, and brought the topic of prison sex to the national forefront (CNN, 2000; *USA Today*, 2000).

According to Tewksbury and West (2000), the study of prison sex is important for three reasons. First, researchers must understand the institutional culture and inmate experiences that derive from that culture. For example, inmates are often deprived of heterosexual outlets while incarcerated. This deprivation may cause "extreme emotional, psychological, and perhaps physical distress" (Tewksbury and West, 2000: 369). Because of this deprivation, inmates may engage in homosexual activity with either consenting or coerced partners.

One alternative method to homosexual activity in which inmates can release pent-up frustrations and stresses in prisons is masturbation. Experts on prison sexuality have recently recommended to prison administrators that masturbation be tolerated as a natural part of life. In addition, masturbation in prison can reduce the spread of sexually transmitted diseases such as HIV/AIDS. Therefore, it is important for correctional administrators and policymakers to reconsider the definition of masturbation as a violation of institutional rules. Most important, the justification and rationale for instructing inmates that autoerotic activities are "wrong" needs to be revisited and reconsidered.

Second, correctional administrators and society must be concerned with the spread of sexually transmitted diseases including HIV/AIDS within prisons. The rate of confirmed HIV cases in prisons is five times higher than in the general U.S. population (Maruschak, 1999), and, as stated earlier, the rate of confirmed AIDS cases in correctional facilities is six times higher than in the U.S. population. In addition, between 1991 and 1996, one out of every three inmate deaths was attributable to AIDS-related causes (Hammett, Harmon, and Maruschak, 1999). Therefore, "health issues related to the sexual activity among the imprisoned become both institutional and public health care concerns" (Tewksbury and West, 2000: 369). Thus, it is imperative that prisons begin to distribute condoms to consenting sex partners to prevent the spread of sexually transmitted diseases (Hensley, 2000, 2001; Saum et al., 1995). As previously mentioned, only six correctional systems in the United States allow condoms behind institutional walls.

Third, there is often a link between sex and violent behavior in prison (Fleisher, 1989; Lockwood, 1980a; Wooden and Parker, 1982). According to Struckman-Johnson, "Sex in prison is a major cause of violence . . . of upset and turmoil" (Lockwood, 2000: B1). Sylvester, Reed, and Nelson (1977) argue that violence in prisons has a clear homosexual underpinning. They found that one of the leading causes of inmate homicides was homosexual activity in prisons. Therefore, in order to better understand inmate behavior and experiences, researchers must continue to investigate the dynamics of the various subcultures found in correctional institutions. Hence, preventing sexual violence within our prisons can make these facilities safer for both inmates and correctional staff.

To suppress such violent behavior within the prison setting, correctional administrators need to establish some type of control initiative. A few prison officials and state departments of corrections have recognized that conjugal visits serve this purpose by controlling the behavior of the inmates (Hensley, Rutland, and Gray-Ray, 2000b; Hensley et al., 2000). Goetting (1982b) argued that conjugal visits could be used as a mechanism for controlling inmate behavior. To participate in these visitation programs, an inmate must not have any behavioral or misconduct reports; it is assumed that inmates receiving conjugal visits tend to follow the rules and regulations within the institution.

In one of the few studies that has addressed the effect of conjugal visitation programs on prison violence, Hensley et al. (2000) found that inmates who did not participate in the Mississippi conjugal visitation program were more likely to exhibit violent behavior than those inmates who did participate. In addition, results from the inmates indicated that 90 percent of the participants in the conjugal visitation program and 80 percent of the nonparticipants agreed that the program did reduce violence and tension within the prison. Therefore, it is argued that correctional administrators across the United States must provide married inmates a "normal" outlet for sexual release.

In addition, research on prison sex provides correctional administrators and staff with a more complete picture of their correctional institutions. Every form of sex, including autoeroticism, consensual sex, and coerced sex, is typically illegal and forbidden in prison. According to Saum et al. (1995), sex is forbidden "so that correctional officers can fulfill their objective of a safe and secure environment" (414). Because of the severe deprivations placed on inmates, prison sex becomes a commodity that can then fuel an "underground economy" (Saum et al., 1995; Silberman, 1994). Thus, correctional administrators and staff must be aware and concerned about the amount of sexual activity occurring in their institutions so that they may provide additional safety and security to their inmate populations as well as society. Tewksbury and West (2000) stated, "It should be of institutional concern to understand sexual expression among inmates who are safe and discreet, and to control unsafe and unwanted sexual expression among inmates who use sex as a weapon" (375).

The study of prison sex also advances the knowledge of sex and gender in diverse populations. For example, during their study of sexual behavior of the human male, Kinsey, Pomeroy, and Martin (1948) examined inmates' sexual behaviors. Although inmates were included in the study, they were excluded in the final rates of sexual frequency.

The researchers felt that inmates were in a "special situation" because of their deprived status. Even so, from this study as well as others on sexual behavior in society, we have learned a great deal about human sexuality.

Finally, research on prison sexuality is important because most inmates in prison are eventually released. Therefore, knowing more about sex in prisons and preventing sexual violence can aid in a more productive and psychologically balanced individual returning to society. One must consider the experiences that our prisoners face. Inmates currently being released feel more alienated and frustrated toward society. In addition, with the increasing rates of HIV/AIDS within our correctional facilities, it is quite plausible that infected inmates are transmitting the virus to their spouses or partners once they are released from prison. This is possibly a death sentence for both the inmates and their significant others.

CONCLUSION

Aside from a few exceptional studies on prison sexuality, we still know very little about the subject. The present undertaking examines various issues related to prison sexuality including prison argot and sexual hierarchy, nonconsensual sexual behavior, corrections officers' attitudes toward prison rape, the treatment of sexual assault victims, staff training for inmate sexual assault, HIV/AIDS, consensual sexual behavior, masturbation, and conjugal visitation programs. Although the primary focus of this book is the examination of the male prison subculture, several chapters address the unique differences that female inmates face once they are incarcerated. The ideology behind this project is to bring awareness to correctional administrators, correctional staff, and society regarding the healthy ways (masturbation and conjugal visitation programs) to promote normal sexuality in prison and decrease sexual violence.

2

ARGOT ROLES AND
PRISON SEXUAL HIERARCHY

Tammy Castle, Christopher Hensley,
and Richard Tewksbury

The rapid and continued growth of prison populations in the United States since 1980 has brought with it increasing attention and concern about whether and how U.S. society can afford (financially, politically, and culturally) to maintain the correctional industry. However, while a great deal of attention has been directed toward these macro-level issues, attention to micro-level issues such as programmatic operations and inmate culture has been largely neglected. This neglect is clearly a shortcoming of the penological literature. Without a thorough under-standing of how institutions operate on a day-to-day basis, it may not be possible to fully and adequately address larger-scale issues such as finances and the place of prisons in the political and social structure of society.

Understandings of the micro-level operations of correctional institutions are the world of the prison inmate. Inmates, obviously, live very differently from their counterparts in free society. Prison inmates live in a "total institution" (Goffman, 1961). Total institutions are closed, single-sex societies separated from society both socially and physically. Inhabitants of total institutions have essentially all decisions about the structure and content of their daily lives made for them, and they share all aspects of their daily lives within these types of institutions. However, one area in which occupants of total institutions do retain some degree of control is in their individual and collective abilities to develop unique values and norms and means for exercising social control over such. Central to this cultural construction is the delineation of specific social roles that are accompanied by rigidly proscribed behavioral expectations. These distinct values and behavioral roles are referred to as the prison subculture.

Newly arriving inmates entering into a correctional facility who seek to ease their social transition must learn the values, attitudes, and behavioral expectations that structure the operations of the institution. According to Einat and Einat (2000), "The norms and values of the inmate code form the core of an inmate subculture, providing its members with informal means to gain power and status and, thereby, a way to mitigate their sense of social rejection and compensate for their loss of autonomy and security" (309). Once the new inmates have accepted the prison lifestyle and criminal values, they have been "prisonized." Any inmate whose behavior violates the values and behavioral codes and traditions faces the likelihood of sanctions from other inmates and/or staff. Official sanctions imposed by staff range from verbal chastisement to time in solitary confinement and loss of earned "good time." However, for most inmates, the more serious forms of sanctions are those that come from other inmates. Peer-imposed sanctions range from ostracism to physical and sexual assault and occasionally death.

Prison researchers who have studied prison life have found that inmates use a special type of language or slang within the prison subculture that reflects the "distorted norms, values, and mores of the offenders" (Dumond, 1992: 138). As such, the vocabulary and speech patterns of prison inmates—what is known as prison argot—are largely distinct from those of noninmates. Language, as is well known, provides the parameters of understanding and possibilities for constructing a social and cultural milieu. Perhaps nowhere is this clearer than in correctional institutions, where inmates live, think, and function within the framework defined by the argot (Bondesson, 1989). Thus, the argot is centered on the functions that it serves for inmates. Einat and Einat (2000) document six functions of argot roles: (1) the need to be different and unique; (2) alleviation of feelings of rejection and refusal; (3) facilitation of social interactions and relationships; (4) declaration of belonging to a subculture or social status; (5) a tool of social identification leading to a sense of belonging to a group; and (6) secrecy (310–311).

One critical component of correctional institution culture that builds on argot roles is the prison sexual hierarchy. Sexual behavior among inmates does occur, although the sexual activities of individual inmates and with whom an inmate engages in sex is governed by a hierarchical system of roles and relationships. Within this structure the roles, activities, and actors involved in sexual activities are assigned unique, institutionally specific labels. According to Dumond (1992), "While the terms may have changed somewhat over the decades, prison slang defines sexual habits and inmates' status simultaneously, using homosexuality as a means of placing individuals within the inmate caste system" (138). These "sexual scripts" define an inmate's position within the prison society. Dumond (1992) also found that argot roles "help to define the treatment which an inmate is likely to receive from other inmates and corrections officers" (138). Labels, then, are central elements in the structuring of social interactions.

Previous research has attempted to describe the inmate subculture, including sexual argot roles and the prison sex hierarchy. However, inmates in prison today face myriad new challenges, many of which are at least indirectly related to sexuality issues. Overcrowding, fears of contracting HIV, and widespread influence of gangs are just some of the issues inmates confront as they enter and become integrated into the prison subculture. Understanding the prison subculture is not only important but also necessary to inmates' survival while incarcerated. Yet in recent years, there have been very few studies focusing specifically on argot labels and the sexual hierarchy that exists in prisons. The purpose of this chapter is to describe the sexual roles and hierarchy that exist in prison, with special emphasis on sexual argot at the start of the twenty-first century, and to assess how these factors have transformed prison subcultures.

EARLY SEXUAL HIERARCHY AND ARGOT ROLES OF MALES

In 1934, Joseph Fishman conducted one of the first ethnographies on sex in male prisons. Fishman found that homosexuality was an offense in many communities and that men were arrested and sent to prison for this offense. The Penitentiary at Welfare Island in New York was a prison where men were commonly sent for offenses such as soliciting members of the same sex for money, indecent exposure, and attempting to corrupt a minor. Fishman noted that men who came into this prison for these offenses were often passive and were known by other inmates as "punks," "girls," "fags," "pansies," or "fairies." These men had feminine characteristics and often wore makeup in prison. Other men, known as "top men" or "wolves," took advantage of these homosexuals. In other words, such sexual argot roles marked the prisoner as an appropriate target for sexual assault.

In studies of social roles in male prisons, Sykes (1958), Kirkham

(1971), Sagarin (1976), and Donaldson (1993a) found that inmates engaging in homosexual activity were divided into three categories. The first category contained those inmates who played an active, aggressive (masculine) role in homosexual relations. Inmates referred to these men as "wolves," "voluntary aggressors," or "daddies." The second and third categories contained inmates who played a more passive and submissive part. These men were known as "punks" and "fags." The stress on masculinity in prison contributed to inmates adopting the role of wolf. Wolves adopted an aggressive role and often preyed on inmates through coercion. Although wolves engaged in homosexual behavior with fags, the goal for wolves in these relationships was nothing more than physical release. However, raping punks reinforced the wolves' masculinity and maintained their high position in the status hierarchy. Through aggressive behavior, wolves also managed to escape the stigma of being labeled a homosexual.

Fags engaged in homosexuality because they were born that way (Donaldson, 1993a; Kirkham, 1971; Sagarin, 1976; Sykes, 1958). In other words, a fag adopted the same role in prison as he would have in the free community. The fag was known by his exaggerated feminine mannerisms, often wearing makeup and dressing in women's clothing. The fag fulfilled the stereotype of the homosexual in the free community and was viewed by inmates as playing a "natural" role. Fags were defined as having "pussies" not "assholes," and they wore "blouses" not "shirts" (Donaldson, 1993a). They were considered gender nonconformists and posed little threat to the masculinity of other inmates. According to the inmates in these studies, fags, "effeminates," or "queens" held more status than punks in the hierarchical division of homosexual roles.

In contrast, punks or "jailhouse turnouts" initially engaged in homosexual behavior through coercion. Inmates viewed punks as cowards who were morally weak and unable to defend themselves. Thus, they were also often targets of sexual attacks. Punks did not display feminine characteristics. Donaldson (1993a) argued that punks had some common characteristics including being younger, inexperienced first-time offenders, middle class, white, and physically smaller in size. They were viewed as having lost their masculinity as a result of submitting to a more aggressive inmate. Punks often chose to engage in homosexual behavior in prison for protection or for goods and services. Kirkham (1971) called punks who engaged in homosexual activities for goods and services "canteen punks." Kirkham (1971) and Sykes (1958) also discovered that punks were on the lowest rung of the hierarchical division. Punks were considered slaves, and wolves used them as commodities.

Buffum (1972) also made the distinction between true homosexuals and those who engaged in "situational homosexuality." Those who engaged in situational homosexuality fell into two categories: victims and rapists. Victims were referred to as "made" homosexuals and were stigmatized as effeminate men. Rapists, however, were referred to in the masculine term of "jockers." Jockers remained consistent with their masculine role and escaped stigmatization in prison.

In 1982, Wooden and Parker expanded on previous research concerning argot roles. They suggested that argot roles were adopted based on the distinction between the dominant partner (the inserter) and the submissive partner (the insertee). Homosexuals and vulnerable heterosexual "kids" were categorized as feminine and were encouraged or forced to exhibit feminine characteristics. This group took the role of insertee. They were often referred to as "broads," "bitches," "queens," and "sissies." The homosexuals usually conformed to this role and adopted feminine names. However, this role was imposed on those who were not true homosexuals and had been "turned out."

The dominant partner maintained his masculine identity. This type of inmate was known as the "jocker," "stud," or "straight who uses." The jocker's sexual behavior was viewed as situational homosexuality. The jocker exploited the vulnerable homosexual or heterosexual inmate in prison and treated his sexual partner as a surrogate female. In this way, jockers were attempting to replicate their sexual roles outside of prison.

Wooden and Parker also discovered that sissies were tolerated by inmates as maintaining their natural role. Heterosexual kids were also tolerated as long as they did not attempt to change the role specification and accepted the scripts of the inmate subculture. Submissive men, however, were not respected or seen as real men. They were viewed as commodities that jockers often used to satisfy a need, whether sexual or economic.

Fleisher (1989) found that many terms were used to designate effeminate homosexuals at the United States Penitentiary at Lompoc, California, including "skull-buster," "punk," "queen," "fag," "homo," "bitch," "faggot," "fruiter," "broad," "kid," and "ol' lady." However, four dominant categories and associated argot roles were found at the prison. These included "fags," "fuck-boys," "straights," and "turnouts."

Fags and fuck-boys were the female sex-role players in the institution. Both groups claimed homosexuality and were described as homosexual by other inmates, but some differences were evident between the two. Fags were effeminate homosexuals who were often distinguishable by their gait, dress, hair, and speech. Fuck-boys were not distinguishable by these traits.

Straights and turnouts were the male sex-role players in the institution. They did not consider themselves homosexual, nor did the other inmates define them as homosexual. Straights "used" fags for sexual gratification. However, some straights developed long-term sexual relationships with other straights and these relationships were guarded by privacy. Turnouts took a passive strategy by seducing inmates with commissary privileges or other items.

THE NEW SEXUAL HIERARCHY AND ARGOT LABELS OF MALES

The most recent research on the prison sexual hierarchy came from a study of three male prisons in Oklahoma conducted by Hensley in 1998–1999. During the 174 face-to-face interviews with inmates from minimum-, medium-, and maximum-security correctional facilities, Hensley noted that inmates continued to discuss the three "traditional" sexual roles found in male prisons (wolves, fags, and punks). However, inmates at these facilities did make two very surprising revelations about the roles that inmates assumed while incarcerated and the structure of the hierarchy itself.

Inmates discussed that there were two subcategories within both the wolf and fag roles. Inmates labeled the two subcategories of wolves as the "aggressive wolf" and the "nonaggressive wolf." The aggressive wolf was depicted as someone of African American descent who was both physically and verbally "tough." These inmates entered prison with a heterosexual orientation and maintained their masculinity by sexually assaulting younger, weaker inmates (punks). Raping a punk had more to do with power than sex. They maintained their masculine identification by participating in active roles during the sexual act (i.e., received oral sex from punks and played the inserter role during anal sex). When asked about their current sexual orientation, all of the self-described aggressive wolves maintained their heterosexual identity.

Nonaggressive wolves (or "teddy bears"), on the other hand, typically did not sexually assault their sex partners. Rather, they sought sexual relationships with other inmates ("fish" or "closet gays") who were willing to engage in consensual homosexual activity while in prison. They tended to be Caucasian men who entered prison with a heterosexual identity and maintained their masculine role by participating in active roles during sex. However, when asked about their current sexual orientation, over half of the nonaggressive wolves answered that they were now bisexual. Thus, many of these inmates—because of the lack of heterosexual sex in prison—had changed their self-concepts regarding their sexual orientation.

The two subcategories of fags included the fish and the closet gays. Fish (thought previously to be newly entering inmates) were typically African American males who took on a feminine role and appearance. Although it violated institutional rules and regulations, they wore make-up, displayed female mannerisms, and took on female nicknames. Fish entered into prison life homosexual and maintained their homosexual identity by assuming the passive role during sexual activity (i.e., performed oral sex and played the insertee role during anal sex). Some fish "sold" themselves for canteen goods and cigarettes whereas others developed relationships with nonaggressive wolves.

Closet gays were typically Caucasian males who entered prison with a "hidden" homosexual identity. Closet gays had the ability to take on both the active and passive role during sexual activity. They did, however, try to maintain masculine appearances and mannerisms. They typically sought other closet gays in hopes of forming a "true love" relationship.

According to previous studies, there is a clearly defined prison sexual hierarchy with wolves on top, fags in the middle, and punks on the bottom. Yet Hensley's Oklahoma prisons research of 1998–1999 pointed to a newly defined hierarchy. According to the inmates, the status that fags received in prison had progressed upwardly to equal that of the wolves. Fish and aggressive wolves were the most respected and feared groups within the prison sexual hierarchy. Many inmates feared fish because they were known for their aggressive behavior. For example, two incidents were reported by the inmates in the maximum-security facility of fish killing other inmates because the other inmates had referred to them as punks. In addition, fish were also known for their jealousy. Inmates were often scared to engage in homosexual behavior with the fish's sex partners.

Closet gays and nonaggressive wolves typically maintained equal status with each other, but they were slightly beneath the fish and aggressive wolves on the pecking order. Punks continued to remain at the bottom of the prison sexual hierarchy. Inmates continued to view

punks as cowards who were physically and morally weak. Because
punks often sold themselves for protection, inmates saw them as inferi-
or to other inmates within the correctional facility.

EARLY SEXUAL HIERARCHY AND ARGOT ROLES OF FEMALES

Up until the 1960s, minimal sociological research existed on the
amount of homosexual activity in female prisons and the roles associated with such behavior. In 1962, Halleck and Hersko conducted one of
the first studies on homosexual behavior in a correctional institution for
adolescent girls. Their research exhibited little differentiation into masculine and feminine roles. Yet one argot role was distinguished among
those females who engaged in homosexual activity. They noted that
some females attempted to change their grooming and attire to suggest
a masculine appearance. These females were known as "butches." In
the adolescent correctional institution, butches held high status and pop-
ularity among the other females.

Ward and Kassebaum (1964) and Giallombardo (1966) were also
early researchers who endeavored to study homosexual behavior in
female prisons. Their study uncovered two major distinctions among
homosexual roles at the Frontera Correctional Institution in California
and the Alderson Federal Penitentiary in West Virginia. The inmates
defined these argot labels as the "true homosexual" or "lesbian" and the
"jailhouse turnout" or "penitentiary turnout."

The inmates defined the true homosexual as a woman who was a
homosexual before being incarcerated. These women typically participated in homosexual activity in prison and remained homosexual upon
their release. The jailhouse turnout was introduced to homosexual
behavior while in prison. Estimates by staff and inmates suggested that
the majority of homosexual activities in female prisons involved the
jailhouse turnout.

Whether a female represented a true homosexual or a jailhouse
turnout, other distinctions in argot roles existed, too. Ward and
Kassebaum (1965) and Giallombardo (1966) noted that one role was
known as the "butch," "stud," "stud broad," or "drag butch." The butch
maintained the dominant role in the homosexual relationship by being
the aggressive sexual partner. The butch manifested many masculine
characteristics including short hair, a lack of makeup, and a masculine
gait. Ward and Kassebaum (1964) also established a variation in the
butch role in which the female did not manifest masculine characteris-

tics. However, the female did maintain the dominant role in the homosexual relationship. Females who were seemingly unattractive or who
were already inclined toward masculine habits were more likely to designate themselves butch.

The complementary role to the butch was known as the "femme."
The femme maintained her feminine characteristics while taking a passive and submissive role in the homosexual relationship. The
butch/femme couples in prison mirrored patriarchal, heterosexual relationships that existed in the free community. The butch provided protection and economic stability while the femme provided passive sexual
relations and housekeeping services.

Giallombardo (1966) also discovered two further distinctions
between the "femme"/"mommy" and the "stud broad"/"daddy." The use
of the terms mommy and daddy emphasized the familial aspect of the
homosexual relationship and its similarities to the patriarchal heterosexual relationship. Relationships in the Alderson Federal Penitentiary
were highly sought after by the inmates. Giallombardo's research concluded that the goal of female inmates who engaged in homosexual
activity was to establish a sincere relationship. Therefore, the inmates
looked down upon transitory relationships. Two of the groups who participated in such relationships were known as the "trick" and the "commissary hustler."

The trick was a woman who allowed herself to be exploited for a
variety of reasons. Rather than establishing a sincere relationship, the
trick was typically involved in several unstable relationships. The trick
was usually exploited economically, especially as a source of labor.
Inmates frowned upon these weak women. The inmates had a name for
the women who exploited the tricks. These women were known as commissary hustlers. The commissary hustler maintained a traditional
homosexual relationship with another inmate, while establishing other
sexual relationships with females for economic reasons. Therefore, any
woman involved with the commissary hustler other than the main
femme was labeled a trick. The commissary hustler provided the trick
with a list of items needed from the commissary. The trick often com-
plied because she anticipated that the stud would leave her wife and
become involved in a serious relationship with her instead. Inmates
reported that this often occurred because the trick would be better off
economically due to her commissary account.

Another role that existed at Alderson was known as the "chippie"
role. Giallombardo (1966) implied that the chippie was a woman who
exploited each situation for material or sexual gratification. Unlike the

commissary hustler, the chippie did not establish one sincere relationship. Therefore, the chippie was often labeled the prison prostitute. The chippie was promiscuous and the inmates often scorned this type of behavior.

Contrary to the chippie role, there were women who were promiscuous solely for sexual gratification. These women were known as "kick partners." The inmates reported that some women chose to enter into this role for a variety of reasons. One reason given was that some women preferred to become kick partners rather than assume the responsibilities of a permanent relationship. Kick partners also included a group of women who exchanged partners and maintained friendly relations. The inmates at Alderson did not look down upon the kick partners because they usually were very discreet.

Giallombardo (1966) also learned of three other distinctions at the Alderson Federal Penitentiary. Inmates distinguished between the punk, fag, and turnabout. The punk in the female prison was someone who manifested feminine characteristics while assuming the stud role. Women who played the stud role in prison were expected to exhibit male characteristics. In Alderson, punks were despised and ridiculed by inmates for playing a false part.

Fags in female prisons were considered sincere by the inmates because they were true lesbians. The fag was justified because the inmates rationalized that they were born that way or something happened to them in their life that made them become a lesbian. Since the stud role resembled their true identity in the free community, the inmates viewed it as natural for the fag to adopt in prison.

The turnabout in Alderson Federal Penitentiary was so labeled due to her claimed expertise at assuming either role in prison. Based upon the benefits associated with the role, the turnabout could play either the male or female role. Thus, the inmates held the turnabout in low esteem. Inmates reported that they preferred a woman to choose her role and remain in that role. Inmates valued the structured setting, and deviation from that structure was frowned upon.

There were two argot labels for those women who had not yet engaged in homosexual behavior while in prison. The first was known as the "square." The square refused to engage in homosexual behavior. Inmates joked that someday the square may "see the light" or "come around." Unlike the square, the "cherry" had simply not engaged in homosexual activities. Inmates viewed the cherry as having not yet been turned out. The cherries were considered by inmates to be a reserve for potential mates. Thus, inmates favored the cherries over the squares. Giallombardo (1966) also found that cherries might not engage in homosexuality due to short sentences, not wanting to become emotionally involved, or not considering the lifestyle desirable.

In order to develop a perspective of the major argot labels used in the Women's Reformatory of the District of Columbia in Occoquan, Virginia, Heffernan (1972) interviewed correctional staff who had extensive contact with the inmates. Information about the roles and the patterns of association of each role were discussed. Interviews with the inmates supplied additional information concerning the roles. The major argot roles of "the square," "the cool," and "the life" referred to members of the inmate subsystems who were affiliated through their criminal convictions. The squares were females who had no previous criminal record but were convicted for homicide or assault. White collar convictions of embezzlement or forgery committed during employment also afforded an inmate the title of square. Sentence time for squares ranged from one year to fifty years. The square just wanted to do her time, obey the rules, and did not care about gaining any status among the other inmates. The square chose esteem rather than control of other inmates. This was gained by "recognition of work, respect of staff, affective relations with friends, and moral standing as a good woman" (143). While 31 percent of the squares participated in make-believe families, only 9 percent of the squares reported "playing" (engaging in homosexual activity).

Inmates with an arrest record including burglary, robbery, check stealing, and forgery were considered cools. If an individual was convicted of drug dealing but was not an addict, she was also considered to be a cool. The cools usually had shorter sentences and when released were not rehabilitated. The cools adhered to both the code of the inmates as well as the policies of the staff. The cools were the operators and conformists within the prison who sought status through channels provided by the prison administration (inmate council positions, working on the newspaper, etc.) and interrelations with other inmates. Interestingly, 32 percent of the cools reported playing, while 48 percent mentioned their participation in "familying" even though cools felt that "close" relationships in prison should be avoided. In other words, this was viewed as an economic outlet, not an affectionate one (Heffernan, 1972).

The lifes were habitual offenders who were drug addicts or alcoholics convicted for such crimes as prostitution, shoplifting, or larceny. Most of the life inmates had juvenile records of incarceration. The lifes had long and indeterminate sentences. These inmates were manipulative of staff and inmates for both legal and illegal goods and services. The lifes reported that 57 percent played and 58 percent were family members in order to maintain their addictive habits (Heffernan, 1972). Although each of these roles differed in ideology, various members of all three sub-systems shared not only emotional and economic ties but interracial family and conjugal roles to sustain them during their incarceration.

THE NEW SEXUAL HIERARCHY
AND ARGOT LABELS OF FEMALES

Greer (2000) conducted the most recent study addressing argot roles in women's prisons. For this study, Greer interviewed thirty-five female inmates in a Midwestern correctional facility. Her research indicated that the nature of interpersonal relationships in female facilities had changed over time. In this facility, intimate sexual relationships were formed on the basis of "playing games" and economic manipulation. The study also noted less use of labels and specifically defined argot roles, showing the changing nature of female prisons.

From personal interviews with inmates, Greer (2000) found that females in this facility did not seem to be strongly invested in any particular social roles. Contrary to previous research, inmates in this study did not seem to portray specific feminine or masculine characteristics when involved in a homosexual relationship. Only a couple of women referred to other inmates as adopting a masculine role, which they described as "bulldogging." However, inmates suggested that women often engaged in sexual relationships for economic gain. The inmates with the highest status in the facility were the ones who had the most money in their accounts. The women who sought sexual relationships for this reason were consistently referred to as "canteen whores" or "commissary whores."

Greer's (2000) research suggested that the label of "lesbian" still applied to those women who identified themselves as such before incarceration. Women who only engaged in homosexual behavior while in prison were referred to as "turnouts" or "bisexuals." Inmates reported that lesbians often formed the most stable relationships if they chose to participate in them while in prison. Lesbians were viewed as engaging in sincere relationships, while most other sexual relationships were marked by mistrust and manipulation.

CONCLUSION

Inmates within correctional institutions have developed an inmate code. An inmate code consists of norms and values that structure the informal patterns of life among inmates. In 1958, Sykes outlined five universal aspects of the inmate code: (1) Don't interfere with inmate interests; (2) don't fight with other inmates; (3) don't exploit other inmates; (4) be strong; and (5) don't trust the staff. According to Einat and Einat (2000), "[This] code is directly linked to the process of socialization and adaptation to prison life" (309). In other words, the inmate code is universal across all correctional facilities because the normative society, its attributes, and its delegates are inherent opponents of prisoners. The language (argot) that inmates use within prisons is one of the principal elements of prisonization and the development and perpetuation of the inmate code.

As one can see from the previous discussion, there are similarities in the early research of sexual argot roles in male and female correctional facilities. Inmates who engage in homosexual activity are labeled based on the sex role they portray in the interaction. In both female-female and male-male relationships in prison, one individual will take on the characteristics and mannerisms of the opposing sex. The female who adopts masculine characteristics in these relationships holds the highest status in the prison. Conversely, the male who maintains his masculinity while engaging in homosexual activity holds the highest status in the prison.

Differences in early research on sexual argot roles reflects the socialization and norms for individuals at the time of the writing. Most of the homosexual relationships in female facilities are laden with emotional attachment and family-like commitment. However, emotional attachment in male facilities is frowned upon and considered a threat to masculinity.

Recent research on sexual argot roles in female and male facilities suggests that the nature of these relationships is changing. In male facilities, wolves originally held the highest status in the prison sexual hierarchy. However, Hensley's (1998–1999) study indicates that the status of fags is now equal to the status of aggressive wolves. In female facilities, Greer's (2000) research suggests that relationships are often based on economic manipulation and that the designated sex roles in previous research are almost nonexistent.

Sexual argot roles in prison reflect the organization, language, and status hierarchy of the prison subculture. To survive in prison, inmates must learn to reject the norms of free society and adopt the new normative order. It is also important for correctional administrators and staff to learn the organization of the prison subculture. Learning the language and normative codes help staff maximize the efficiency of the prison, as well as the safety of other staff and inmates. Therefore, by identifying the sexual status and associated roles, it is possible that correctional administrators and staff can minimize the number of sexual assaults within their prisons, especially male correctional facilities. The next chapter will explore many of these sexual scripts by examining the dynamics and motivations that surround nonconsensual sexual activity in both male and female correctional facilities.

3

NONCONSENSUAL SEXUAL BEHAVIOR

Julie Kunselman, Richard Tewksbury, Robert W. Dumond, and Doris A. Dumond

For decades, a cancer has gone untreated and has overtaken the ability of U.S. corrections institutions to provide safe and humane treatment for its charges—in direct opposition to the Constitution's Eighth Amendment guarantee against cruel and unusual punishment. In early 2001, startling headlines flooded the national media with cries of concern and calls for reform. Morse (2001) argued that "savage prison gang rapes turn many run-of-the-mill prisoners into violent felons in waiting" (21). Lehrer (2001) opined that "prison rape may be America's most ignored crime problem" (24).

In April 2001, the Supreme Court of Canada rebuked the U.S. criminal justice system by unanimously ruling to block the extradition of four men accused of a multimillion-dollar telemarketing scam in the United States. The Court held that the reason for this action was that Pennsylvania prosecutor Gordon Zubrod had violated the Canadian Charter of Rights guarantee to life, liberty, and security of the person in 1997 by threatening, "You're going to be the boyfriend of a very bad man if you wait out the extradition" (a reference to sexual abuse in prisons) (Bailey, 2001: A8).

Two international organizations also raised the alarm about sexual violence in U.S. prisons. Amnesty International (2001) issued *Broken Bodies, Shattered Minds: Torture and Ill-Treatment of Women,* and Human Rights Watch promulgated *No Escape: Male Rape in U.S. Prisons* (Mariner, 2001). What is most disturbing about these two reports is not simply that they document horrific sexual violence upon inmates by other inmates but by correctional custodial staff as well. Until 1999, as noted by Goering (2001) "sexual abuse of prisoners

27

by correctional officials was not even a criminal offense in 14 states" (18).

Adding to this concern has been the flood of incarcerated inmates pouring into U.S. correctional institutions, derailing any attempt at providing sound, safe, therapeutic environments. Sadly, the United States currently ranks first worldwide in the number of inmates it incarcerates and ranks first in its imprisonment rate per 100,000 people (Beck and Harrison, 2001; Gardner, 2000; Walmsley, 1999). On December 31, 1999, the overall number of incarcerated persons in the United States was an astounding 2,026,596 persons, a 39.2 percent increase since 1990 alone (Beck and Harrison, 2001).

INMATE SEXUAL ASSAULT

In dealing with the issue of inmate sexual assault, one must be aware that the definition of what this actually means is itself a problem. How is "sexual assault" defined? Can a man be raped? Is forced oral or anal sex considered rape? These kinds of questions reflect the general confusion and misunderstanding that exists. Over the years, the definitions of terms such as "rape," "sexual assault," "sodomy," "sexual abuse," and "coercive sex" have taken on expanded meanings, which can even differ depending upon the perspective (medical, legal, etc.) being employed. Although there has been an attempt to more accurately define rape and sexual assault in order to reflect a more precise understanding of this phenomenon, these definitions continue to confound and frustrate efforts to effectively intervene with victims.

In both common language and in the medical arena, there has been a transition from a singular definition of rape—"sexual intercourse with a woman forcibly against her will" (Book Essentials Publications, 1987)—to one that is gender neutral (can be male or female) and generally includes the following specific elements that must be proven beyond a reasonable doubt to support a conviction: (1) unlawful, (2) penetration of any orifice, (3) against a person's will, and (4) with the use of threat or force (Brown, Esbensen, and Geis, 1998).

However, in the legal arenas, there is still no consensus on the definition of rape. Although many states employ the four elements noted above (such as Massachusetts General Law, Chapter 265, Section 22), not every state utilizes this definition or any of its elements, nor does the United States Penal Code. Brown, Esbensen, and Geis (1998), using an adaptation of Klotter (1994), note that the common-law definition and elements of the crime remain "the act of having unlawful carnal knowledge by a man of a woman, forcibly against her will," whose elements include "1. unlawful; 2. carnal knowledge (or sexual intercourse); 3. by force or fear; and 4. without the consent or against the will of the female" (37). Even the Federal Bureau of Investigation has maintained this archaic definition of rape in the Uniform Crime Reports, which has been the standard for the reporting of criminal offenses by local police, organized by states, since 1930. Such discrepancies in definitions result in the inability to establish national standards for arrest and prosecution of rape cases in the community and especially in incarcerated settings.

If an inmate sexual assault occurs in a city or county jail or a state prison, the criminal justice professional should consult the specific statutes of the state, as state law takes precedence. Researchers, though, continue to struggle to determine exact, systematic definitions of sexual assault and may wish to utilize the specific language employed by Struckman-Johnson and Struckman-Johnson (2000a, 2000b) as well as Struckman-Johnson et al. (1996).

The discussion of sexual assault is further confused by the dynamics of life within a correctional institution. Unfortunately, many inmates come into the prison environment without an adequate understanding of the complex sociopolitical structure. As such, many inmates may find themselves in jeopardy. An inmate may unwittingly take items from other inmates, not realizing they will now be indebted to the provider of these goods (Bowker, 1980; Scacco, 1982). Repayment for the used goods, which are often doubled or tripled, can then become problematic. The new inmate must repay their benefactor with sexual favors. In addition, some inmates may be coerced into trading sexual favors for protection, known as "hooking up" in prison jargon (Cotton and Groth, 1982; Dumond, 1992; Wooden and Parker, 1982). While some observers argue that inmates who trade their bodies for protection do so willingly, most analysts agree that protective pairing is anything but consensual (given that outside the coercive conditions of confinement, these individuals would never agree to such an arrangement). We can then conceptualize sexual assault within correctional institutions as a continuum, from consensual sexual conduct to gang rape. In the following sections, we will review the scarce history of sexual assault research in male and female prisons.

Sexual Assault Research in Male Prisons, 1930–1989

The focus on nonconsensual prison sex has been limited due to societal indifference and intolerance, causing the importance of this research to be overlooked. The importance, as it relates to the general public, is best summarized by Fishman (1968): "The man in jail today is the man who will be out tomorrow. . . . If the treatment which they receive in jail, and the surroundings forced upon them are such as to turn them out with criminal tendencies which were lacking or dormant when they went in, you, Mr. Average Citizen, may be the one to suffer" (249). The importance, as it relates to prison populations, "cannot be overemphasized. . . . Everyone in the prison environment is affected in varying degrees by the influence [of sex]" (Clemmer, 1940: 249).

Sex in prisons, both coerced and noncoerced, is associated with increased health risks of inmates (Blumberg, 1989; Cotton and Groth, 1982; Gido, 1989), increased chances that the victims become victimizers (Chonco, 1989; Lockwood, 1980a, 1982; Smith and Batiuk, 1989), and increased institutional violence (Cotton and Groth, 1982; Fleisher, 1989; Lockwood, 1980a). Further, the lack of research also implicates future measurement problems in that research design and methodology have not been perfected, in addition to not providing support for policy initiatives. For example, even completed prison sex research admits that findings must be regarded as conservative (Davis, 1968), "inconsistent and inconclusive" (Saum et al., 1995; Smith and Batiuk, 1989), or simply unknown (Cotton and Groth, 1982).

Although research on sexual assaults in prison since the 1930s is limited, a handful of authors have engaged in prison sexual assault research to provide others with knowledge of the incidence of sexual assault in prison, as well as the dynamics surrounding nonconsensual prison sex. In one of the earliest studies on prison sex, Clemmer (1940) suggested that sex in prisons has probably always existed and that prison culture really "fosters and tolerates" sexual behavior among inmates. From a self-drop sample of "a few inmates who were aware of the writer's objective interest," Clemmer estimated that about 60 percent of the prison population were "normal," 30 percent were "quasi-normal," and 10 percent were "frankly abnormal" (257). Inmates fitting the normal category did not participate in any type of sexual contact and those who fit the quasi-normal category included inmates who participated in prison sex but used their participation to gain status. Inmates known as "wolves," "jockers," or "daddies" were categorized into this quasi-normal group. Inmates included in the abnormal category included "inverts" (inmates having feminine characteristics) and sexual psychopaths.

In another early study, Davis (1968) reported that 2,000 male inmates were raped while confined in (or being transported to) a Philadelphia jail during a twenty-six-month period. This, however, represented only 3 percent of the 60,000 inmates who were examined by Davis. Some authors suggest Davis's findings are a conservative estimate (Donaldson, 1995; Nacci, 1978), and Davis (1971) agrees, reporting, "Sexual assaults are epidemic in some prison systems" (n.p.).

In the first major study to assess same-sex sexual activities in federal prisons, the focus was on the dynamics of sexual assault. Nacci (1978) randomly selected and gathered data from 330 male inmates from seventeen different federal institutions. Although forty inmates (12 percent) reported they had sexual contact in their current facility, only two inmates (0.6 percent) reported they were victims of nonconsensual sex. So, although nonconsensual sex does occur, at least according to self-report data, it is far less common than consensual sex among inmates.

In his book *Men Who Rape: The Psychology of the Offender*, Groth (1979) advanced understandings of nonconsensual sex in prison by differentiating characteristics between institutional and community sexual assault against males. His sample included twenty offenders and seven victims who participated in rapes while in prison. All of the offenders committing sexual assault in prison reported they either forced their victim to perform fellatio or penetrated the victim both orally and anally. Further, and most noteworthy as the most differentiating of characteristics between community and institutionalized male rape, was that 80 percent of the prison sexual assaults were gang rapes versus 32 percent gang rapes in the community.

During a yearlong study completed by Moss, Hosford, and Anderson (1979) of 1,100 inmates from a federal correctional institution, only 1 percent (twelve) were identified by correctional officers as having sexually assaulted other inmates. All inmates identified by staff as sexual aggressors were either black (seven) or Chicano (five), whereas all but two of the victims of the assaults were white. Moreover, in all of the cases of sexual assault, the victims and offenders were of different races. The authors, therefore, suggested that the incident rate of sexual assault in federal prisons "may not be a frequent problem," but that the "racial compositions of the assaulters and victims" might be (823).

The findings of Moss and colleagues were also supported by the work of Carroll (1977). As an observer in a prison housing 200 prisoners, Carroll did not notice any acts of sexual assault even though informants estimated at least forty sexual assaults occurred per year. However, in his observations and via informant suggestions, Carroll notes the "biracial character of sexual assaults" and the supposition that racial hostility forms an underlying current for such assaults (418–419). The interracial nature of nonconsensual prison sex was one of the most strongly established facts of early prison sex research.

At approximately the same time, Lockwood (1980a) and Bowker (1980) published their well-known research on violence in prisons. Lockwood drew on a sample of male inmates from New York State prisons. In one portion of his research, eighty-nine inmates were selected at random from two institutions (Coxsackie and Attica). Of the seventy-four inmates who agreed to an interview, 28 percent reported they were targets of sexual aggressors in prison, though only one target reported he had been a victim of a completed assault. According to Lockwood (1980a), these same inmates reported fifty-one total incidents of sexual assault or other physical violence (35 percent of total incidents) and ninety-seven incidents of less aggressive behaviors. Further, almost one-half of the violent incidents involved "fairly high levels of force, i.e., sexual assault, stabbing, clubbing, or beating" (21). In simple terms, inmates were fairly forthcoming in reporting regular violent victimizations, but not so for sexual victimizations.

Bowker's (1980) research focused on the broader issue of violence and victimization in prisons. He, too, found that violence is a rather common occurrence and not infrequently involved older inmates offering protection to younger inmates in exchange for sexual favors. However, what ties these two pieces of research together are their conclusions that violence of all forms in prisons can be either for purposes of obtaining desired rewards (instrumental violence) or for communicating a position of strength to others (expressive violence).

Wooden and Parker's (1982) survey of 200 inmates from a medium-security California prison resulted in their expression of alarm based on their findings of 14 percent of inmates being sexually victimized. Furthermore, 52 percent of the inmates responded they had been pressured into having sex. The authors also interviewed a sample of eighty self-identified homosexuals, of which 40 percent had been forced to have sex while incarcerated, 95 percent had performed oral sex, and 98 percent had had anal sex while in prison.

Nacci and Kane's (1983, 1984b) research on sexual victimization drew on interviews with 330 randomly selected inmates and 500 correctional officers from the Federal Bureau of Prisons. Twelve percent of inmates reported they had participated in at least one homosexual act during their current incarceration; more than twice as many inmates (29 percent) had been propositioned for sex. Seven percent responded they were pressured into sex through some seductive means (i.e., offering of gifts or favors), and only one respondent stated he was a willing participant (to avoid a violent assault). Two (0.6 percent) of the inmates stated they were coerced to perform sexual acts in prison, and only one (0.3 percent) reported he was raped while in a federal institution.

The 1980s ended with Tewksbury's (1989a) study of 150 Ohio inmates. This study focused on reports of sexual assaults, forceful sexual approaches, and sexual propositions provided by inmates. Interestingly, none of the offenders reported having been sexually assaulted or raped even though 14.4 percent reported having been approached for sex with force. Yet Tewksbury found that the measure of nonforceful or consensual sex patterns of the inmates yielded a much higher percentage of participation (between 25 and 40 percent).

Throughout the 1980s, research on sexual assault in prisons provided criminologists and correctional practitioners with a breakdown of incident rates and patterns of coerced sex. The variability in measurement of sexual assaults in these studies is also noteworthy because even with more than thirty years of studies, researchers are not able to accurately portray the nature of the problem (Dumond, 1992). However, the research is not limited to unsuccessful portrayal of sexual assault incidents. Much of the research did successfully record the dynamics of nonconsensual prison sex (i.e., participant demographics and actions leading up to the assault). Focus on these issues of prison sexual assault will be addressed later in the chapter.

Sexual Assault Research in Male Prisons, 1990–2000

Research on prison sex in the 1990s was limited. Yet one of the primary themes in this literature (in addition to HIV/AIDS) was the incidence of sexual assaults (Tewksbury and West, 2000). More recently, *The Prison Journal*, a leading publication in the field of criminal justice, dedicated an entire volume in December 2000 to issues of sex in prison.

In 1995, Saum et al. interviewed 101 inmates in a medium-security state prison over a one-year period to assess inmates' perceptions of sexual assaults. Forty percent of these inmates reported personally knowing of forced sexual assaults taking place, and only 4 percent reported they had personally seen a rape occur during the previous year. More interesting is that although the majority of offenders (60 percent) reported "not knowing of sexual assaults taking place," 38.7 percent of the inmates responded they "thought that rape takes place once a week or more" and 15.9 percent believed "rape to be a daily occurrence" (423). These data suggest we should question why there is such a discrepancy between what the inmates in this study reported "knowing," and how frequently they believed rape was occurring.

In a study of 528 inmates (486 males and 42 females), Struckman-Johnson et al. (1996) estimated that 20 percent of inmates in one institution were coerced into having sex and usually on more than one occasion. In fact, victims of sexual assault were coerced into sex an average of nine times. One-third of the inmates reported being a victim of coerced sex one time, whereas 4 percent reported being assaulted an alarming fifty-one to 100 times! Most commonly, male victims were forced to engage in anal sex (52 percent of victims), and three female victims were forced into genital touching or attempted sexual contacts.

In a subsequent and larger study, Struckman-Johnson and Struckman-Johnson (2000a, 2000b) examined sexual coercion in prison, drawing on data from 1,788 inmates in seven male prisons. Both the incidence of sexual assault and the worst-case incident rates of sexual assault were recorded by individual inmates and correctional officials. The results of this study showed that 16 percent of the inmates report they had been sexually coerced during their current incarceration. However, the rate of sexual coercion varied widely across institutions, ranging from 4 to 21 percent. As in the earlier study by Struckman-Johnson et al. (1996), when inmates were asked to report on how frequent they believed sexual assaults to be occurring, overestimating of sexual assaults was found. For example, both staff and inmates from one of the prison facilities estimated that sexual coercion took place at a far greater rate than was actually recorded by the facility. Again, this discrepancy highlights the problem of inaccurate recording or failure to report incidents of sexual assault; it also suggests potential problems regarding the validity of data obtained with different methodologies.

Sexual Assault Research in Female Prisons

Mainly because research is limited, this section briefly explores the area of coerced sex among women inmates. The following excerpt from *Crucibles of Crime: The Shocking Story of the American Jail* is one of the first to document the problem of inaccurate recording of sex acts — in this case consensual sex — in a female prison (Fishman, 1968):

> Mrs. O'Hare complains in her pamphlet of the appalling amount of homosexuality which exists in the women's section of the Missouri Prison, and states that in her opinion fully seventy-five per cent of the inmates are abnormal or subnormal.[1] This figure is entirely too high,

but Mrs. O'Hare was naturally led into such an exaggeration because, having no previous personal knowledge of prisons, she was swept off her feet to find that such things existed. She was utterly amazed when I told her that homosexuality was a real problem in every prison. (101–102)

It is interesting to note that it was a female inmate making the observation of "the appalling amount" of sex among inmates and that in her opinion "fully seventy-five per cent of the inmates" were homosexuals. Meanwhile, although Fishman suggests that 75 percent is too high, he does conclude that consensual sex is a real problem in all prisons, including female prisons.

Studies of sexual coercion among female inmates are scarce. There have been only three studies completed on sexual coercion in female prisons from the mid-1990s through 2000. The first studies, completed by Struckman-Johnson et al. (1996) and Struckman-Johnson and Struckman-Johnson (1999), found that 7 percent of the women surveyed (n = 93) in three prisons reported incidents of forced sex. However, and in contradiction to the responses from male inmates (discussed above), the female respondents estimated that the incidence of coerced sex was lower (3 percent) than the reported rate. What might this mean? It could suggest that female inmates are passive to sexual aggressors to avoid confrontation and violence but are not actually condoning the sexual encounter like the female inmate respondents are suggesting. Or, this could suggest that women in prison are less aware of sexual coercion in their institutions.

Using a different approach, Alarid (2000a) sought to describe the incidence of, and issues related to, sexual assault and sexual coercion of incarcerated women by conducting a content analysis of one female inmate's prison letters over a five-year period. Similar to the studies of sexual assault and coercion in male prisons, Alarid discovered an underreported rate for sexual assaults in female institutions. In fact, Alarid states, "For some women, being a target of sexual coercion by a few female perpetrators was a daily experience" (396). Further, in discussing the occurrence of rape at the prison over the five-year period, she states, "Rape occurred at a much lower rate than other forms of sexual behavior. However, when rapes did occur among women offenders, there were multiple perpetrators rather than a single female offender" (399).

This study goes a step further and also discusses the probable relationship between sexual coercion and later incidents of physical violence and sexual assault among the female inmates.[2] Again, this might suggest that female inmates are passive to sexual aggressors in order to avoid confrontation and violence. It also provides reasoning for much of the disparity in sexual coercion rate reporting, as will be discussed in the next section.

REASONS FOR DISPARITIES IN PRISON SEXUAL ASSAULT RATES

Although one reason for inconclusive findings might be the lack of an established and agreed-upon definition of nonconsensual sex (for measurement), a failure to report such incidents is probably the greater problem. Male inmates might fail to report sexual assault because of the perceived stigmas that are associated with being raped, such as being weak or unable to defend one's manhood. It might also be that male inmates fear a more violent assault (whether physical or sexual) as a consequence of reporting a victimization incident. This section utilizes several examples from the research described above to discuss these possible reasons for disparities in sexual assault reporting.

Limitations in methodology and research design clearly have some affect on the disparity of reported rates. For example, characteristics of the sexual assault often are not mutually exclusive to survey categories, which creates a problem for participants to respond accurately. What is more, sexual acts might not be defined clearly, thereby leaving inmates unsure of what acts relate to the definition. And finally, some researchers have consistently used self-administered surveys to measure the incidence of sexual coercion. The problem with this is that approximately 60 to 75 percent of U.S. prison inmates are illiterate (Herrick, 1991; Ryan, 1990), but knowing that such a high percentage of the inmate population is illiterate is sometimes not accounted for in the methodology of prison sex research. For example, Wooden and Parker's (1982) survey on sexual behavior in prison is a twenty-item questionnaire with the following directions: "This is an anonymous survey. Please answer each question by filling in the blank or circling the appropriate response. *Do not* write your name on this paper" (237–238).

The ability of all inmates, especially the illiterate inmates, to complete this self-administered document is questionable. Therefore, one must consider the problems associated with the validity of this survey and how these problems might be associated with under-reporting or inaccuracy of reporting sexual assault. Moreover, by not including this dimension of the prison population, researchers are not able to get an accurate representation of the aggregate prison population.

Failure to completely define research terminology also presents problems that can lead to highly dispersed incident rates. Although many authors cite in their literature reviews a high percentage of non-consensual sex—28 percent is often used from Lockwood's (1980a) research—in actuality this is a very broad interpretation of the research. Lockwood actually reports that only one inmate out of eighty-nine was actually raped (1.3 percent). The 28 percent was attempted but not completed sexual assaults. The following excerpt (Saum et al., 1995) describes the problem of definitional clarity:

> A large majority of studies do not make any effort to define the sexual terminology either to the inmates who are being interviewed or to the readers who must interpret the researchers' findings. Some analyses have measured rape in the broadest sense, as any act of coercion. Other studies break down these acts of coercion into categories such as forcible rape, sexual assault, sexual aggression, sexual solicitation, and attempted sexual acts. Perhaps even more damaging, researchers have failed to distinguish between consensual acts and acts of rape. (418)

This lack of definitional clarity hinders researchers from accurately reporting the incidence of prison sexual assault.

Victims of sexual assault might also fail to report their victimization due to concerns with repercussions that might arise from reporting sexual assault. These repercussions may be from both inmates and correctional officers (Moss, Hosford, and Anderson, 1979; Wooden and Parker, 1982). Cotton and Groth (1982) suggest that reporting a sexual assault puts the victim in a "no-win" situation and that this becomes the primary reason for not reporting the victimization. For example, one-half of the no-win situation could stem from staff members' discomfort in dealing with the sexual assault, which might lead to poor communication between the staff and the victim, or it might simply be that because of the actions staff need to take after having a sexual assault reported, they regret that any action has to be taken at all. The second half of the no-win situation involves the victims' options after the report has been made. That is, the victim is usually either sent to protective custody or transferred to another facility (Chonco, 1989). In either case, the victim is further victimized via segregation from the general population or by being transferred to another facility where the "I've been raped and reported it" label is sure to follow.

Another reason for nonreport of sexual assault is that inmate victims might be embarrassed to admit they were forced into a sexual act or raped. Often these victims are harassed with labels of "homo" or of being a "punk" (Smith and Batiuk, 1989). There is a stigma that is primarily associated with male inmates who are victimized. A desire to avoid this negative label might cause an inmate to not report a rape in order to avoid being labeled as a "snitch" (Eigenberg, 1994). Victims might also fail to report their victimization because they would be admitting weakness to the sexual aggressor (Toch, 1977). Often prison subcultural norms and codes of conduct serve as a barrier to reporting sexual assault. For example, Wooden and Parker (1982) stated:

> The prison subcultural norms and codes of conduct are rigid and traditional. Based primarily on power and dominance with the physically strong preying on the weak, the convicts settle their own disputes and handle their own social problems. The guards and prison officials encourage this rule. . . . Patterns of intimidation, exploitation, and even sexual assault are likely not brought to the attention of the guards. (33)

Building on this idea, Smith and Batiuk (1989) discussed underreporting of sexual assaults as an effect of the "inmate code of conduct": "This pervasive fear of sexual victimization leads to a performance which emphasizes strength and masculinity and de-emphasizes characteristics which are considered weak or feminine. The new inmate learns quickly that there are a wide range of behaviors and emotions which he must not communicate" (32).

STRATEGIES USED BY VICTIMS
TO PROTECT AGAINST FORCED SEX

Inmates who might be considered targets for sexual assault might fight off possible assaults by showing strong masculine behavior, or "fronting," by physically fighting back or by attempting to sexually assault another inmate (as a way to display their own strength). To defend against unwanted sexual attacks, the targets might present, or front, a strong masculine, even macho demeanor. This masculine presentation of self is often believed to mask what might be considered by other inmates as feminine (or "femme") characteristics or simply boy-like features. In Smith and Batiuk (1989), two inmates discussed the need to front their masculinity and not portray any signs of weakness or emotions:

> You can't show any fear, they pick up on that. You gotta show strength. You gotta say it in a strong way and look 'em in the eye. Never look down, like you're afraid to look 'em in the eye. That's a sign of weakness. I'd never hug a friend. Let's say he got a parole and I was happy for him. I'd still play it cool with him. You can't do any physical contact. . . . If you show people that you care about them or are Mr. Niceguy, that will get you in trouble. They will come after you to get whatever you got, like vultures swooping in. Another thing is to never show fear or any kind of weakness. You gotta be a man all the time, and a man according to the standards in here. (33)

Masking of feminine or boylike characteristics might not be as easy as putting up a tough front, however. Some targets for sexual assault turn to violence as a way to protect themselves from being victimized (Chonco, 1989; Lockwood, 1980a).

One way some potential targets might strive to present a tough, masculine image is to use tough talk, physical aggression, or violence toward others to discourage forced sexual attacks. Tough talk means learning and using the prison argot. Physical aggression or violence might be in the form of using a knife to attack an aggressor, attempting to turn the tables and physically or sexually assault an inmate who attempts to victimize them, or simply standing up to an aggressor. Sykes (1958) identified an inmate's need to fight back as a form of protection early on, writing: "Sooner or later he will be 'tested' — that someone will 'push' him to see how far they can go and that he must be prepared to fight for the safety of his person and his possessions. If he should fail, he will thereafter be an object of contempt, constantly in danger of being attacked by other inmates who view him as an obvious victim" (77–78).

In an inmate interview, Chonco (1989) also identified the need for a potential victim to fight back to avoid victimization:

> If an inmate has to survive in prison, he has to learn to fight or else he will be a faggot until he leaves the joint. The image of a faggot is not a good one because if he leaves a joint still chickening out to fight, if he comes back again he will be a victim. . . . (This guy) told me that if any guy wants to fuck me or fucks with me I must stick him up. "If you do so," this guy says, "no son of a bitch will bother you." I took his advice and no guys ever bothered me again. (78)

In the instance when the target inmate (i.e., potential victim) uses violence/force against the aggressor, the victim then becomes the victimizer. Examples of the victim becoming the victimizer are illustrated in the following excerpts from two separate studies. First, Wooden and Parker (1982) provided an example of a homosexual victim's violent response to sexual intimidation: "A newly arrived homosexual, using a razor, slashed the face of a black jocker who had been intimidating him" (42). Additionally, Groth (1979) showed that coerced sex in prison might be revenge or retaliation, the idea that the victim becomes the victimizer. He highlighted a revenge case utilizing the story of Carlos, a twenty-five-year-old Puerto Rican who raped a twenty-three-year-old inmate.

> He was talking about my race, calling me a Puerto Rican pig and a punk. He made comments about my mother. I told him I'd get him when I had the chance. . . . I cornered him in the showers. . . . He was real scared. . . . I told him, "You're going to give me some ass," and I fucked him. It wasn't for sex. I was mad. I wanted to prove who I was and what he was. (127–128)

Thus, victims who become victimizers might not limit their violent response to physical forms of assault but might even respond with forced sexual assaults. In the example above, the victim of verbal sexual assault becomes quietly aggressive as a coping strategy, and this manifested into the behavior of a sexual perpetrator (Cotton and Groth, 1982). Some inmates, however, unwilling or unable to fight against sexual aggressors, consent to sexual victimization to avoid additional and more severe forms of victimization, including economic exploitation, rape, or murder (Nacci and Kane, 1983, 1984b). This leads into our next discussion on strategies used by aggressors to coerce inmates into having sex.

STRATEGIES USED BY PERPETRATORS TO PRESSURE OR FORCE SEX

Reasons and strategies used by perpetrators to pressure or force other inmates into sexual activities include using a "set-up team" (Chonco, 1989), creating power relationships (Cotton and Groth, 1982), and exploitation (Lockwood, 1982). The goal of sexual aggressors is to show who is in control—that is, to show aggression in a power relationship (Cotton and Groth, 1982). This is not unlike sexual assault in the free community. Inmates who sexually assault other inmates might also engage in sexual assaults or gang rapes as a means to demonstrate their status or gain some group/gang affiliation (Groth, 1979). An inmate might also become a sexual aggressor as a means of gaining status, dominating others, or even (as we saw above in the victim becoming the victimizer) revenge (Cotton and Groth, 1982).

A set-up team includes a group of inmates that plays certain roles, from targeting a victim to completion of the victimization in a planned sexual assault. Several inmates are needed to play the roles of "observers, contacts, turners, and pointmen" for the different stages of "observation, selection, testing, approaching, and actual victimization" (Chonco, 1989: 75). Inmates' discussion of the steps involved in a planned sexual assault have been reported as:

> *Observation:* A guy who knows nothing about prison is followed around by these guys who think they know a lot. They tail him so that they pick something about him they think will make their mission easy. . . . I mean screwing him.
>
> *Selection:* Guys who are usually selected for victimization are those whose background information is weak. I mean the guys who consciously showed fear, and in trying to suppress that fear he talks too much and tries to be nice or friendly to inmates he meets.
>
> *Testing/Approaching:* Some other guys like to make friends with newcomers, especially those guys who know nothing about the joint. Them guys give the newcomer things, and the newcomer, without using his mind, accepts the fucking favors. An inmate who is a fool enough to trust the guys in the joint gets stung when his buddy turns against him. I mean when the other guy asks the other dude to produce. . . . I mean when he asks him to sleep with him. (Chonco, 1989: 75–78)

During the actual victimization stage, the target is usually assaulted in what is referred to as a "trouble spot" or a location such as a bathroom, shower, gymnasium, or cell, where correctional officers and others who might intervene are unlikely to be watching (Chonco, 1989: 76). As Chonco explains, "The pointman stands guard and watches whether the target does sexual favors for other inmates or whether he has a record of being sexually assaulted by other inmates" (76).

Using a set-up team is only one example of sexual assaults being completed as a group effort. There is also the possibility that inmates will be gang-raped. In the following excerpt, one inmate provides his personal experience of being gang-raped in prison when four offenders sexually assaulted him and his cellmate as a means of showing the victims "who's boss" (Groth, 1979):

The two of us were in our cell, and four black dudes came in. They said, "We're the Black Power." . . . One guy pulled out his cock and told me to suck him or he would kill me. . . . While I was blowing him, I had to massage another guy's cock; then this guy screwed me up the ass. All four guys took turns on me and my cellmate. When they were finished, they said, "Now you know who's boss. If you rat on us we'll break your arms and legs." (129)

The notion of showing the victim who is in control is not limited to these two examples of coerced sex by groups of aggressors. Instead, aggressors on an individual level often use control or a power relationship to force sex. Moreover, an individual inmate knows that by sexually assaulting or simply degrading another inmate, he can gain status for himself.

VICTIM AND PERPETRATOR CHARACTERISTICS

Characteristics of victims and perpetrators of sexual assault are well documented in criminal justice and corrections literature. Being able to recognize characteristics that might be helpful in targeting potential victims or aggressors of sexual assault is important from a policy and a programming standpoint. For example, Donaldson (1995: n.p.) suggests, "If most (victim characteristics) apply, rape becomes a probability."

In general, perpetrators of sexual assault are more likely to be older than their victims yet younger than the general population of the institution (Chonco, 1989). Furthermore, although many researchers characterize perpetrators to be race-defined, one should note that this simply makes the probability of being a sexual aggressor more or less likely. It does not mean or even suggest that all perpetrators are African American, nor in the same vein does it prove that all victims are white. In fact, Chonco (1989) suggests that findings of race-defined characteristics are due to the fact that black inmates start criminality at a very early age and are likely to be more familiar with institutional life and culture. However, Chonco suggests that this is probably also a true characterization for white inmates who are aggressors.

What is more, one should recognize that all inmates who possess many of the characteristics described are susceptible to being sexually assaulted. In fact, very recently a judge in Tampa, Florida, exercised her discretion in sentencing to keep a probable target for sexual assault out of prison and instead sentenced the offender to probation. According to a transcript from the sentencing hearing, the judge suggested, "He's a small, thin, white man with curly dark hair, and I suspect he would certainly become a target in the Florida state prison system" (*Pensacola News Journal*, January 7, 2001: 2A). However, after less than one month, the judge publicly apologized for making the statement, saying, "Race is never an issue in [my] courtroom" (*St. Petersburg Times*, January 27, 2001: 3B). One might argue the issue seems to be that the judge would have used the same reasoning and discretion in sentencing if the offender had been small, thin, and nonwhite. Again, this shows the importance of recognizing that all inmates who possess many of these target characteristics are susceptible to being sexually assaulted.

EMOTIONAL AND PHYSICAL CONSEQUENCES OF INCIDENTS

It is well known that victims of sexual assault, whether in prison or not, experience a wide range of negative emotional and physical consequences. Victims are likely to experience "physical, emotional, cognitive, psychological, social and sexual" problems associated with sexual assault (Cotton and Groth, 1982: 51). Victims who physically fight back in an attempt to avoid rape are additionally susceptible to being injured or even murdered. Furthermore, the possible health risks associated with sex in prison are staggering. The implications related to inmate sexual assault are confounding not only for the inmates themselves but also for the entire inmate population and the general public.

When focusing specifically on sexual assault of male prison inmates, a number of researchers have argued that the majority of the emotional and psychological consequences of sexual assault concern the masculinity, or loss thereof, of the victimized inmate (Cotton and Groth, 1982; Scacco, 1982; Sykes, 1958). Psychological and emotional stresses may also precede an actual sexual assault. Prior to a "successful" victimization, many targets find it necessary to constantly present a masculine front, always be watchful of potential attacks, and also be wary of the prison culture. In essence, in their attempts to prevent being targeted for sexual victimization, inmates suffer under persistent emotional stresses. Dumond (1992) recognized the need to study the psychological and emotional implications of sexual assault at the individual victim level: "Not only does the terror, trauma and victimization impact upon the victim, but the additional components of one's identity and sense of self must be considered. . . . There is an increase of fear, loss of status and feminization, including the threat of continued revictimization" (141). Additionally, the threat of victimization is one that the victim will have to deal with both prior to victimization and after it (Chonco, 1989; Lockwood, 1978). That is, once an inmate is a victim of sexual assault (also known as being "turned out"), that inmate will probably always be a target for sexual aggression (Donaldson, 1995; Lockwood, 1980a).

Victims who physically fight back to fend off sexual aggressors are susceptible to being significantly injured, in addition to having to deal with the stressors associated with imitating an aggressor. In fact, when analyzing homicides at the federal institution in Lewisburg, Pennsylvania, Nacci (1978) reported that five out of eight homicides (62.5 percent) were motivated by homosexual activity. That is, "unre-quited love, adultery, and pressuring for sex" were suggested as causes of the homicides (30). In this example, the victims who became victim-izers would then have to face both the legal (e.g., additional sentence) and social consequences of their violent actions. Hence, when victims or potential victims fight back, there exists the potential for loss of inmate safety, in addition to heightened personal trauma (Moss, Hosford, and Anderson, 1979).

Health risks associated with prison sex, namely HIV/AIDS, were a major focus of prison sex research in the 1980s and 1990s (Tewksbury and West, 2000). The majority of the HIV/AIDS research looked at "identifying rates of infection among inmates, patterns in the rates of infected inmates, and information about how potential vectors of trans-mission could be controlled in prisons and jails . . . [and] management issues that HIV/AIDS presented for correctional administrators" (Tewksbury and West, 2000: 370–371). Again, the implications associ-ated with the spread of HIV/AIDS among prisoners, whether they are raped or are involved in consensual sex relationships, reach far beyond the prison walls. Very simply, most inmates who are, or become, infect-ed while incarcerated will be released from prison. Many of these inmates might have families to return to when they are released. The risk of HIV/AIDS is simply one element that should focus the need for, and move toward, prevention of prison sexual assault.

POLICY RECOMMENDATIONS AND FUTURE RESEARCH

Policy recommendations related to nonconsensual sex in prison have been limited because most such incidents are never reported. This lack of reporting has hindered the ability of correctional officials to proactively address the issue (Cotton and Groth, 1982), yet this need not be the case. This section identifies a number of policy suggestions that may aid correctional administrators in the prevention of prison sexual assaults and the provision of victim services.

Prevention of prison sexual assault must be a two-pronged approach of intervention (or social programming) and administrative enforcement of institutional rules such that the two entities are complementary and form a complete prevention package. Using only a social approach for inmates will not affect the lack of concern by staff, which might not solve the problem of protecting targets in assault situations. For example, inmates in the Wooden and Parker study (1982: 120) suggested that as a means of "humanizing the plight of these sexual victims" (a social aftercare program), staff attitudes must change (administrative regulation). The two-pronged approach encompasses what Smith and Batiuk (1989) call looking at the prison setting "holistically" to show that the threat of sexual violence dominates all facets of the prison.

Prevention programming and victim services are important on an individual level so that inmates might be educated on how to cope with rape trauma and the range of consequences of being raped. Intervention programming could teach psychological and coping strategies that might help inmates manage sexual assault peacefully instead of violently. Lockwood (1982) highlights the need for programs to help inmates deal peaceably with attacks of verbal and physical aggression. He states, "Programs aimed at reducing violence can train participants to respond assertively to unwanted approaches in ways that diminish subsequent escalation" (259). Such programs are examples of human relations training. Goals of the training are to increase interpersonal skills, relieve interpersonal or group tensions, develop individual and group problem-solving skills, and applying these skills to daily life (Lockwood, 1982). Additional educational and vocational training programs, treatment-oriented interventions, and cooperative work experiences might all be utilized as individual or inmate-group strategies to prevent both sexual and physical assaults in prison.

Although there exists a need for prevention, intervention, and victim services for inmates, there is also a need for correctional administrators to implement additional and advanced training for institutional staff. Training should include education on the dynamics and implications of sexual assault (e.g., victim rape trauma) and training on how to both identify and moderate high-risk situations. These are not new ideas. Cotton (Cotton and Groth, 1982) suggests the need for staff to be comfortable dealing with sexual assault and that the facility should develop a model protocol for crisis intervention and train staff members accordingly. Further, increased surveillance in high-risk areas, such as showers, recreation room, and dorms, is imperative (Cotton and Groth, 1982). Training focused on prevention programming targeted at correctional officers should present a proactive approach that also strives to reduce the possibility of victims becoming victimizers. Finally, in a discretionary decision, administrators might also study the implications of segregating inmates who are at high risk of being a target of sexual assault. Inmates themselves have suggested the need to segregate young and passive inmates (Wooden and Parker, 1982). Administrators may also evaluate whether the segregation of nonviolent and violent inmates might reduce the possibility of sexual assaults.

Policy recommendations to prevent prison sexual assaults must provide both a social service component (prevention, intervention, and victim services) and an administrative component (education, training, and facility rule development and enforcement). Only policies that implement this two-pronged approach are likely to be proactive in preventing prison sexual assault.

CONCLUSION

Nonconsensual sexual behavior pertains less to sex and sexuality and more toward violent behavior, power, and control. Therefore, nonconsensual sex in prison is a major policy issue for correctional administrators, an important and common area of concern for inmates, and yet a relatively infrequently studied and discussed issue. Research specifically addressing nonconsensual sex among prison inmates has been infrequent and often plagued by methodological difficulties. However, scholars and practitioners alike have some understanding of the rate at which such instances occur, who is likely to be involved, and typical dynamics of sexually assaultive incidents.

The fact that nonconsensual sex happens, and happens with some frequency, in U.S. correctional institutions is one of the most serious problems that plagues the criminal justice system. This is a problem that, while it may not be realistic to totally eliminate, can be reduced and controlled. The challenge for practitioners is to use the research that is available to develop prevention, intervention, and victim services to better manage this dilemma. The challenge for scholars is to find ways to produce valid and reliable research concerning nonconsensual sex in prisons. Both challenges are considerable, but both are also very important.

NOTES

1. Mrs. O'Hare is an inmate at the institution and was convicted under the "special legislation enacted during the war" (Fishman, 1968: 97).

2. In this study, the author distinguishes between sexual coercion (verbal pressure tactics) and sexual assault (rape, forced anal, or oral sex).

4

PRISON STAFF AND MALE RAPE

Helen M. Eigenberg

I first began to study correctional officers' attitudes toward male rape in prison in the early 1990s. One important factor that contributed to my interest in this area was my prior experience working in the field. I was employed for approximately five years in the 1980s in a relatively safe, federal, medium-security male facility. As a former correctional officer and case manager, I was acutely aware of the nonresponsive nature of staff to inmate-on-inmate rape. I remember watching young men who smelled awful because they would not go near a communal shower and men who stayed up all night, every night, watching television because they were afraid to go to sleep in the dormitory-style housing unit. Although I was acutely aware that many of these men were either in danger or felt unsafe, I had no solutions to offer them. Instead, I remember all too well counseling inmates who were being targeted for victimization that they had two choices. In the prison vernacular, we told them to "fight or fuck." At the same time, we would caution them that fighting was a rule violation and that they would be punished—possibly losing good time or parole dates as a sanction for "their" violence. I am ashamed that I actually used these words but also recognize that I, like other staff, had been provided with no tools to deal with the problem.

I also remember instances where staff took a more active role in contributing to the problem. For example, I recall the constant barrage of insults handed out to inmates who had "chosen" to submit to sexually coercive behavior. Both staff and inmates ridiculed them, calling them by female pronouns and using other derogatory names for them (e.g., punks, bitches, and queens). I remember rare occasions when staff would use housing assignments to punish inmates by placing them in secure cells with known predators. I also remember numerous instances where other officers and/or I stumbled upon inmates engaged in sexual activities with each other and chose to ignore it. Embarrassed to confront the situation, (many of us justified looking the other way by assuming that these acts were consensual) (because of no overt signs of coercion) and concluded that two grown adults should not be punished for engaging in same-sex behavior. I now wonder how many of these acts were truly consensual. These experiences working in the field led me to hypothesize that correctional staff were part of the problem—that in some ways, both covertly and overtly, they contributed to a rape-prone atmosphere in male prisons. This hypothesis, however, also led me to believe that correctional staff, especially correctional officers, can be part of the solution. My research has led me to explore these ideas in a more systematic fashion.

This chapter reviews the literature associated with correctional officers and male rape in prison.[1] It concentrates on correctional officers for several reasons. First, correctional officers supposedly have some influence over inmates because of the amount of contact between the two groups (Guenther and Guenther, 1974; Peretti and Hooker, 1976; Philliber, 1987).[2] Second, literature on female rape victims in the community suggests that police response has an impact on reporting (Feldman-Summers and Palmer, 1980; Field, 1978; Karmen, 1990; Weis and Borges, 1973; White and Mosher, 1986). Therefore, it is reasonable to assume that correctional officers, like police officers, may affect reporting practices of inmate victims. For example, it seems likely that inmates will refuse to report rapes if the administration refuses to treat the issue seriously and/or take actions against perpetrators. Finally, correctional administrators can develop strategies that influence how correctional officers respond to rape. Although affecting change is always problematic, it would seem logical to assume that the actions of correctional officers are more directly amenable to administrative control than are those of inmates. Thus, if officers appear to be part of the problem, if they appear to facilitate stigmatization of victims, or if their actions facilitate victimization, then administrators may be able to devise strategies to rectify the problem.

RESPONSES BY CORRECTIONAL OFFICERS

It is odd that research on male rape in prisons has basically ignored the role of correctional officers given their critical role in the institutional hierarchy. The influence that officers have over inmates can occur as a result of both formal and informal means of social control. It is clear that correctional officers are the police of the prison (Crouch and Marquart, 1980; Lombardo, 1981; Poole and Regoli, 1980) and that formal rule enforcement is one of their primary functions. Officers affect formal sanctions because they are the individuals who largely are responsible for introducing a case into the prison disciplinary system. In prisons, both consensual homosexual acts and rapes are prohibited and subject to disciplinary sanctions, and correctional officers are responsible for charging violators when this type of behavior is encountered. Yet it is not clear whether most officers regularly report these infractions or whether they use their discretionary power and ignore some violations.

At one end of the continuum, proactive, well-trained officers might recognize the symptoms of inmates who have been raped and take appropriate actions such as making medical and psychological referrals, even if an inmate will not self-identify as a rape victim. Vigilant officers with good observational skills might identify inmates who are being targeted and take preventative actions such as increasing their patrols of the area or requesting that an inmate be transferred to another cell block. Hence, officers might be able to prevent some rapes or at least make sure that victims get adequate services. At the other end of the continuum, some officers may use rape or the threat of sexual violence to control inmates, or officers may tolerate coercive acts because they facilitate division among inmates, making them more manageable.

There is very little research that actually examines officers' responses to rape in prison. One of the earliest studies conducted by Davis (1968) examined male rape in the Philadelphia prison system. Although Davis reportedly interviewed 561 custodial employees, he provided little detail about any findings derived from officers. He did, however, report that interviews with more than 3,000 inmates suggested that correctional officers' responses were nonresponsive. He stated that inmates reported a lack of confidence in administrative responses. Specifically, inmates claimed that correctional officers failed to adequately supervise inmates and urged inmates not to press charges against their assailants. Inmates felt that officers would be unable to protect them from retaliation if they reported the rape and the most common response by the officers would be placing the victim in protective custody where they generally ended up staying for their entire sentence. Davis (1968) also reported that many "homosexual liaisons" developed after inmates were gang-raped or threatened with gang rape, and argued that prison officials are "too quick to label such activities 'consensual'" (70). As such, Davis was one of the first researchers to acknowledge that rape is often redefined as homosexuality and treated like sex rather than aggressive behavior.

Wooden and Parker (1982) also interviewed more than 200 inmates and a handful of correctional officers (7). The small number of officers makes this information highly suspect. Nonetheless, Wooden and Parker reported that officers tended to demonstrate a lenient approach toward homosexuality. Furthermore, the inmates in the study claimed staff were insensitive to the problems of homosexual inmates and did not try to protect them.

Lockwood (1980b) concentrated on studying inmate victimization in New York State prisons. In contrast to his rigorous analysis of victims, Lockwood provided no quantitative data on his study of correctional officers. Nonetheless, he concluded that staff knew about many incidents of sexual assault but that "staff who achieve solutions must often be persistent, vocal (and to other staff, obnoxious) advocates of prisoners' welfare" (130). He also reported that officers sometimes ignored or encouraged fighting when inmates were defending themselves against rape or coercive sexual pressure.

A survey of federal correctional officers was one of the first studies to report empirical data regarding correctional officers' response to rape in prison. Nacci and Kane (1983, 1984a, 1984b) surveyed 500 correctional officers in seventeen federal institutions. They found that inmates reported feeling less risk of rape when officers were satisfied with their jobs (1983: 49). Officers also indicated they were slightly more willing to prevent rape than to deter homosexuality (which is especially problematic if some rapes are being committed under the guise of consenting homosexual acts). And although some research indicates that bisexual and homosexual inmates are victimized more frequently (Lockwood, 1980b; Nacci and Kane, 1983, 1984a, 1984b; Wooden and Parker, 1982), officers in the Nacci and Kane survey reported that they were more willing to protect heterosexual inmates from rape. The authors interpreted these findings as evidence that officers equated bi/homosexuality with voluntary participation.

More recently, research on 166 correctional officers employed by the Texas Department of Corrections (Eigenberg, 1989, 1994) found that the overwhelming majority of officers (97 percent) believed that they should try to prevent rape. The majority of officers (73 percent) also indicated that inmates were unwilling to report rapes to correctional staff. Officers were just as likely to report that they should protect heterosexuals (73 percent) as they should homosexuals (71 percent).

Most of them endorsed proactive responses to rape such as writing disciplinary reports when possible (92 percent), refusing to manipulate cell assignments to expose inmates to the threat of rape (93 percent), and making referrals to protective custody (69 percent). Interestingly, only about half of the officers (48 percent) indicated that they should talk to new inmates about the risk of sexual assault.

A study of 209 correctional officers employed by a Midwestern rural state in 1991 indicates similar patterns (Eigenberg, 2000b). Officers were asked to respond to five statements that examined their responsiveness to consensual sexual acts and another five statements addressing rape to determine if they were more lenient toward consensual same-sex sexual acts. Officers generally indicated a willingness to respond to both types of acts, but they were consistently less apt to endorse proactive responses to consensual homosexuality than to rape. The overwhelming majority of officers (96 percent) reported that they should do everything they could to prevent rape, including patrolling areas (98 percent), issuing disciplinary reports (99 percent), and encouraging inmates to report sexual assaults (98 percent). Likewise, the vast majority of officers (85 percent) recommended that officers should do everything possible to prevent consensual sexual activities, including patrolling areas (93 percent), issuing disciplinary reports (94 percent), and encouraging inmates to report these activities (81 percent). However, here again, officers were reluctant to talk to inmates about either types of acts. About 40 percent of the officers did not think they should talk to inmates about the risk of sexual assault, and 36 percent believed they should not discuss consensual sexual acts with inmates in an attempt to discourage this behavior.

In this same study, officers were also asked several questions to determine whether they had ignored any type of sexual activity in the past five years and whether they had actual experiences writing incident reports for this type of behavior. The majority of the officers had never written an incident report involving sexual activity, although 8 percent of them admitted ignoring some type of sexual behavior in the preceding five years. Officers were most apt to have written a disciplinary report for prostitution (57 percent) or consensual sexual acts (38 percent) and least apt to have written reports for rape (14 percent).

In sum, research suggests most officers report that they should or would respond to acts of homosexuality and rape (Eigenberg, 1994, 2000a; Nacci and Kane, 1983, 1984a, 1984b). This finding is in direct contradiction to the literature based on inmate populations, which contends that correctional officers are *not* responsive and that they contribute to rape in prisons (Davis, 1968; Lockwood, 1982; Wooden and Parker, 1982). There are several possible explanations that may account for this apparent contradiction.

First, officers may report that they respond to rape because they believe they are supposed to say they take actions to ensure the safety of inmates. Second, perhaps officers are quite willing to respond to acts of rape, but like police officers in the community, they are unable to respond to most sexual assaults because of the hidden nature of the assault. Translated, correctional officers are not able to catch many inmates in the act. As a result, officers may end up responding only to those assaults that are reported by victims, and many (most) inmates may fail to report their victimization. Finally, officers may consider themselves proactive in their responses but may not respond to acts of rape because they fail to define many types of sexual assaults as rape. Officers' definitions of rape are key because officers cannot write disciplinary reports or secure crisis intervention services for inmates if they fail to define them as victims in the first place. In other words, it will be difficult to understand how officers react—both formally and informally—unless we have a better understanding of their definition of the situation.

OFFICERS' DEFINITIONS OF RAPE

There is some evidence that correctional officers' definitions of rape may blur the lines between rape and consensual homosexuality. This is reflected in the following excerpt from one interview with an officer: "Q: Do you feel that homosexual acts between consenting adults are wrong? A: No, as long as no force is used" (Wooden and Parker, 1982: 196). As this quote clearly demonstrates, it may not be easy to distinguish rapes from consensual sexual assaults because rape in prison often relies upon extortion techniques where coercion is more important than outright force. Thus, some officers may fail to define some acts of rape simply because a knife is not at a man's throat during the sexual act. When rape is defined as consensual sexuality, victims are not really victimized and rape is just sex.

The tendency to define rape as consensual sexuality has a rich tradition in the literature on prison homosexuality, which historically relied upon the concept of situational homosexuality. This body of literature asserted that situational homosexuality occurred when heterosexual men engaged in sex with other men because of the situational nature of their sexual deprivation. Researchers also discussed how some hetero-sexual inmates are seduced into situational homosexuality (Fishman, 1951; Scacco, 1975; Vedder and King, 1967; Weiss and Friar, 1974). This process was described according to the following scenario: New inmates are offered protection, loans, gifts, or commissary. Shortly thereafter, these inmates are approached sexually. Aggressive inmates then require the recipient of these gifts to participate in sexual acts unless the recipient repays the loans, reimburses inmates for the com-missary, or gives up the protection. Thus, more sophisticated inmates coerce or physically threaten other inmates into participating in sexual behavior. However, the literature failed to label this process rape and instead described it as situational homosexuality. Any discussion of truly consensual situational homosexuality or bisexuality was rare (Eigenberg, 1992).

This literature on situational homosexuality describes two very dif-ferent categories of participants: victims and rapists. Victims are referred to as punks (Kirkham, 1971; Sykes, 1958), made homosexuals (Buffum, 1972), involuntary recruits (Sagarin, 1976), and jailhouse turnouts (Sagarin, 1976). They are highly stigmatized as effeminate men and homosexuals (which for many people are one and the same). In contrast, rapists are referred to in exaggerated masculine terms such as wolves (Kirkham, 1971; Sykes, 1958), jockers (Buffum, 1972), and voluntary aggressors (Sagarin, 1976). Therefore, those men who act consistently with the masculine role—as sexual aggressors—are described as real men who need sex and lose control of their sexuality. These men escape stigmatization as the attitude that boys will be boys prevails.

This body of work also defines prostitutes (men who engage in homosexual behavior to gain certain goods) as situational homosexuals. These men also are stigmatized but less so than men who are raped. After all, at least prostitutes sell their bodies instead of being forced into sexual acts, although it is not clear whether all, or even most, pros-titution is voluntary. Some prostitutes may be willing entrepreneurs, but the seduction process described previously also indicates that some of these men are unable to protect themselves from rape and sexual exploitation. Therefore, perhaps some prostitutes are rape victims who simply choose to "make the best of a bad situation" by accepting gifts or commissary from their rapists (Eigenberg, 1992).

The literature also suggests that some men look for protection by hooking up with a more powerful protector (Wooden and Parker, 1982). Targets of sexual aggression make an alliance with dominant men who are perceived as heterosexuals and trade their bodies in exchange for protection from the larger inmate population. In other words, a weaker inmate who is afraid makes an alliance that he will submit to a single perpetrator rather than taking a chance of being victimized by other (even more apprehensible) predators or of being gang-raped. In exchange for sex and other favors (often mimicking those of a traditional female role—e.g., ironing clothes, doing laundry, and keeping his cell clean), the more powerful inmate provides protection from assaults by other inmates, at least until the protector tires of the weaker inmate's services. At that time he may, without notice, trade him to another protector or replace him with a younger "wife."

This body of literature, then, suggests a strong tendency among inmates to blur the lines between consensual sexuality and male rape in prison. It also appears that much of the rape in facilities occurs by the use of coercive tactics. It is not clear, however, whether correctional officers exhibit these same tendencies.

A study of 209 correctional officers employed by a Midwestern rural state in 1991 provides insight into officers' definitions of rape (Eigenberg, 2000b). Six vignettes were used to determine what type of acts officers viewed as rape. The use of vignettes made it possible to examine the situational context of victimization by asking officers to apply their definitions of rape to concrete situations. These vignettes involved two inmates: Smith and Jones. In the first situation, inmate Jones physically overpowers inmate Smith and has sex with Smith. In the second situation, inmate Jones threatens to kill inmate Smith unless he engages in sexual acts. In the third situation, Jones threatens to tell other inmates that inmate Smith is a snitch (informant). In another situation, Smith is identified as a snitch and Jones offers to provide protection in exchange for sexual acts. The fifth situation is identical to the prior (fourth) situation, except that Smith demands cigarettes when he "agrees" to participate in sexual acts in exchange for protection. Finally, in the last vignette, Smith borrows cigarettes and cannot pay off his debt. Jones tells Smith that he can get beat up or participate in sexual acts. Each of these scenarios ends with the statement, "Smith has been raped." Officers who evidenced high agreement with these statements embraced a more proactive definition of rape and recognized that rape may occur in response to physical threats or force, but they also defined rape when more sophisticated means of coercion were used.

The overwhelming majority of officers believed that an inmate had been raped when he was physically overpowered or threatened with bodily harm (95 percent and 96 percent, respectively). Yet officers were less sure when coercion was used to accomplish rape. About three-fourths (74 percent) of the officers believed it was rape when an inmate threatened to identify another inmate as a snitch in order to secure sexual acts. Likewise, most officers (73 percent) defined the situation as rape when an inmate was forced to choose between paying off a debt with sexual acts or receiving a beating. Interestingly, officers appeared to be less willing to define acts as rape when the victims were identified as informants. About two-thirds (64 percent) of the officers defined the situation as rape when a snitch engaged in sexual acts in exchange for protection, and only slightly more than half (56 percent) believed it was rape when the inmate informant demanded cigarettes after engaging in sex in exchange for protection. Thus, a considerable proportion of correctional officers in this study were not willing to define assaultive acts as rape when these acts were coercive in nature.

In addition to these vignettes, officers in the study were asked a variety of questions relating to their definitions of homosexuality and prostitution. Interestingly, their definitions of prostitution demonstrate confusion regarding whether it is a coercive enterprise. The overwhelming majority of officers (84 percent) reported that prostitutes in prison *willingly* participate in sexual acts in exchange for material goods. Likewise, almost all officers (93 percent) indicated that inmate prostitutes engage in sexual acts of their own free will. Ironically, however, almost all of them (98 percent) reported that prostitutes engage in sexual acts for protection. Finally, the overwhelming majority (96 percent) of officers reported that it was sometimes difficult to tell whether inmates were being forced to participate in sexual acts or if they were willing partners in consensual sexual activities. Therefore, some empirical evidence shows that officers' definitions of rape are not clear, especially when the assault relies upon coercion rather than force.

CORRECTIONAL OFFICERS' ATTITUDES TOWARD VICTIMS

The research on correctional officers' definitions of rape is particularly informative when compared to research on the rape of women in the community. This body of research on women suggests that definitions of rape are highly situational and dependent upon a variety of factors, including the relationship between the offender and the victim and the behavior of the victim (see Scully, 1990). Furthermore, this literature also finds that police officers' responses to rape are affected by these situational variables. Police officers are often skeptical of female victims who fail to report the crime immediately following the rape (Amir, 1971; Bienen and Field, 1980; Burgess and Holmstrom, 1974c; Gager and Schurr, 1976; LeDoux and Hazelwood, 1985; Weis and Borges, 1973). Women who are raped are supposed to appear victimized. They are to be upset and show "signs of violence and resistance: dirty and torn clothes, bruises, and other evidence of forceful intercourse" (Weis and Borges, 1973: 102). Victims are less likely to be believed by officials if they have had prior social contact with their rapists, if they consume alcohol or drugs at the time of the rape, or if they refuse a medical examination (Feldman-Summers and Palmer, 1980; Russell, 1984; Weis and Borges, 1973; White and Mosher, 1986).

Unfortunately, victims who fail to conform to the expectations of police officers may have less credibility. Hence, police officers may fail to define these assaults as rape and refuse to act accordingly. In other words, police officers do not respond to some acts of rape because they fail to define certain kinds of rapes as sexual assaults (Amir, 1971; Bienen and Field, 1980; Burgess and Holmstrom, 1974c; Campbell and Johnson, 1997; Feldman-Summers and Palmer, 1980; Gager and Schurr, 1976; Russell, 1984; Weis and Borges, 1973; White and Mosher, 1986).

Like police officers, correctional officers' definitions of rape may be highly situational and may be affected by more general social attitudes about victim precipitation. Moreover, officers' definitions of rape may be impacted by victim blaming because the very concept of victim precipitation shifts the focus from the coercive nature of the act and emphasizes the ways in which the victim has participated in a consensual act of sex. Thus, just as female victims in the community have had rape redefined as consensual sexual activity, male rape victims are also rendered invisible when sexual assaults are redefined as consensual homosexual behavior.

There is some empirical evidence that correctional officers are willing to blame at least some men for their victimization, and there is a tendency to create "legitimate" victims. For example, in the study of Texas correctional officers (Eigenberg, 1994), about half of the officers (46.4 percent) believed some victims deserved to be raped. Approximately one-third (33.7 percent) of the officers believed rape victims were weak, and about one-sixth (14.9 percent) of them believed male rape victims were homosexuals. These findings also were supported by research on officers in a Midwestern state (Eigenberg, 2000b). Although officers in that study appeared to be somewhat less apt to blame victims, there were areas of concern. Twelve percent of the officers believed that some inmates deserved to be raped because of the way they acted. Likewise, 16 percent of officers indicated that homo-sexual inmates got what they deserved if they were raped, and 17 per-cent reported that inmates deserved to be raped if they dressed or talked in feminine ways. Almost one-fourth of the officers believed that inmates deserved to be raped if they previously engaged in consensual sexual acts in prison or if they took money or cigarettes for consensual sexual acts prior to a rape (23 percent and 24 percent, respectively).

The study on correctional officers in Texas also suggested that they endorsed somewhat rigid definitions of victims (Eigenberg, 1989). Officers were asked whether they were likely to believe an inmate who told them they had been raped. Officers were most apt to believe that an inmate had been raped if the inmate was young or in debt.

The tendency to believe young men is consistent with victimization data that suggest that young men and inmates with no prior prison expe-rience are more frequently victims of rape (Lockwood, 1980b; Nacci and Kane, 1983, 1984b; Scacco, 1975; Vedder and King, 1967; Weiss and Friar, 1974). It also is consistent with research that describes how men are tricked into coercive sexual relationships through loans. Young and naive inmates may, in fact, be more vulnerable to victimization. However, it also is possible that officers are more willing to define these men as victims, which affects who reports and who is believed when they report. This statement may also apply to officers' beliefs about the victimization of muscular men. Stereotypes and conventional wisdom dictate that rape victims are effeminate—not hypermasculine or muscular. Victimization data also indicate that individuals with femi-nine traits are frequently viewed as high-risk targets for victimization (Lockwood, 1980b; Nacci and Kane, 1983, 1984b; Scacco, 1975; Vedder and King, 1967; Weiss and Friar, 1974), yet it is possible that officers are simply unwilling to believe that "real men" get raped.

In fact, it would be remarkable if male rape victims were not viewed as emasculated, because in our culture the very definition of masculinity does not allow for men to be raped. Although researchers traditionally concentrated on the homosexual nature of male rape in prison, more recent research has focused on rape in prison as an expres-sion of power and control (see Eigenberg, 1994). However, this litera-ture generally ignores gender in a more complex theoretical manner. In other words, it disregards the ways in which rape is associated with tra-ditional definitions of masculinity and femininity. As a result, the litera-ture fails to fully extrapolate why it is essential to portray male rape victims as weak, homosexual, and effeminate. Men are those individu-als who possess and manipulate power and control, especially as it relates to the use of sexual aggression, and women are generally the recipients of this violence. The very thing that separates rape victims from perpetrators in the larger culture is gender. Hence, men who are raped in prison take on the status of women. They are weak and effeminate, then, by definition. Real men would fight to the death rather than be raped. Unfortunately, most of the literature on rape in prisons has ignored the contribution of research that links gender and gender socialization to rape.

THE IMPACT OF BELIEF SYSTEMS ON OFFICERS' UNDERSTANDING OF PRISON RAPE

There is reason to believe that officers' attitudes toward male rape and their willingness to respond may be impacted by belief systems that are formed outside of the prison environment. For example, a great deal of literature finds that men are more apt than women to blame female rape victims who are raped in the community (Deitz and Byrnes, 1981; Field, 1978; Fulero and Delara, 1976; Jenkins and Dambrot, 1987; Kanekar and Nazareth, 1988).[3] And at least one study using a hypothetical scenario reports that male college students are more likely than females to blame male victims who are raped in jail (Whatley and Riggio, 1993). Hence, it is possible that a largely male correctional staff is already somewhat predisposed to blame victims if gender is related to acceptance of the concept of victim precipitation.

Other studies also indicate that attitudes toward women may have a significant impact on officers' attitudes toward male rape in prison. Research finds that people with traditional (conservative) attitudes toward women are more apt to accept rape myths as they apply to the rape of women in the community (Burt, 1980; Field, 1978). Therefore, officers who endorse conservative attitudes toward women may be less willing to respond to rape in prison because of broader social definitions about rape and the role of women in society. In other words, officers who believe a woman's place is in the home and who endorse victim-blaming attitudes toward rape victims would seem to be more predisposed toward blaming male rape victims because they have a cultural framework in place that is merely adapted to the prison environment. If officers believe that women who are in bars alone or dress seductively get what they deserve if they are raped or were asking for it, then it would not be surprising to find that these same officers also believe that men who act effeminate or who get in debt are somehow culpable for their victimization.

In a similar vein, general attitudes toward homosexuality may affect how officers respond to same-sex relationships in prison. Officers with liberal attitudes toward homosexuality may be less inclined to enforce the regulations prohibiting consensual sexuality out of a belief that there is nothing wrong with same-sex relationships. In contrast, officers with conservative attitudes toward homosexuality might be less compassionate toward gay victims, concluding that they were "asking for it" because of their sexual orientation.

Some of these assertions were examined in the research on correctional officers in a Midwestern state (Eigenberg, 2000b). A path model was used to examine the relationship between a variety of attitudinal variables and officers' definitions of rape. Demographic variables (age, sex, race, education, and religiosity) and organizational characteristics (shift, stress, job satisfaction, experience, role conflict, and attitudes toward inmates) entered the model first and functioned as control variables. Additional attitudinal scales were included to test theoretical relationships among attitudes toward women, attitudes toward homosexuality, acceptance of victim blaming, and officers' definitions of rape. Demographic variables and organizational characteristics had no direct effect upon officers' definitions of rape. Both attitudes toward women and homosexuality had an indirect effect upon definitions of rape (and the direct effect of attitudes toward women approached significance, p = .055). Officers with less egalitarian attitudes toward women or officers who condemned homosexuality were more inclined to blame victims. Moreover, officers who blamed victims were less apt to define assaultive situations as rape.[4] This study provides support for the notion that attitudes toward women, attitudes toward homosexuality, and beliefs about victim blaming provide a cultural framework that affects officers' definitions of rape. These findings suggest that if we are to adequately understand male rape in prisons, we must also understand attitudes toward rape in the larger social structure.

CONCLUSION

Future research on rape in prisons should draw more from the vast research on rape in the community. The research on rape in prisons tends to ignore this larger body of literature and operates on the assumption that rape in prison is somehow drastically different from the rape of women in the community, despite evidence that indicates that there are important conceptual links. These similarities should be explored in more depth.

It also is important that we do not get so caught up in counting the incidents of assault that we neglect research insights into correctional responses. Victimization studies are useful, but their limitations require that any estimates of male rape be evaluated with caution (see Eigenberg, 1989, 1992, 1994). First, many of the studies rely upon small, convenience samples. Second, researchers often fail to clearly distinguish between consensual homosexuality, prostitution, and rape in their conceptual schemes. Third, researchers and administrators have been reluctant to acknowledge that inmates may fail to report rape.

Most of the data suggest that victimization is rather rare and that as few as 1 percent of the prison population have experienced a rape (Maitland and Sluder, 1998; Nacci and Kane, 1984a, 1984b; Saum et al., 1995; Tewksbury, 1989a). Other studies report higher rates, such as 14 percent (Wooden and Parker, 1982) and 20 percent (Struckman-Johnson et al., 1996). It is crucial, however, that researchers and administrators acknowledge that these figures may still under-represent the amount of rape in prison (see Eigenberg, 1989, 1994, 2000b). It is also important to acknowledge that research on inmate populations indicates that fear of rape is a central defining characteristic of the prison experience (Jones and Schmid, 1989; Maitland and Sluder, 1996; McCorkle, 1993a) and that at least some correctional officers are not responsive (Davis, 1968; Lockwood, 1980b; Struckman-Johnson, et al., 1996; Tewksbury, 1989a; Wooden and Parker, 1982).

These concerns bear remarkable similarity to the concerns of female rape victims in the community. Research has demonstrated that women's experiences of rape have not been reflected in official estimates of rape (see Eigenberg, 1990; Koss, Gidycz, and Wisniewski, 1987; Russell, 1984). The literature also discusses the many ways in which the fear of rape (and other sexual victimization) defines women's reality and influences women's daily experiences (see Stanko, 1985, 1993), and it has examined the ways in which police responses have inhibited the reporting of rape (Feldman-Summers and Palmer, 1980; Field, 1978; Weis and Borges, 1973; White and Mosher, 1986). Therefore, the literature on rape of women in the community suggests that there is a need for additional research before rejecting inmates' perceptions about the nature of rape in prison.

Additionally, research indicates that there are significant concerns as they relate to correctional officers and their responses to male rape in prison. Studies reveal that officers do not clearly distinguish between consensual sexuality and rape, especially when rape is accomplished by coercive tactics. Research also shows that officers have trouble differentiating between homosexuality, prostitution, and rape. Officers have a tendency to equate victimization with weakness and, consequently, are unlikely to believe men who fail to meet their definitions of rape victims. Their definitions of rape and victimization also appear to be influenced by larger social attitudes about rape and victim precipitation. And although most officers say they will respond to rape, their actions indicate that they have little experience actually doing so. Furthermore, many officers are uncomfortable or unwilling to take even the simplest proactive response—talking to inmates about the problem. These findings then suggest that officers are at least part of the problem. This statement is not intended to blame officers for reflecting values of the larger social structure or for their inability to deal with situations that the prison system itself would rather ignore. Instead, it points to the need for better administrative responses and increased training for officers.

The literature suggests that a wide variety of programs and administrative tactics might be used to combat rape in prison. These solutions include implementing conjugal visits and furlough programs (Hensley, Rutland, and Gray-Ray, 2000b; Ibrahim, 1974; Karpman, 1948; Lee, 1965; Nice, 1966; Scacco, 1975; Vedder and King, 1967); placing victims in separate housing units (Bowker, 1980; Ibrahim, 1974); providing vocational, educational, psychological, and athletic programs (Davis, 1968; Ibrahim, 1974; Lockwood, 1980b; Wooden and Parker, 1982); and normalizing the prison environment by increasing the number of female officers (Ibrahim, 1974; Scacco, 1975). None of these strategies is based on empirical data, and many are based on questionable theoretical assumptions (i.e., that rape in prison occurs in response to sexual deprivation) or lack of any conceptual basis whatsoever (e.g., educational and vocational programs). An interesting exception, though, is the research conducted by Struckman-Johnson and her colleagues (1996). They report that both inmates and correctional officers believe that rape would be reduced if (1) better screening and classification procedures were used to segregate potential targets and victims; (2) supervision was better and that there was more of it; (3) punishment of perpetrators was faster; (4) single cells were used more often; and (5) training for inmates and staff was improved.

It is disturbing that so little attention has been given to administrative responses to male rape in prison. Although the first protocol to deal with male rape (Cotton and Groth, 1984) was developed for the San Francisco County Jail in 1979 (Dumond, 1992), other prisons and jails have been slow to develop policy in this area. One notable exception is the Federal Bureau of Prisons. By 1995, it had adopted a policy on sexual assault prevention and intervention (U.S. Department of Justice, 1995). Another organization also has been involved in efforts to change administrative responses. The Safer Society Press, an organization governed by the New York State Council of Churches, developed a series of prisoner education tapes and a manual for administrators who wish to address rape in prisons. This project was completed by Stephen Donaldson (1993b), a former inmate who was raped in prison and went on to form the Stop Prison Rape organization.[5]

Each of these sources places emphasis on prevention. They require or encourage training that would enable staff, especially correctional officers, to recognize the physical, behavioral, and emotional symptoms of rape; to understand the referral process that is to be followed when victims are identified; and to have a basic understanding of the dynamics of rape in prison. Inmate education is also stressed. Strategies inmates can use to protect themselves include making inmates aware of treatment options and informing them about reporting procedures. These policies and protocols also concentrate on intervention efforts, such as providing for the medical, psychological, and safety needs of victims. Administrators are advised to aggressively investigate rapes so that they can be addressed by both the prison disciplinary system and by the criminal justice system.

These policies and administrative protocols are definitely a step in the right direction. Yet there is still much to be done. For example, the Safer Society Press states that their project is "prisoner-oriented" because "in reality, prisoner rape is most effectively prevented and controlled by the prisoners themselves. In the absence of administrative attention, it is the prisoners who tolerate sexual assaults, fail to protect their peers, and fail to protect themselves" (Donaldson, 1993b: 7). The project goes on to advise inmates who are experiencing attempted rapes to try to negotiate with their perpetrators to perform oral sex instead of anal sex, which is more dangerous in terms of exposure to HIV/AIDS. It also recommends the distribution of condoms and instructs inmates how to fashion makeshift condoms out of plastic bags or gloves as a measure of last resort in order to try to protect themselves. These types of suggestions are offered in a sincere attempt to help inmates in desperate situations. But we, as a society, should be ashamed. We can and must do better.

One also anticipates that any effort to respond to male rape victims in prison will be hampered by a social structure that continues to blame female victims for precipitating their victimization. Likewise, it will be difficult to affect change as long as society continues to believe that harsh punishment is appropriate for all offenders. The widespread use of humor to make jokes about men dropping the soap in the prison shower suggests that for too many Americans, rape in prison is considered just desserts.

NOTES

1. This study does not examine the rape of women in women's facilities. Traditionally and historically, violence against women has been committed by men, not by other women. As a result, one would anticipate that the dynamics of rape in women's prisons would be very different from rape in men's prisons (see Propper, 1981).

2. Unfortunately, the complexity of the relationship and the nature of any interactions between the two groups have yet to be adequately researched (Philliber, 1987).

3. There also is contradictory evidence suggesting that gender is not associated with victim-blaming attitudes.

4. There were also some interesting findings relating to the indirect effects of attitudes toward inmates and their impact on definitions of rape. (To examine these effects in detail, see Eigenberg, 2000b.) The impact of these variables does not affect the overall discussion of the findings presented in this chapter.

5. More information on this organization is available online at www. igc.apc.org/spr/.

5

THE TREATMENT OF
SEXUAL ASSAULT VICTIMS

Robert W. Dumond and Doris A. Dumond

Within U.S. jails and prisons, inmate sexual assault is a devastating and overwhelming scourge that remains largely unabated, under-reported, and ignored. Although the problem has been known for centuries, there has been an inconsistent response among all correctional professionals, including medical and mental health practitioners. Very early in the correctional history of the United States, many observers began to identify the problem of sexual violence being perpetrated against inmates. The Reverend Louis Dwight, founder of Boston's Prison Discipline Society, was one of the first to investigate conditions in state prisons in the first half of the nineteenth century. Considered one of the best sources of information about prison life in that era (Allen and Simonsen, 1998), Dwight presented a report on April 25, 1826, in which he stated that after visiting "most of the prisons . . . between Massachusetts and Georgia," he found "melancholy testimony to establish one general fact, viz., that boys are prostituted to the lust of old convicts." Dwight further pleaded: "Nature and humanity cry aloud for redemption from this dreadful degradation" (Katz, 1976: 27). Since then, many voices have been raised in indignation and concern.

Since the mid-1960s, there has been considerable attention to systematically identify inmate sexual assault (Cotton and Groth, 1982, 1984; Davis, 1968; Dumond, 1992, 2000; Lockwood, 1978, 1980a, 1992; Nacci and Kane, 1983, 1984a, 1984b; Scacco, 1975, 1982; Struckman-Johnson and Struckman-Johnson, 1999, 2000a, 2000b; Struckman-Johnson et al., 1995, 1996; Toch, 1992a, 1992b; Wooden and Parker, 1982). Despite these examinations, the incidence of inmate sexual victimization in U.S. correctional institutions remains unknown and the treatment of inmate victims has been largely ineffective and, in many cases, nonexistent. The impact of this terrible crime upon its unwitting victims is catastrophic and pervasive. All correctional staff must respond with timely, comprehensive, and effective treatment to help in healing these wounded victims.

The predominant ethic among staff is the care, custody, and control of inmates. This often involves a depersonalization and cultivation of an "us" versus "them" mentality (which is also mimicked by inmates). Among inmates, those individuals for whom society holds the greatest contempt (e.g., murderers) command the highest respect and fear. Such settings are also dominated by the realization that perception is reality. It does not matter what is accurate. It is what the institution (staff and inmates) perceives that dictates the interpersonal and social dynamics (Dumond, 1992).

Changes in inmate population, especially in size and composition, have made the correctional officer's job more difficult and life threatening (Tonry and Petersilia, 2000). The increasing commitment of younger, more violent, more radical and unpredictable prisoners has heightened the danger level in all prisons (Ross, 1991). Incarcerated settings are societies that value aggression, power, and loyalty—many of the attributes often associated with masculinity in society (Dumond, 1992; Nacci and Kane, 1983; Scacco, 1982; Wooden and Parker, 1982). Correctional staff often adopt an attitude that is similar to that of machismo—in its negative connotation: appearing impenetrable, unaffected by violence and fear, and capable of maintaining the facade of control. Prison is a place where kindness is weakness and where all of the players, both staff and inmates, share the environment of confinement and isolation from the rest of community life.

Ross (1991) noted that U.S. prisons today are a dangerous place to work and live, more so than in any other time. There were seventy-nine homicides in 1998 and sixty-eight homicides in 2000 in adult prisons nationwide and 8,094 inmate-on-inmate assaults requiring medical attention (Camp and Camp, 1998, 2001). More troubling about these statistics is the recognition that inmate violence is routinely underreported (Reid, 1991). Additionally, corrections officials note with increasing concern the spillover effect of gang violence from the community into the institutions themselves.

THE PRISON SUBCULTURE—LIFE BEHIND BARS

The prison setting is a closed society with both formal and informal stratification and role expectations. Zimbardo and his colleagues (1973) dramatically illustrated the role that prisons have in shaping behavior, even in a mock prison environment. After six days, the study was discontinued when five of the ten "prisoners" developed psychological symptomology and the group as a whole developed a "perverted" symbiotic relationship. How more profound and overwhelming is the real world of incarceration, a subculture with its own language, hierarchy, and stratification?

Prison stratification is complex. It includes a combination of personal characteristics, the crime for which one is convicted, and the perceptions of others. The patterns and perceptions about an inmate will often shape the treatment that they will receive from other inmates and correctional staff. The sexual identity of an inmate also helps to define the inmate's orientation within the prison society (Bowker, 1980; Dumond, 1992; Knowles, 1999; Wooden and Parker, 1982). There is a general joining of social status and sexual behavior in prison that leads many inmates to choose, albeit unknowingly/unwillingly, the role of either victim or aggressor, as a means of survival in the subculture of incarceration (see Dumond [1992, 2000] for a discussion of this issue).

THE EFFECTS OF SEXUAL ASSAULT/VICTIMIZATION

The crisis of being a sexual assault victim is pervasive, devastating, and global. It affects the victim physically, emotionally, socially, and spiritually. Sexual victimization causes a psychological disequilibrium from a situation that cannot be avoided and for which a person cannot use their normal problem-solving resources. Burgess and Holmstrom (1974a, 1974b, 1975) developed the first working model to understand the physical and psychological annihilation of sexual assault. They identified the "rape trauma syndrome" (RTS), characterized by an acute phase of disorganization, followed by reorganization and resolution, which has since been adopted as a nursing diagnosis by the Fourth National Conference on the Classification of Nursing Diagnoses (Burgess, 1985). The sequela of sexual victimization has physical, cognitive, social, behavioral, and psychological components, yet during incarceration, sexual victimization has additional effects on victims. This model has been an important adjunct to understanding the impacts on sexual assault victims as well as improving the response of practitioners treating them.

The first psychiatric formulation of traumatic stress was developed by Mott (1919) to describe shell shock and battle fatigue experienced by combat veterans in World War I. The American Psychiatric

Association adopted "general stress reactions syndrome" to describe the reaction to extreme stress that evoked fear in otherwise normal individuals in its first *Diagnostic and Statistical Manual of Mental Disorders* (1952). The reaction was considered fleeting and reversible, and no specific symptoms were described. The syndrome was eliminated from the *DSM-II* (1968) but was reintroduced in the *DSM-III* (1980) as "post-traumatic stress disorder" (PTSD) to describe the reactions of individuals to a wide range of traumatic events, including war, combat, and victimization. Future refinements in diagnostic precision in future editions of the *DSM* (1987, 1994, 2000) have improved our understanding of PTSD. Both diagnoses are currently in use—PTSD being usually diagnosed by psychiatric and psychological staff while RTS is being used by nursing professionals.

Each diagnosis provides aspects of the victimization experience that are essential to treating the problem. PTSD tends to focus on the cognitive and psychological aspects, while RTS includes behavioral aspects as well. Both describe the same phenomenon, which is vital to understanding the complexity of the experience. The rape survivor endures a life-changing event whose impact is destructive (Ruch, Chandler, and Harter, 1980) and may even include a lifetime of pain and suffering after only one event (Allison and Wrigthsman, 1993). It should also be noted that victims may suffer from PTSD/RTS even in incidents when a sexual assault has only been attempted (Ruch and Leon, 1983).

For victims of any traumatic assault, there is always the lack of control accompanied by physical pain, suffering, and threat of further harm or death that is concomitant with the assault. Victims often articulate shock and disbelief, panic, and fright. The major task during the attack is survival. A host of coping strategies can be employed by victims, including fighting back, bargaining, focusing on the rapist, mental escaping, and compliance. Although these may aid in some cases, they may equally exacerbate the situation. Understanding the victim's coping strategies is invaluable to treatment, as it can improve the recovery time of the rape survivor (Lennox and Gannon, 1983). It is important to understand the range of strategies that victims may employ, because what a victim appears to do may in no way reflect their actual intention or motivation. These are crucial issues in educating staff, who may conclude erroneously that a victim submitted voluntarily to a sexual assault, when, in fact, the victim's actions were motivated by survival needs.

Victimization in Prison

The effect of sexual victimization in prisons and jails has been shown to be even more devastating due to the unique structure of incarceration that increases the impact on victims. In situations of captivity, the perpetrator often becomes the most important person in the life of the victim. Ironically, as noted by Mariner (2001), sexual assault victims may be coerced, threatened, and intimidated into long-term sexual slavery and continuous degradation in order simply to survive. Over time, the perpetrator's actions and beliefs profoundly influence the psychology of the victim (Herman, 1992). Especially in incarcerated settings, victims may experience a systematic, repetitive infliction of psychological trauma, as well as the continuation of terror, helplessness, fear, and lack of autonomy. Toch (1992a) identified the double bind facing inmates. Although an inmate who fights earns respect from other inmates and staff, the inmate is seen as a troublemaker, and that may affect his parole. These pressures produce confusion, disorientation, and discomfort, especially in potential victims.

Prisons are so volatile that fear alone has been identified as a chief measure of well-being (McCorkle, 1993a). Even reports of rape in prison have a dramatic impact on inmates, especially those new to prison (Jones and Schmid, 1989). The worry and constant alert to being assaulted—and being victimized—can result in a whole host of psychophysiological conditions that can lead to asthma, ulcers, colitis, and hypertension (McCorkle, 1993a, 1993b). For youth in prisons, in particular, daily survival and avoiding victimization become the predominant activities in the prison jungle (Eisikovits and Baizerman, 1982; Maitland and Sluder, 1996; Rideau, 1992).

Groth, Burgess, and Holmstrom (1977) identify three major methods used to assault victims: entrapment, intimidation, and physical force. These tactics have been described more extensively by Struckman-Johnson and Struckman-Johnson (2000a, 2000b) and Struckman-Johnson et al. (1996) as either force tactics or pressure tactics. Force tactics include threat of harm, being scared by perpetrator size/strength, being physically held down, and having a weapon present. Pressure tactics include persuasion, bribes, blackmail, threats to withdraw love, and use of alcohol/drugs. Most inmate targets of sexual coercion reported the use of at least one force tactic (Struckman-Johnson and Struckman-Johnson, 1999, 2000a, 2000b; Struckman-Johnson et al., 1996).

Perpetrators also utilize five major psychological components to engage victims: (1) conquest and control, (2) revenge and retaliation, (3) sadism and denigration, (4) conflict and counteraction, and (5) status and affiliation (Groth, Burgess, and Holmstrom, 1977). This information is vital to comprehending the seductive and manipulative nature of the "grooming," and communicating these strategies to potential victims is a key preventative strategy.

SEXUAL VICTIMIZATION AS A MALE

In addition to the ravages of prison, male sexual assault victims face additional humiliation, which further complicates their potential for recovery. Dumond (1992) reviewed nine key studies that examined the impact of sexual victimization on males in particular. The vast majority of these studies were conducted in prison/incarceration settings because few male victims report such abuse in community life. Male victims of sexual assault experience not only the more traditional rape trauma syndrome as described by Burgess and Holmstrom (1974a, 1974b, 1975), with its concurrent features of post-traumatic stress disorder, but also a number of other issues that exacerbate the victimization experience (Anderson, 1981; Calderwood, 1987; Mezey and King, 1989).

The rape trauma syndrome identified that rape victims can manifest two response styles: expressive and controlled (Burgess and Holmstrom, 1974a, 1974b). Kaufman et al. (1980) noted that 79 percent of the men sexually assaulted in free society manifested a controlled response, characterized by being calm, controlled, and/or subdued. This can be very deceptive to correctional staff, who may assume that the overwhelming crisis of a rape should precipitate a more expressive response. These staff may subsequently interpret a subdued, emotionless response as evidence that a forced sexual assault did not take place. However, given the dynamics of the prison subculture and the emphasis on control, aggression, and masculinity, it is entirely consistent that most male rape victims in incarcerated settings would be guarded in their overt manifestation of trauma (Donaldson, 1993b; Wooden and Parker, 1982).

The devastation of sexual assault is profound and life changing for both men and women. However, the male sexual assault victim faces some specific challenges that need to be identified and addressed:

- Male victims experience higher rates of fear, anxiety (especially while incarcerated), suicidal thoughts, social disruption, and attitudinal change.
- Male victims have an increased likelihood of having been the victim of multiple assaults by multiple assailants, experiencing more physical trauma, and being held captive longer.
- Most male victims experience concern about their masculinity, and, in the prison community, fear of reprisal and loss of social status.
- Male victims appear to suffer more dramatic victimization, especially in incarcerated settings, in part because of the devaluation of the two primary areas of male identity: sexuality and aggression.
- Male victims appear to experience a devalued sense of their manhood, that is, their sexuality, as well as competence and security.
- Traditional gender role stereotypes contribute to lack of responsiveness toward male rape victims, and gaps in services often prevent men from getting the services they need.
- Social institutions often are involved in a second assault experience on male victims in their denial of the legitimacy of their experiences and the reinforcement of harmful gender role socialization.

With younger male victims, there may also be considerable confusion regarding their sexual identity. One of the strategies that predators often use is to attempt to get the victim to ejaculate. A common myth about male rape is that men cannot become excited or ejaculate under coercion. Groth and Burgess (1980) have demonstrated that men can be physiologically sexually aroused by a variety of emotions, including pain, fear, and anger. When this occurs, as noted by Groth, Burgess, and Holmstrom (1977) and Struckman-Johnson (1991), there is considerable confusion and questioning of the victim's sexual orientation. Additionally, victims in such situations are more likely to blame themselves and feel intense guilt and shame.

IMPEDIMENTS TO DISCLOSURE OF SEXUAL ASSAULT

Without even considering incarcerated settings, disclosure of sexual assault for any victim is a most difficult endeavor. Many patients are reluctant to discuss victimization with health care providers because of two primary reasons:

1. Victims often perceive that providers are not knowledgeable or sympathetic to the problems they experience, and they fear that disclosure will add to further victimization, humiliation, shame and a sense of blame.
2. Victims, in discussing the assault, may experience discomfort, pain, and panic symptoms, re-experiencing the helplessness of fear of assault. (Fruend, 1991)

This is further compounded by factors related to the ecology and ethos of incarceration. It has often been believed by inmates and staff alike that there are few real "victims," that most sexual behavior in incarceration is consensual. The literature that examines sexual victimization often does not clearly distinguish between consensual homosexuality, prostitution, and rape (Eigenberg, 1994). Struckman-Johnson et al. (1995) have identified that "incarcerated inmates who are sexually assaulted may be viewed as somewhat deserving or responsible for their fate because of the crimes committed against society" (3).

A poll of 400 registered voters in Massachusetts conducted by KRC Communications Research, and reported in the *Boston Globe* on May 17, 1994, noted that 50 percent agreed that society accepts inmate sexual assault as part of the price criminals pay for committing crimes (Sennott, 1994). Herein lies one of the most difficult issues to confront. It is the case that incarcerated inmates do engage in sexual behavior willingly and that it is sometimes difficult to differentiate the validity of an inmate's complaint of sexual victimization. Nonetheless, medical and mental health practitioners must be extremely careful to create the environment for disclosure by inmate victims and not create the chilling effect that apparently continues to exist in incarcerated settings.

Struckman-Johnson et al. (1995, 1996) reported that of the target victims identified, only 29 percent of the inmates told at least one staff person in either an administrative or nonadministrative position. (It is interesting to note that 18 percent reported their assault to counselor/clergy and 10 percent to medical staff.) When asked to identify the reasons for their nondisclosure, target victims identified, in order of importance: (1) fear that perpetrator(s) would kill or injure them; (2) the feeling that staff would not believe them, would laugh at them, or would do nothing about it; and (3) shame and embarrassment. Other reasons identified were the belief that reporting would cause more problems and make prison life more difficult, and the fear of being placed into protective custody. Follow-up studies by Struckman-Johnson and Struckman-Johnson (1999, 2000a, 2000b) revealed similarly low rates of disclosure to prison officials.

It is critical, therefore, that practitioners avoid what Symonds (1980) calls the "second injury" to victims: the perceived rejection by or lack of support from staff and/or the institution and the conscious and/or conscious/unconscious projection of feelings of blame onto the victim. Lockwood (1995, 1996) and Toch (1992a, 1992b) also emphasize the necessity for custodial staff to learn and understand the grave problems experienced by inmate victims and refer these inmates to medical and mental health staff.

MEDICAL INTERVENTION IN SEXUAL VICTIMIZATION INCIDENTS

Recognizing that there is the potential for serious, even lethal injury to all victims of sexual assault, especially in incarcerated settings, the first priority must be to treat imminent injuries and minimize life-threatening events. The immediate initial focus of correctional staff when managing an inmate victim must be to address the sequelae of brutal victimization, which can include bleeding, head trauma, anal tears/fissures, oral gagging/vomiting, venereal diseases(s), HIV/AIDS, shock, and suicidal thoughts/tendencies. Each correctional institution has its own particular protocol in responding to medical emergencies. Large state prisons and jails, for example, may have well-equipped and -staffed medical facilities that are able to respond to medical emergencies. Smaller prisons and jails, however, may be unable to provide appropriate medical care. As such, emergency medical care may be required from a local or designated community hospital, which requires an established procedure for medical transfer of inmates.

Transporting an inmate could potentially complicate the medical intervention of incarcerated victims. Security is a key factor to be considered when any inmate is removed from the incarcerated setting, for there is an inordinately high incidence of inmates attempting or completing escapes from emergency rooms (Topham, 1999). As a result, enhanced security procedures initiated to intervene with victims may compromise the privacy and confidentiality of the victim/patient.

Correctional security staff should adopt the model of confidentiality and professional respect in their monitoring of inmate victims in external medical settings.

For purposes of discussion, medical and mental health treatment will be divided into four distinct phases: (1) immediately upon disclosure after the assault, (2) within seventy-two hours, (3) short-term intervention, and (4) long-term intervention. Table 5.1 outlines the key action steps to be undertaken by medical and mental health staff following identification and/or disclosure of inmate sexual victimization.

Emergency room practitioners should perform a comprehensive medical examination on the inmate victims and execute the appropriate treatment for injuries sustained as a result of the sexual assault. All sexual assault victims face medical risks that include sexually transmitted diseases, other communicable diseases, and HIV/AIDS (Beers and Berkow, 1999; Cotton and Groth, 1984). Be advised, however, that while the presented action steps are based upon the experience and training of a number of researchers and clinicians, correctional staff must conform to the established protocols of their own institutions.

Sexually Transmitted Diseases

Because inmates tend to have higher risk lifestyles and behaviors, preventative STD testing and treatment are vital (Widom and Hammett, 1996). Powelson and Fletcher (2000) note the variety of sexually transmitted diseases that are present in incarcerated populations and identify some of the tests involved. For example, the Raid plasma reagent test is a blood test used to detect syphilis, to which some inmates are reluctant to submit. However, the Ligase chain reaction test used to detect gonorrhea and chlamydia is a urine test that is less invasive (Powelson and Fletcher, 2000). Therefore, using less invasive tests and making prisoners aware of the procedures and risks are necessary for the inmate's peace of mind.

Other Communicable Diseases

Unfortunately, other communicable diseases abound in prison, including tuberculosis (TB) (MacIntyre, Kendig, and Kummer, 1999) and hepatitis B (DeNoon, 1999). Ninety to 95 percent of primary TB infections go unrecognized (Beers and Berkow, 1999). This appears especially true in correctional settings as well (MacIntyre, Kendig, and Kummer, 1999). Hepatitis C virus has also been identified as a major public health risk, with 30 to 40 percent of the 2 million inmates poten-

Table 5.1   Key Medical and Psychological Intervention, Defined by Time

	Key Responsibilities
Immediately upon disclosure/following sexual assault	• Triage: Determine level of trauma—if life threatening or acute, immediately secure victim, medically stabilize, and secure emergency transfer to emergency medical facility. If non–life threatening, secure victim, treat injuries, and provide treatment within institutional hospital.
	• Attention should be focused on bleeding, head trauma, treating ancillary injuries suffered during the attack (including anal tears/fissures and vaginal tears/injuries), oral gagging and vomiting, shock, and suicidality. Records should carefully document both general and genital trauma, objective clinical findings, subjective victim statements, and behavioral observations. Evaluation, testing, and prophylactic treatment for sexually transmitted diseases (STDs), pregnancy (females), and HIV-positive/AIDS should also be initiated.
	• If external medical agency is used, secure appropriate medical/psychiatric historical information from victim's medical record for assessment/consideration by hospital staff. Recommendations and treatment of external facility should be followed by institutional medical staff upon inmate's return to prison/jail facility.
Within seventy-two hours	• Complete sexual assault evidence collection kit, including securing authorization, collection of foreign materials, undergarments, clothing, debris, pubic hair combings, pulled pubic hairs, vaginal swabs and smears, rectal swabs and smears, oral swabs and smears, pulled head hairs, known saliva and blood samples, careful anatomical drawings, detailed history, and assault information. Preserve evidence appropriately using proper collection techniques, maintaining closely scrutinized and documented chain of custody. Photograph all injuries.
	• Perform complete mental status examination, noting affect, behavior, verbal responses, body language, cognitive processing, and emotional responses. Carefully assess suicidal risk. Inquire specifically about prior suicide attempts and current feeling states. Note confusion, shock, disbelief, or severe depression. If necessary, secure psychiatric consultation and prophylactic psychiatric medication as required. Contract for inmate safety and prepare victim for PTSD/RTS symptomology. Perform crisis counseling and supportive services. Carefully record all findings, preserve inmate safety, especially upon return to setting.
	• If medically necessary, negotiate in-patient hospital admission, addressing security issues.
	• Negotiate family contact/notification and other ancillary support as appropriate (clergy, etc.). All clinical staff should preserve inmate confidentiality, treat inmate victims with respect, provide encouragement and reassurance, and follow through on commitments to patients.
Short-term follow-up	• Provide ongoing medical follow-up treatment as required—continue medications, change dressings, evaluate healing of wounds, continue medical treatment initiatives as necessary.
	• Provide follow-up on results of STD and HIV-positive testing and provide continued prophylaxis. Initiate supportive counseling and education to patient regarding STDs and HIV-positive/AIDS.

(continues)

Table 5.1　continued

	Key Responsibilities
Long-term follow-up	• Continue close mental health supervision, including ongoing crisis counseling to focus on self-identity, survival and coping skills, and ventilation of feelings and life goals and issues. • Continued assessment of suicidality, depression, PTSD symptoms, and mental status. Mental health staff should be available regularly; psychiatric evaluation/monitoring should continue. • Continue monitoring of medical issues, including STD evaluation and six-month HIV/AIDS testing up to eighteen months following sexual assault. Continue appropriate medical treatments. • Continue mental health intervention, including ongoing counseling and support, with attention to PTSD symptomology, mental status, sexual identity, and coping skills responses. • Differentiate treatment for inmates incarcerated for short-term period vs. long-term period. • Ensure continuity of medical and mental health care for inmate victims within institutions and upon inmate's transfer to other institutions. • Make appropriate follow-up clinical referrals for inmates upon release to community.

tially infected, most prior to incarceration (Reindollar, 1999). These diseases are affected by high-risk behaviors (drug use and high-risk sexual behaviors). Medical staff should evaluate the presence of these diseases in inmate sexual assault victims and treat accordingly.

HIV/AIDS

HIV and AIDS continues to represent a deadly threat to inmate sexual assault victims. DeGroot, Hammett, and Scheib (1996) note that the HIV serepositivity rate is ten- to 100-fold higher among inmates than in the general population, with the rate of female inmates higher than male inmates. Maruschak (1999) reported that 3.5 percent of all female state prison inmates were HIV-positive, compared to 2.2 percent of male state prisoners. More recent evidence (DeGroot, 2001) has suggested that incarcerated women are three times more likely to be HIV-infected than incarcerated men, representing an "epidemic behind the walls." The most recent HIV incidence data available indicate that 25,483 U.S. state and federal prisoners were HIV-positive in 1998 (Cusac, 2000).

In 1999, AIDS accounted for 10.1 percent (324) of all the inmate deaths in adult state and federal prisons (Camp and Camp, 2001). For at least some inmates, sexual assault while incarcerated was the precipitating cause of their contracting HIV and facing a foreshortened future as a result (*Corrections Compendium*, 1995). The potential for an "unadjudicated death sentence" as a result of sexual assault is an extremely troubling and disturbing consequence (*Corrections Compendium*, 1995: 14).

Due to legal and ethical requirements, responding medically to the potential risk of HIV/AIDS requires the inmate victim's consent to test for the disease. Medical staff should carefully advise and inform the patient of their rights and instruct about the risks and benefits of pursuing HIV/AIDS testing and prophylactic treatment. Following supportive counseling and upon the informed consent of the victim, medical staff should suggest the collection of blood samples during the initial examination, to be followed up ninety and 180 days later (Beers and Berkow, 1999; Huffman, 2000).

SEXUAL ASSAULT NURSE EXAMINERS INITIATIVE

The last (but certainly not the least) medical consideration involves the process of collecting forensic evidence from sexual assault victims in order to potentially prosecute inmate predators. The sexual assault nursing examiner initiative was created nearly thirty years ago to build a system of quality care that is consistent, humane, and supportive (Mawn, 1999). Nurses are specially trained and certified to provide crisis intervention, patient evaluation, collection and documentation of forensic evidence, and provision of necessary treatment. These nursing specialists also provide victim advocacy, referrals to ancillary care, and provide expert court testimony in criminal prosecutions, if they are pursued.

Standard medical protocol requires patients to be acquainted with the process, to have the steps carefully illustrated, and to secure appropriate informed consent from sexual assault victims. The use of standardized sexual assault evidence collection kits (also referred to as rape kits) are a vital ingredient to successful prosecution and are seen as especially valuable in prison/jail sexual assaults, which are often not successfully prosecuted because of lack of appropriate evidence (Cotton and Groth, 1982, 1984; Fagan, Wennerstrom, and Miller, 1996; Nacci and Kane, 1984a, 1984b). Ninety percent of the city, county, state, and federal law enforcement agencies, crime laboratories, and hospital personnel use sexual assault evidence collection kits manufactured by Tri-Tech, Inc., of Southport, North Carolina. This has greatly increased standardization and reliability of sampling and evidence collection.

However, due caution is also required. Correctional medical personnel have the primary duty of treating inmate victims—requiring institutional correctional staff to perform the tasks of collecting forensic evidence may actually contaminate the integrity of the relationships between inmate victims and medical staff. As a result of this concern, the National Commission on Correctional Health Care (1997) has promulgated standards of care in cases of sexual assault. The standards specifically prohibit correctional institutional medical (and mental health) staff from participating in forensic evidence collection, citing that subsequent staff credibility, neutrality, and caring may be severely compromised. The commission suggests two alternatives: the use of external agencies to perform such tasks or the use of institutional staff (with permission of the inmate victim) who will not be involved in a therapeutic relationship with the inmate (National Commission on Correctional Health Care, 1997).

Because sexual victimization is a profound and devastating event in the inmate's life, medical staff may uncover previously untreated medical and/or psychiatric problems. For a variety of reasons, such symptomology may not have been identified earlier, and the inmate victim has been untreated. Careful attention must be paid to counterbalancing the need for ongoing treatment for the identified medical/psychiatric problems; the victim's willingness, ability, and consent for such treatment; and even communicating these findings to medical/mental health staff at the institution where the inmate victim will be housed.

It is vital that clearly defined and clinically appropriate strategies be implemented to ensure the continuity of care between the hospital providing treatment to inmate victims and the institution to which the inmate victim will return. In some cases, there is even a concern for the ongoing safety of the victim upon return to the institution, and this is an issue that must be carefully reviewed and appropriate action initiated.

Several models may be appropriate for adoption. The Federal Bureau of Prisons (1997) has established an extremely thorough protocol, *PS 5324.04 Sexual Abuse/Assault Prevention and Intervention Programs* (updated December 31, 1997), that city/county/state correctional departments may wish to examine. The Massachusetts Department of Correction (2001a) has also established a comprehensive strategy to address these issues. Its *103 DOC 520 Inmate Sexual Assault Response Plan* is a carefully designed protocol that outlines specific action steps to be taken by correctional staff in responding to alleged incidents of inmate sexual assault in conjunction with the designated medical setting.

Additionally, ongoing dialogue has been established to resolve difficulties that may result from some of the aforementioned issues. This is especially important because medical and mental health staff cannot make the immediate, practical decisions that custodial administrators can regarding housing, inmate placement, movement to a new facility, and so on.

MENTAL HEALTH INTERVENTION ISSUES

There are several major mental health issues that can follow inmate sexual assault: suicide; PTSD; and other psychiatric disturbances, including exacerbation of existing mental illnesses and dissociative disorders. Each of these issues represents a major area of concern for correctional medical and mental health staff.

Suicide

Called the "crisis behind bars" (Danto, 1981), suicide is the most serious concern following an inmate sexual assault. Suicide in jails is the second leading cause of death following illnesses/natural causes (excluding AIDS), with 283 deaths by suicide in 1993 (Perkins, Stephan, and Beck, 1995). In prisons nationwide, suicide was the third leading cause of death in 1999, with a total of 324 inmate deaths by suicide (Camp and Camp, 2001). Toch and Kupers (1999) maintain that the situation of inmate rape, coupled with the overcrowding, brutality, and violence, constitutes a mental health crisis for all inmates, but particularly for the mentally ill.

An increasing number of mentally ill inmates continue to enter U.S. prisons and jails. In fact, Harrington (1999) notes that between 60,000 and 100,000 of the annual jail admissions in the United States are mentally ill. Torrey (1997) has identified that in some states, the number of mentally ill who are incarcerated exceed the number of mentally ill who are institutionalized in state psychiatric hospital facilities. As suggested by Harrington (1999), confinement institutions of all types (lockups, jails, and prisons) have become the new "Bedlams" of the twenty-first century.

A number of researchers have documented that suicide is the option for some sexual assault victims to cope with the increased fear, stress, and anxiety, especially for men (Bland et al., 1990; Dooley, 1990; Haycock, 1991; Lockwood, 1980a; Wiggs, 1989; Wooden and Parker,

1982). Recent research conducted by Struckman-Johnson and Struckman-Johnson (1999, 2000a, 2000b) and Struckman-Johnson et al. (1995, 1996) in Midwestern prisons continues to document the manifestation of suicidal ideation among inmate sexual targets. Given the dynamics of incarcerated settings, such observations are predictable. If an inmate victim believes they will continue to be sexually targeted and victimized, and, if no tangible relief exists, suicide may appear to be the only rational option to some inmates. For this reason, inmate sexual assault victims (and targets) should be considered at imminent risk of suicide until seen and evaluated by mental health professionals (Donaldson, 1993b). Throughout the intervention, the mental health practitioners should carefully assess and inquire about suicidal ideation in inmate victims in each and every interaction, for the full impact of the sexual victimization may not be manifest until some later period.

Post-traumatic Stress Disorder/Rape Trauma Syndrome

Many sexual assault victims experience the debilitating effects of post-traumatic stress disorder/rape trauma syndrome as a direct result of their victimization. In fact, about one-third of all female rape victims developed PTSD at some point in their lifetimes following victimization, with female rape victims being 6.2 times more likely to develop PTSD than women who had not been abused (Boudreaux et al., 1998). Even though this data describes female victims, there is ample evidence that male rape victims experience similar degrees of PTSD (Anderson, 1981; Calderwood, 1987; Cotton and Groth, 1982, 1984; Groth and Burgess, 1980; Kaufman et al., 1980; Lockwood, 1978; Mezey and King, 1989). Donaldson (1993b) has noted that correctional settings may employ mental health practitioners who are conversant and knowledgeable about treating mental illness and offenders but who may be unaware of the nature of sexual victimization and its impact on inmates. Anecdotally, several victims have reported that when they have consulted correctional mental health practitioners, many of these professionals were inadequately prepared to meet the psychological needs of sexual assault victims. As a result, many victims have reported that what should have been an opportunity for coping and healing has actually resulted in further alienation and isolation.

Mental health practitioners should become familiar with RTS and treating PTSD, employing the most current recommended techniques to help ameliorate the problem. Several researchers have emphasized the role of victim coping strategies and defenses as having a dramatic impact upon recovery (Lennox and Gannon, 1983; Marton, 1988). Consequently, clinicians should utilize an educational approach in their therapeutic interventions, tangibly helping inmate victims to master sensible and manageable coping strategies and understand their unique character style and associated defenses. Cognitive-behavioral therapy has also been shown to be extremely helpful in assisting victims manage and modify PTSD symptomology, as elucidated by Foa and Rothbaum (1997) and Rothbaum (2000).

Finally, because PTSD symptomology can be global and devastating, conjoint therapeutic interventions may be the most effective. The efforts of the Post-traumatic Stress Disorder Alliance has established concrete protocols that show great promise and are valid especially in correctional settings (Beyzarov, 2000). Foa, Davidson, and Frances (1999) recently promulgated expert consensus guidelines on the treatment of PTSD, which included psychotherapeutic as well as psychopharmacological interventions.

Other Psychiatric Disorders

As previously noted, there is a growing number of inmates in U.S. correctional facilities who already have been diagnosed with mental illness. Ditton (1999) has noted that the estimated rate of mentally ill inmates may be as high as 16 percent in state prisons and jails and more than 7 percent in federal prisons. Chelala (1999) reported a total of 283,800 inmates in U.S. prisons who had some form of mental illness. Mental health clinicians should carefully review inmate victim medical and mental records and scrupulously inquire about prior mental health treatment, psychiatric hospitalizations, prior suicidal attempts, and psychiatric medication. Careful attention should be noted to prior diagnoses of major depression (recurrent), PTSD, and psychoses. Also important is the recognition of the number of inmates reporting incidents of prior abuse (physical and sexual). Harlow (1999) has documented the relatively large number of inmates (18.7 percent state prison, 16.4 percent jail, and 9.5 percent federal) reporting abuse prior to their incarceration, including between 7 and 16 percent of inmates reporting prior sexual abuse. Prior physical and sexual abuse can exacerbate the traumatic experience of sexual assault victims and can complicate their recovery (Burgess, 1985; Burgess and Holmstrom, 1974a, 1974b).

Many inmate victims may have personal characteristics and/or have committed crimes that have made them less sympathetic and credible. Without even realizing it, correctional mental health practitioners may not adequately confront their own transference/countertransference issues, and they may exacerbate the psychological injury to inmate victims (Donaldson, 1993b). Therefore, all correctional mental health practitioners must be well versed in the impact of sexual victimization on inmates, as well as the complex relationship of treatment within the confines of a correctional setting. It is often the case that appropriate treatment cannot occur independently of providing for the safety and security needs of the victim. Clinicians may be required to intervene with security, classification, and administrative staff on behalf of their inmate victims to ensure the basic safety needs of their patients (Dumond, 1992).

Furthermore, if inmate victims will be moved from one incarcerated setting to another, it is essential that there be ongoing continuity of care. This can sometimes be difficult in institutional settings that may not always notify mental health officials in a timely fashion. Strategies must be initiated to include mental health in the classification process and the transition to new institutional settings to ensure that continued care will be afforded to victims.

Other clinical issues are important to consider. As noted by Herman (1992) and Turner (1992), reactions to sexual torture over an extended period of time may elicit a variety of responses in victims. For example, in victims who experienced childhood sexual victimization, revictimization during incarceration may exacerbate and reinitiate the feelings of helplessness and hopelessness, and increase suicidal ideation. In addition, some victims may experience dissociative reactions when there has been extreme, long-term victimization.

Care should also be taken to identify the premorbid psychiatric condition of patients. Those who have had prior psychiatric disturbance are likely to re-experience symptomology (Burgess and Holmstrom, 1974a, 1974b). Clinicians should carefully monitor patient behavior, affect, and feeling states, be aware of symptoms of acute decompensation, and treat patients accordingly. This may also be manifest in victims who have experienced repeated, ongoing victimization, either with the same perpetrator or with additional perpetrators. To survive, victims may anesthetize themselves with substances, and experience pathologic changes in identity (Herman, 1992), sexual disturbances, depression, and lack of wholeness (Turner, 1992). The emotional "processing," as identified by Turner (1992), requires a calm, unhurried approach that often exceeds the traditional fifty-minute hour session.

Anticipatory preparation and behavioral rehearsal are key ingredients to the healing that incarcerated victims require. All sexual assault victims experience symptomology that may leave them feeling as if they are going crazy. By helping to prepare for such experiences, victims may be empowered to better manage their responses to victimization and to minimize the likelihood of revictimization. Use of strategies such as those identified in the manual and tapes of the *Prisoner Rape Education Program* (Donaldson, 1993b, 1997) are important adjuncts to therapeutic intervention.

Regarding an inmate victim's sentence status, individuals who will be released within a short period of time will need information on securing support in the community, dealing with family and friends regarding their victimization experience, and learning how to reintegrate their lives and sexual identity. If the inmate victim will be serving an extended period of incarceration, careful attention should be paid to assisting the inmate victim to learn the skills and techniques of managing their incarceration safely. Additionally, depending on the individual circumstances of the inmate victim, there may need to be extended mental health intervention and continued emotional processing. Should the tragic experience of HIV/AIDS transmission be experienced, there may even be the need for hospice work (Dubler, 1998).

INTERDISCIPLINARY INTERVENTION

The management of inmate sexual assault victims cannot be effectively undertaken without the active and positive involvement of all correctional staff, including administrators, security, classification, and other members of the correctional team (Cotton and Groth, 1982, 1984; Donaldson, 1993b; Dumond, 1992; Fagan, Wennerstrom, and Miller, 1996). Everyone plays an integral role in the process, and all members are vital to ensuring a just and efficient response to inmate victims. Table 5.2 provides guidelines particularly to correctional security and investigative staff, as well as classification staff, in supporting and strengthening the response to inmate sexual assault victims.

Correctional staff must participate in pursuing prosecution (when appropriate) and in ensuring the ongoing safety and security of inmate victims. Each staff member is key to the process—everyone, from administrator to correctional officer, plays an important role in mediating the often destructive impact of inmate sexual assault. It is only with

Table 5.2 Key Correctional and Classification Interventions, Defined by Time

	Key Correctional and Investigative Responsibilities	Key Responsibilities of Classification
Immediately upon disclosure following sexual assault	• Identify the victim, initiate emergency first aid if necessary, remove victim to a safe, secure environment until able to transfer to medical unit within facility. Notify administration. • Secure medical treatment as soon as possible. • Get basic information and document same. • Secure crime scene; begin evidence collection (cells area, physical evidence, victim's clothing, medical evidence) with careful attention to labeling and chain of custody. Photograph. • Isolate and secure aggressor(s), keeping victim and offenders separate. Collect evidence from suspect, clothing, weapons, with careful focus on labeling and chain of custody. Photograph. • Gather witness statements (inmate and staff) and document carefully. Mirandize alleged offenders and begin interrogation procedures.	• Evaluate needs of victim in terms of most appropriate placement; initiate classification review process and recommend short-term placement options to preserve victim safety. • If alleged offenders are identified, note inmate record regarding enemies and ensure that placement not jeopardize inmate victim in this/another institution. Negotiate securing of victim's property from cell, especially if victim is to be held in another location or transferred to the hospital or another prison setting. • Assist victim in notifying family and/or friends for support and assistance; help secure other institutional support from clergy, property, etc.
Short-term follow-up	• Determine appropriate placement conjointly with victim, attempting to not be punitive. • Ensure victim safety and security at all times. • Cooperate with law enforcement and refer to prosecuting attorney for case disposition. • Maintain confidentiality and avoid victim stigma. • Carefully document all findings for prosecution. • Evaluate ongoing risks to inmate victim and promote environmental changes as necessary.	• Determine appropriate placement with inmate victim, and assess options (i.e., protective custody, housing/setting transfer) and implications of placement. • Always ensure victim safety and security. • Convene disciplinary board to respond to complaints against alleged offenders. • Assist victim to secure all necessary services to ensure optimum coping. • Ensure thorough documentation of events to reduce future victimization.
Long-term follow-up	• Preserve inmate safety during incarceration. Facilitate successful completion of prosecution. • Develop long-term placement plans and negotiate safe environments for inmate victims upon release to the community.	• Continue to maintain inmate safety. • Monitor inmate placement throughout institution. • Support victim through prosecution. • Make appropriate discharge referrals.

professionalism, dedication, and knowledge that true improvement in correctional management can be undertaken.

CONCLUSION

Effective management of inmate sexual assault continues to be a challenge, and due to the complex and changing nature of corrections, it may actually be more difficult at the dawn of the twenty-first century. Issues such as dramatic increases in inmate populations, the increase in mental illness, substance abuse, HIV/AIDS, and continued overcrowding and scarcity of resources have all contributed to the problem.

Despite years of research, the actual incidence of inmate sexual abuse in U.S. correctional settings remains unknown. Recent research, however, employing large sample sizes and universal surveying of state correctional systems, may provide a reasonable and sound assessment of the incidence. The effects of inmate sexual assault are global, devastating, and pernicious. Multiple victimizations, continued confinement, sexual slavery, and lack of treatment may increase the impact of victimization. Many sexual assault victims experience suicidal ideation, posttraumatic stress disorder, rape trauma syndrome, and increased psychiatric disturbances. However, positive and active interventions can help to mediate and effectively treat these symptoms.

All correctional staff play an important role in the process. Each member of the correctional team brings their own unique skill, experience, and function to the process. By utilizing empirical data, fostering state-of-the-art interventions, establishing clear, concise protocols, and increasing staff training and communication, it may be possible to effectively respond to the crisis of inmate sexual assault.

6

TRAINING STAFF ON INMATE SEXUAL ASSAULT

Robert W. Dumond and Doris A. Dumond

At the opening of the twenty-first century, the U.S. corrections system faces challenges that are unparalleled in its history. Added to the quandary is the revelation that rape in prison has become "an accepted fact of prison life" (Lewin, 2001: 1). A groundswell of concern is demanding a national response to end what the *Washington Post* (2001) has called the "cruel and usual" punishment of prison rape (A14). The *New York Times* (2001) observes that "America's two million prison inmates have been lawfully deprived of their liberty, but they have not been sentenced to physical and psychological abuse" (16). To remedy this abomination, we may need to initiate legislative, policy, and operational initiatives (Mariner, 2001). The most critical component of the solution, however, is training at all levels of the correctional hierarchy. It is to this endeavor that this chapter is devoted. Staff training is one of the most vital ingredients to promoting correctional institutional safety and security and ensuring the humane and constitutional care of inmates committed to custody (Smith, 2000).

Despite a decade of constructing correctional institutions in the 1990s, the incarcerated population continues to explode (Beck, 2000). Prison construction has simply not been able to keep pace with the burgeoning of the national inmate population (Masci, 1999). At midyear 2000, state prisons nationally were 1 to 17 percent above capacity, while federal prisons were 32 percent above their rated capacity (Beck and Karberg, 2001). Tonry and Petersilia (2000) argue that since the early 1970s, prisons have changed a great deal, including changes in inmate and staff subcultures and changes in inmate-staff interaction.

They posit that education of correctional officers needs to be augmented to effectively manage these transformations.

There are a number of reasons for these changes. Legislative and judicial policy changes since the mid-1970s have significantly lengthened the sentences of inmates (Petersilia, 1999). The resultant aging of the inmate population will further exhaust correctional assets (Champion, 2001; Tonry and Petersilia, 2000). The increased number of inmates with significant health problems, including HIV/AIDS (DeGroot, 2001; Maruschak, 1999) and mental illness (Chelala, 1999; Ditton, 1999), continues to tax medical, mental health, and programmatic resources within jails and prisons nationally (McDonald, 1999). To meet the dynamic future needs of managing prisons and jails effectively, correctional administrators must have the vision to anticipate these challenges and proactively prepare for them (Stinchcomb and McCampbell, 1999).

IGNORANCE OR INDIFFERENCE AMONG CORRECTIONAL OFFICIALS?

Despite a well-documented association between homosexual behavior and inmate rape, U.S. correctional officials have manifested either ignorance, misunderstanding, or more alarmingly, deliberate indifference. In the first national study of male sexual assault in U.S. prisons, Human Rights Watch (Mariner, 2001) found that most correctional authorities deny that sexual assault is a serious problem. Conducted from 1997 through 2000, the study surveyed all fifty states' department of corrections and the Federal Bureau of Prisons to determine the reported rate of inmate sexual assault. Forty-seven corrections departments responded, but only twenty-three departments reported that they maintained separate statistical information on the number of inmate sexual assaults (Mariner, 2001). The number of inmate sexual assaults disclosed was stunningly low: Only four states, Texas, Florida, Ohio, and Illinois (ranking second, fifth, sixth, and seventh in size, respectively), and the Federal Bureau of Prisons (ranking third in size) acknowledged receiving more than fifty incidents of inmate sexual assault. Texas, with a 1999 inmate population of 146,574 inmates, revealed the largest number (237 allegations) of inmate sexual assaults for a reported rate of 162 per 100,000 inmates (Mariner, 2001: 134, 373).

What made this study especially important was the discrepancy of reported incidents with substantiated results from more recent, well-designed empirical studies concerning prison sexual assault. No state indicated a rate of sexual abuse consistent with recent, large-scale analyses by Struckman-Johnson and her colleagues (Struckman-Johnson and Struckman-Johnson, 1999, 2000a, 2000b; Struckman-Johnson et al., 1996). These observations were also at variance with the number of sexual assaults estimated by correctional officers themselves. Eigenberg (1989) found that only 9 percent of the correctional officers in Texas believed that rape in prison was rare (with 87 percent believing it was not), and 73 percent of the officers concluded that inmates do not report such assaults to prison officials. Similar results were found in the studies of Struckman-Johnson and associates. In three Nebraska prisons, correctional officers estimated that 16 percent of the inmates had pressured or forced sexual contact, and only 29 percent of these sexually abused inmates reported their victimization (Struckman-Johnson et al., 1996). Similarly, in seven Midwestern male prison facilities, staff speculated that 14.6 percent of inmates were so abused (Struckman-Johnson and Struckman-Johnson, 2000a), with similar rates of victimized inmates officially reporting to prison authorities (Struckman-Johnson and Struckman-Johnson, 2000b).

Herein lies a major obstacle to initiating substantive change. As noted by Paparozzi and Lownkamp (2000), even a small number of misinformed policymakers can significantly handicap efforts to improve correctional progress. As can be seen, there is currently a significant lack of direction in many state correctional departments about the importance of inmate sexual assault and affirmatively responding to the problem. Only six state correctional departments (Arkansas, Illinois, Massachusetts, New Hampshire, North Carolina, and Virginia) currently provide specialized training to correctional officers in effectively managing inmate sexual assault (Mariner, 2001).

Such a recognition is vital to developing a responsible strategy. Maghan (1997) has proffered that training cannot do what management cannot do. Essentially, correctional management must take the lead in charting the direction of training. Otherwise, it obstructs staff from adequately performing their duties. Staff development efforts must also be grounded in validated, empirical studies that are carefully developed and implemented (Paparozzi and Lowenkamp, 2000; Stinchcomb, 1995; Stinchcomb and McCampbell, 1999).

WHAT SHOULD BE INCLUDED
IN CORRECTIONAL STAFF TRAINING?

Identifying what should be included in correctional staff training has been the subject of considerable debate. A number of researchers and practitioners have advanced sound, responsible recommendations for effective training, and their proposals should be carefully reviewed (Cotton and Groth, 1982, 1984; Dumond, 1992, 2000; Eigenberg, 1989, 1994, 2000b; Lockwood, 1978, 1980a; Nacci and Kane, 1982, 1983, 1984a, 1984b).

Lockwood (1978, 1980a) examined New York State prisons and found that prison staff were aware of inmate victimization. When gangs of assailants bypassed existing security protocols and mechanisms and then subsequently physically dominated their victims, prison rapes occurred. In later analyses, Lockwood (1982) considered the use of human relations and social literacy training, guided by responsible prison staff, and provided insightful assessments of living in protective custody and characteristics of the targets of sexual aggression while incarcerated (Lockwood, 1992).

Cotton and Groth (1982) emphasized that staff must have knowledge of the incidence of sexual assault within their facilities and also information about prison sexuality, victim responses, the dynamics of inmate rape, and associated trauma. Especially helpful was their identification of a three-tiered response model of prevention, intervention, and prosecution, along with a sexual assault service delivery protocol flow chart and the San Francisco Jail sexual assault crisis intervention protocol (Cotton and Groth, 1984).

In studying federal inmates, Nacci and Kane (1983) presented two illustrative models on why inmates participate in homosexual acts and the immediate causes and effects of sexual assaults and prison aggression. In their follow-up study, Nacci and Kane (1984b) presented information that was extremely valuable to help motivate staff to deter consensual activity and protect targets of sexual aggression. In addition, they provided knowledge about the relationship of correctional officer stress and job satisfaction, and then presented crucial information on staff training, such as knowledge of aggressors' cues, target profiles, helping targets to handle pressuring, and systematically responding to suspected and actual incidents through individual and programmatic intervention. They also suggested improved inmate risk-assessment procedures, advancements in prison architecture, and the use of standardized "rape kits" to collect forensic evidence from alleged victims and assailants (Nacci and Kane, 1984a).

Eigenberg's studies (1989, 1994) of correctional officers' attitudes regarding inmate rape and sexual assault were extremely important and should be reviewed. Because correctional staff are not skilled in differentiating between consensual and nonconsensual behavior, Eigenberg

(1994) argued that staff should be trained to vigorously enforce disciplinary standards regarding all sexual activity. She further argued that staff
should receive "sensitivity training" to approach and communicate with
victims in a professional, compassionate manner. In recent analyses,
Eigenberg (2000a, 2000b) examined the willingness of correctional
officers to counter coercive and consensual sexual acts. Consistently,
these officers indicated that they would respond to coercive encounters,
but, in general, were less likely to respond when incidents were consensual or involved homosexuals. These findings are troubling and indicate
that much work needs to be done regarding officers' perceptions and
attitudes.

Dumond (1992) provided a thorough, concise examination of the
issues of male sexual assault and comprehensive strategies for responding to the problem. Included was a discussion of the prison hierarchy,
summary tables on the epidemiology and impact of prison sexual
assault, as well as two very valuable figures illustrating the cycles of
victimization in sexual assault victims. Dumond's (1992) discussion of
strategies for intervention was particularly helpful in training. A more
recent analysis provided a timely encapsulation of the contemporary
issues, for which staff training was a critical response (Dumond, 2000).
Each of the issues raised by these key researchers should be carefully
considered and incorporated in the development of training curriculums
for correctional staff. It is also important to note that sexual relationships occur between staff and inmates and that this issue must be
addressed with correctional staff during their sexual assault training.

STAFF SEXUAL MISCONDUCT

Since 1995, there have been a number of well-documented reports of
sexual misconduct being perpetrated by correctional staff on inmates
under their care (Amnesty International, 1999; Burton et al., 1999;
Human Rights Watch, 1996), which have raised great concerns for the
safety, health, and well-being of incarcerated females. Researchers
studying inmate sexual assault have found, however, that it was not just
male custodial staff victimizing female inmates. In their examination of
Nebraska prisons, Struckman-Johnson et al. (1996) discovered eighteen
incidents of sexual assault by prison staff upon male inmates, and one
incident involved prison employees in the women's prison. In their later
analyses of seven Midwestern male prisons in four different state correctional departments, Struckman-Johnson and Struckman-Johnson (2000a)

found rates of sexual assaultive incidents involving staff ranging between 15 and 28 percent within five institutions for an average of 20 percent. Clearly, then, it is a problem that potentially affects all inmates.

Between 1994 and 1996, Human Rights Watch conducted an examination of five states (California, Georgia, Illinois, Michigan, and New York) and the District of Columbia and found widespread incidents of custodial sexual misconduct by both male and female correctional staff. The organization also found wholesale denial, and lack of appropriate investigative and grievance procedures, and concluded that one of the major barriers to alleviating the problem was its "invisibility . . . and hence its deniability" at the state and national level (Human Rights Watch, 1996: 5). In some cases, accused officers were put in charge of investigating themselves. Class action suits initiated in 1992 in Georgia and 1994 in the District of Columbia were seen as one of the only effective vehicles used to acknowledge and remedy the problem. Unfortunately, correctional officials were often involved in severe retaliation against women who sought such remedies, as noted by Widney-Brown (1998) regarding the Michigan Department of Corrections. She concluded, however, that staff retaliation was largely representative of other corrections departments as well.

The General Accounting Office conducted an examination of staff-on-inmate sexual misconduct in three of the largest correctional departments in the United States (California, Texas, and the Federal Bureau of Prisons ranked first through third, respectively) and the District of Columbia using official sources (Burton et al., 1999). Female inmates made a total of 506 allegations of custodial sexual misconduct, of which ninety-two (18 percent) were reported. The majority of allegations involved harassment, improper surveillance, touching, and "consensual" sex. Only the Federal Bureau of Prisons reported successful prosecution of staff involved, while the other jurisdictions cited the lack of evidence for failure to prosecute. The report highlighted inadequate policies/procedures and the lack of systematic methods for data collection and analysis and concluded that the extent of custodial sexual misconduct in the United States was unknown.

Important to the debate is the notion of consensual sex between inmates and staff. Can sexual contact between correctional staff and inmates ever be considered consensual? Because of the overwhelming power and control that staff exercise over the charges (Human Rights Watch, 1996), it is difficult to take an affirmative position. The more appropriate designation would be to utilize the terms "pseudoconsensual sexual abuse" and "nonconsensual sexual abuse," employed by Calhoun (1996).

Certain groups of inmates seem to be at increased risk of custodial sexual misconduct. The young, mentally ill, inexperienced, lesbian/transgendered, addicted, and first-time offenders are at increased risk (Human Rights Watch, 1996; Smith 1998). A number of factors contribute to the problem, including the unprofessional facility environment, employee character and attitude, poor/absent policies and procedures, poor training, supervisory ignorance, and inappropriate secrecy (Calhoun, 1996; Dennis, 1999; Human Rights Watch, 1996; LIS, Inc., 1996a, 1996b; Phelps, 1999).

Additional issues complicate the eradication of this problem. Staff may have improper allegiance to other staff, be indifferent, or worse, provide tacit support for such behavior. These counterproductive attitudes are dangerous to all correctional environments and underscore a major risk to custodial sexual misconduct. All such incidents compromise the safety and security of the institution and seriously jeopardize staff morale (Dennis, 1999; Phelps, 1999).

To effectively manage this cancer, a number of proposals have been proffered. They include the development of clear policies and procedures, staff training initiatives, systematic investigative techniques, and inmate awareness programs (Dennis, 1999; Human Rights Watch, 1996; LIS, Inc., 1996a, 1996b; Phelps, 1999; Widney-Brown, 1998). Other innovations can be particularly helpful, such as the establishment of confidential hotlines to assist in the reporting of such behavior, use of the polygraph for inmates who allege staff misconduct, and having investigations conducted by independent law enforcement agencies to avoid contamination/subterfuge. Such abuses are intolerable (Dumond, 2000). Dismissal of those staff involved and their swift prosecution must also be initiated in each and every case to send a clear message to all staff that such behavior is never acceptable.

There are several resources that are worthy of note. Competent, reliable policies have been established by a number of state correctional departments. Administrators should consider those promulgated by the state of Georgia (Georgia Department of Corrections, 1994, 1996) and the Commonwealth of Massachusetts (Massachusetts Department of Corrections, 2001b). The Allegations, Investigations, and Personnel Actions System currently being tested by the Michigan Department of Corrections (2000) is another innovation that bears consideration and examination. Because staff training is a vital ingredient of this process, the endeavors of the Virginia Department of Corrections (Hobbs et al., 1998) provide an important model to analyze.

The most comprehensive staff training initiative has been undertaken by the National Institute of Corrections (2000). This curriculum is designed to provide a multiday experience for correctional staff in order to help them understand the complexities of custodial sexual misconduct and should be considered the premier model for other training initiatives. Initial responses to the training have been very favorable, as reported by Moss (2000), which is likely to continue in the future. Problems of this magnitude cannot be ameliorated without a sincere administrative commitment to recognizing the problem and initiating substantive training.

Failure to Respond Can Result in Liability and Penalty

One area that actually may motivate corrections professionals to respond is the realization that failure to respond affirmatively can result in significant liability and substantial compensatory and punitive damages as a result of civil litigation. Scalia (1997) reported that the growth of the prison population between 1980 and 1996 has engendered increases in prisoners' litigation in the federal courts, both U.S. district courts (trial) and U.S. courts of appeal (appellate). More than half of the cases filed in federal courts have been for alleged civil rights violations. Ross (1997) identified that inmates may file lawsuits in federal and state courts under the Civil Rights Statute Title 42 Section 1983 for deprivation of constitutional rights. Between 1970 and 1994, 3,205 correctional liability cases were brought against jail and prison correctional officials for issues such as medical care, administrative liability, conditions of confinement, failure to protect, and cruel and unusual punishment. Increasingly, state and federal courts have held individual officers, superintendents, institutions, and correctional departments liable for compensatory and punitive damages for failing to perform the adequate care, custody, and control of inmates under their supervision.

Four cases may serve to illustrate the severity of such failures and the dramatic consequences to correctional staff, administrators, and departments that can result: (1) *Redmond v. Baxley,* (2) *Smith v. Wade,* (3) *Lamarca v. Turner,* and (4) *Mathie v. Fries.* The most recent substantive case to come before the U.S. Supreme Court, *Farmer v. Brennan,* will also be examined.

Redmond v. Baxley

In this case, a correctional nurse-supervisor and the director of the Michigan Department of Corrections, though aware of the severity of the risk of sexual assault, rendered an inadequate response to an inmate so assaulted. As a result, the incarcerated victim was awarded $130,000 in damages.

Smith v. Wade

In 1976, inmate Daniel R. Wade voluntarily checked into protective custody in the Algoa Reformatory, a Missouri correctional facility for youthful first-time offenders, because of prior incidents of inmate violence against him. Because of disciplinary violations, Wade was transferred to administrative segregation and placed in a cell with another inmate. Later that day, a correctional officer, William H. Smith, assigned a third inmate to the cell, making no effort to determine whether another cell was available (which there was). Following the placement, Wade's two cellmates harassed, beat, and sexually assaulted him. In 1983, Wade brought suit against Smith and four other guards and correctional officials alleging that his Eighth Amendment rights had been violated because Smith knew or should have known that an assault against him was likely under the circumstances.

During the trial, the district judge entered a directed verdict for two of the defendants and instructed the jury that Wade could make out an Eighth Amendment violation only by showing "physical abuse of such base, inhumane and barbaric proportions as to shock the sensibilities." Further, because of Smith's qualified immunity as a prison guard, the judge instructed the jury that Wade could recover only if the defendants were guilty of "gross negligence" (defined as "a callous indifference or a thoughtless disregard for the consequences of one's act or failure to act") or "[e]gregious failure to protect" (defined as "a flagrant or remarkably bad failure to protect"). The jury returned verdicts for two of the three remaining defendants. It found Officer Smith liable, however, and awarded $25,000 in compensatory damages and $5,000 in punitive damages. The district court entered judgment on the verdict, later affirmed by the U.S. Court of Appeals and the U.S. Supreme Court (see

Smith v. Wade, 461 U.S. 30 [1983]). Officer Smith was liable for the damages for his failure to act responsibly.

Lamarca v. Turner

In another case, there were patterns of inmate sexual abuse against a number of inmates virtually ignored by prison officials. This was the situation at the Glades Correctional Institution (GCI) at Belle Glade, Florida, during the early to mid-1980s. Inmate Anthony Lamarca filed a lawsuit in 1982 alleging that he had been harassed and threatened numerous times for sexual favors by other inmates. The allegation was reviewed by U.S. magistrate Peter Nimkoff who began an investigation. A total of ten inmates were identified as having suffered various significant inmate assaults, including five inmates who were raped, usually by several inmates with knives, and the other inmates having been beaten, stabbed, or smashed (Mailander, 1990a). In 1987, U.S. District Court judge James C. Paine adopted the report prepared by Nimkoff and ordered former GCI superintendent R. V. Turner to pay eight inmates $178,500, the highest judgment ever against a state prison warden, for deliberately ignoring the "knowledge: the indices of rape that a prudent administrator would discern" (see *Lamarca v. Turner*, 662 F. Supp 647, [S.D. Fla, 1987]).

Three years later, while conditions appeared to have been improved, Judge Paine noted that homosexual rapes were still occurring at the facility, and he ordered GCI officials to make eighteen major changes at the facility. Among these mandates was the initiation of staff training for all institutional staff. Correctional staff were to be educated about the seriousness of homosexual rape and to more effectively handle rape complaints, while the staff psychiatrist and psychologist were to be trained in rape crisis management (Mailander, 1990a, 1990b).

Mathie v. Fries

There has been increasing awareness of the problem of inmate sexual assault by correctional staff, which is certainly an area of grave concern to all correctional institutions and staff (Amnesty International 1999; Burton et al., 1999; Human Rights Watch, 1996; Mariner, 2001). Such barbaric behavior can result in extraordinary judgments, as noted in *Mathie v. Fries*.

Over a period of four months in 1990, inmate Maurice F. Mathie, then a pretrial detainee at the Suffolk County Correctional Facility in Riverhead, Long Island, was brutally and repeatedly raped by the institution's head of internal security. Sergeant Roy Fries, who had been employed since 1969, had at least one prior known incident of improper conduct with an inmate that had resulted in censure. In August 1996, federal district judge Arthur D. Spatt found that Fries "used his position of Chief of Security . . . to victimize and forcibly sodomize an inmate under his total control in an outrageous abuse of power and authority." The U.S. District Court for the Eastern District of New York awarded Mathie $250,000 in compensatory damages and $500,000 in punitive damages. The finding was appealed to the Federal Court of Appeals for the Second Circuit in New York, which upheld the victory but reduced the punitive damages to $200,000. Suffolk County was correspondingly ordered to pay $450,000 in cumulative damages to the inmate (Stop Prison Rape, 1997). It is clear that prison officials can be held accountable for the wanton brutality of staff sexual assault upon inmates and consequently pay a significant price for their behavior.

Farmer v. Brennan

The most comprehensive case to be brought before the U.S. Supreme Court was the case of a transsexual inmate, Dee Farmer, who had been beaten and raped by another inmate upon being transferred to a federal penitentiary from a federal correctional institution. Farmer argued that his transsexuality made him a clear risk for sexual assault and that federal correctional officials had shown "deliberate indifference" by keeping him in the general population. The Court ruled that prison officials have an "affirmative duty under the Constitution to provide for the safety of inmates" (Justice Blackmun, concurring opinion).

*   *   *

There are a number of other cases in which correctional officials have been held liable and required to pay damages. Pitts (2001) makes the following observation: Successful suits have been brought by inmates against the states of Maryland, Missouri, Arizona, New York, Wisconsin, California, and several others (258). Case awards have ranged from $2,000 to $1 million. Courts in various jurisdictions and at different levels are determined to punish any system or person who allows an inmate to be sexually abused.

Although Mariner (2001: 157) argues that "courts have not proven to be an effective champion of the sexually abused inmate," the preceding cases reveal that correctional officials have been and can be held accountable for their inability to act appropriately and with serious results.

Conclusion

This chapter has examined the range of issues related to correctional staff training regarding inmate sexual assault. Training and staff development are the cornerstones to building an effective response to this complex problem that threatens the safety and security of all correctional institutions. Only a small number of state correctional departments currently engage in staff training, which reflects a deadly malaise among correctional managers and administrators.

Failure to respond affirmatively threatens not only the safety and security of correctional institutions but also compromises staff, who may be held legally and financially accountable for failing to respond appropriately. The issue of inmate sexual assault has been studied in depth, and there are tangible clues as to who is most vulnerable. All correctional staff should correspondingly become familiar with those inmates who are most at risk.

Each member of the correctional team plays a vital role in effectively managing inmate sexual assault. Correctional staff must understand prison sexuality, must develop the proper attitude to respond effectively, and must utilize sound investigative techniques to collect, maintain, and record evidence for prosecution. Classification staff play a pivotal role in managing this problem. They can initially identify potential victims and aggressors and appropriately divert inmates to more appropriate venues. They are also crucial to responding to inmate victims if abuse does occur.

Custodial sexual misconduct is also a major threat to institutional safety and security with which all correctional staff must be aware. Ignorance, indifference, and malaise have contributed to the continuation of this problem, which must be aggressively identified, prosecuted, and eradicated. To prevent sexual violence and the possible spread of HIV/AIDS, all correctional staff must be trained to comprehend the dangers and to ensure that such behavior does not occur.

7

INMATES WITH HIV/AIDS: A GROWING CONCERN

Rosemary L. Gido

In 1996, the Joint United Nations Programme on HIV/AIDS summarized the importance of inmate health care and disease prevention by stating that "prisoners are the community. They come from the community, they return to it. Protection of prisoners is protection of our communities." The group also contended that "failure to provide [prisoners] the basic measures, such as information, education, and the means of [HIV] prevention available on the outside, violates [their] rights to health, security of person, and equality before the law." In other words, by not providing safe sex opportunities, correctional administrators have failed miserably at protecting inmates and their families from acquiring and then transmitting HIV/AIDS. In addition, especially during the 1980s, most correctional facilities failed in addressing the needs of infected inmates. Using personal experiences as the former director of the Office of Program and Policy Analysis in the New York State Commission of Correction (SCOC), I will examine the commission's inability to deal with HIV and how this has been reflective of most correctional systems.

NEW YORK: A STATE WITH LATENT INABILITIES TO DEAL WITH HIV/AIDS

On October 24, 1985, then governor of New York Mario M. Cuomo announced a comprehensive strategy and public information campaign to address the problem of AIDS—acquired immune deficiency syndrome—within the state. Recognizing the significant impact of AIDS on New York's criminal justice system, the governor made specific policy recommendations to each of the five state criminal justice agencies: (1) the Department of Correctional Services (DOCS), (2) the Division of Parole, (3) the Division for Youth, (4) the Division of Probation and Correctional Alternatives, and (5) the State Commission of Correction (Gaunay and Gido, 1986).

The SCOC, as the state's correctional regulatory agency, was legally mandated "to investigate and report . . . on the condition of systems for the delivery of medical care to inmates of correctional facilities" (Gaunay and Gido, 1986: 1). The discovery of the first New York State prison inmate mortality from pneumocystis carinii pneumonia by the commission in November 1981 (Gaunay and Gido, 1986) had gone largely unnoticed. But the annual increase in HIV-positive inmates and deaths due to AIDS uncovered by the commission's monitoring of the disease would lock both the SCOC and DOCS in a struggle to address a complex set of inmate health policy and management issues over the next sixteen years. Bureaucratic inertia and resistance to change characterize much of this case study of the New York State prison system and HIV/AIDS, which illustrates the challenges and barriers to the delivery of humane health care to HIV/AIDS inmates across the United States in 2001.

Drawing on the history of New York State's dealing with HIV/AIDS in its prison system, this chapter illustrates that after twenty years of AIDS, both New York State and U.S. HIV/AIDS correctional populations have been marginalized, the victims of a system reluctant to adopt major strategies of humane treatment, education, and prevention. In 2001, New York still had the greatest number of HIV-positive inmates and inmates with AIDS than any other prison system. Although DOCS health care system improvements have finally been introduced in recent years, these efforts are compromised by a system that still lacks a comprehensive patient education program and links to community public health and criminal justice agency treatment follow-through upon release (Engle, 1999).

CORRECTIONAL HEALTH CARE OVERSIGHT

Drawing on a model of organizational oversight, the SCOC was structurally deficient in the minimal components of monitoring capacity — normative capability, empirical capability, diagnostic capability, and intervention capability (Gilmore, 1985). Typically wanting for resources, the commission lacked the staff to develop minimum standards across all areas of correctional operations (normative capability) and to perform comprehensive field investigations in local and state correctional facilities to ensure their compliance (empirical and diagnostic capability). Hence, the commission's intervention capability came up short time after time.

For example, between August and November 1983, the SCOC staff visited ten large New York maximum-security prisons to investigate the DOCS's health services. The SCOC report issued in June 1984 found deficiencies that included housing of general-confinement inmates in medical services areas and the need to improve health care staffing, deployment, and training (New York State Commission of Correction, 1984: 24). The report further noted:

> The impact of the outbreak of Acquired Immune Deficiency Syndrome (AIDS) upon state facility health services has been profound. Problems involving a uniform approach to screening and diagnosis, outpatient housing, programming, treatment, and education and training have yet to be adequately addressed by DOCS. (24)

In a response characteristic of the antagonism between the two agencies, the DOCS noted that the SCOC had neglected its legally mandated oversight of the department's health services. This "void" had led the department to initiate its own set of health care standards in November 1982 (New York State Commission of Correction, 1984). The commissioner of the DOCS, Thomas Coughlin, further noted that as of June 1984, there were ninety-two diagnosed cases and thirty-three confirmed cases of AIDS in the state prison system. "Therefore, in the best interests of providing adequate care and treatment of AIDS patients, as well as providing for their safety and well-being, DOCS has taken the stand that all inmates diagnosed with AIDS who do not require hospitalization will be housed in facility infirmaries" (3). Over the next two years, the DOCS public relations office would routinely report 100 HIV active cases in the system in response to outside inquiries regarding the frequency of active HIV cases. At the SCOC, the monitoring of inmate deaths from HIV/AIDS suggested a far greater number of cases.

NEW YORK INMATE MORTALITIES FROM AIDS, 1981–1987

In response to the governor's call for HIV/AIDS policy formulations from all criminal justice agencies in 1985, the SCOC staff from the

Office of Program and Policy Analysis and the Bureau of Health Systems Evaluation proposed a research study. Its purpose was three-fold—to: (1) profile demographically inmates who were dying of AIDS each year; (2) outline the disease profile of AIDS in the prison system, including symptoms and time periods of the disease; and (3) present emerging policy and research issues suggested by the data (Gaunay and Gido, 1986; Gido and Gaunay, 1987, 1988b). The research, conducted over a three-year period on each year's "mortality cohort," confirmed that the New York State prison system led the country in the number of inmate mortalities (Gido and Gaunay, 1988b: 3–4):

> Over 50 percent of all DOCS deaths between 1984 and 1987 were due to AIDS. The AIDS mortality rate per 10,000 DOCS inmates has grown steadily. Using a New York City general population mortalities sample (of intravenous drug users) as a comparison group, there has been a decrease in inmate survival rates and a lower mean survival rate of inmate cases compared to this sample. . . . Inmate survival rates were less than half that of the general population sample and declining annually (38).

Opportunistic infection rates in state facilities evidenced an upward trend in the proportion of pneumocystis carinii pneumonia. The typical AIDS inmate mortality in the New York State correctional system was a Hispanic or black, single, male, thirty-four years of age, with a history of intravenous drug abuse prior to incarceration. He was born in the New York City metropolitan area, having lived in this area prior to entering the system. He was typically incarcerated in a state correctional facility. He was likely to have been convicted of robbery, burglary, or drug-related offenses and had been in the system an average of nineteen months prior to death. He was most likely to have contracted the opportunistic infection, pneumocystis carinii pneumonia, and died after an average final hospital stay of twenty-seven days.

Using this enhancement of empirical capability, the commission chided the department for its lack of AIDS management policies and echoed the findings of its 1984 report (Gido and Gaunay, 1987):

> A July, 1987 Commission survey found 362 identified AIDS and ARC patients distributed among 33 state correctional facilities. Of these, a total of 235 were being managed in either facility infirmaries or in population. The conditions of medical management vary among the 33 facilities, but their access to tertiary care medical centers is nearly uniformly limited. Additionally staffing resources have not increased

to meet this need. This, when viewed in conjunction with the increase in deaths at facilities and hospitals (3 in 1984; 4 in 1985; 6 in 1986; and 15 in 1987) and the year-to-year increases in AIDS confirmations only at autopsy (1983–3; 1984–4; 1985–12; 1986–28; 1987–22 [as of 10/31]) suggests that the increased strain on limited DOCS health care resources, both facility and community-based, is having a negative impact on DOCS' ability to achieve nominal results its management of AIDS. (38)

In support of these findings, the SCOC Bureau of Health System Evaluation conducted annual audits of the department's first in-house special needs (HIV/AIDS) medical unit at Sing Sing Correctional Facility (opened in 1983). Summarizing four site visits by two evaluators from 1984 to 1987, the SCOC issued a very critical report in 1988 with thirty-six recommendations for improvement to the Special Needs Unit at Sing Sing (New York State Commission of Correction, 1988). Still, the DOCS resisted the idea that the state prison system shift its mission to include primary responsibility for inmate health care. Further, Commissioner Coughlin responded, "This Department has, and until notified differently, will continue to follow the advice and direction of the [New York] Department of Health" (114). Clearly, the SCOC's intervention was not having an effect.

AIDS Hysteria in U.S. Correctional Facilities, 1981–1990

As inmate AIDS mortalities mounted in the New York State prison system, local, state, and federal correctional systems began to confront the reality of developing policies to manage HIV/AIDS behind bars. Echoing the public hysteria concerning modes of transmission, risks of infection, and mass screening, there were calls for mandatory testing of all incoming inmates, housing segregation for those testing positive, and disclosure of inmate HIV/AIDS status to correctional personnel to ensure the use of proper precautionary measures, such as protective clothing (Basu, 1988; Mahoney, 1988). Early on, correctional administrators wanted answers: "Is the virus being transmitted in prison?" "Should HIV screening be mandatory?" "Should seropositive inmates be segregated?" "Who should have access to files about the HIV antibody status of inmates?" "Should institutions distribute condoms?" (Blumberg, 1990: 193).

In response, the National Institute of Justice, with the American Correctional Association, began an annual survey of all fifty state prison systems, the Federal Bureau of Prisons, and thirty-seven city/county jail systems (Hammet, 1986, 1987, 1988). This survey provided a national picture of the disease across correctional systems, indicating a skewed distribution of cases, with higher concentrations in systems like New York, where large numbers of intravenous drug abusers were incarcerated. A variety of policy responses in correctional settings, some short-term reactions, emerged during this time period.

As the knowledge that HIV transmission occurred only through contaminated blood and semen and the sharing of needles (related to intravenous drug use) became more widespread, the debate still continued as to whether the AIDS virus was being transmitted inside prison facilities (Hammet, 1986: xi–xii). The incubation period of the disease at the time was thought to be as long as seven years, but there were no hard data to document in-prison transmission (Gaunay and Gido, 1986). Over this time period, security issues overshadowed policy recommendations to distribute condoms and provide clean needles (in recognition of widespread tattooing). Most correctional administrators viewed adopting these policies as admissions of security breaches in their institutions. With dissemination of facts about HIV/AIDS transmission, correctional systems soon began to adopt universal precautions for dealing with blood or body fluids (Hammet, 1988: 92).

One reactive housing policy response occurred in California in 1985 with the establishment of a segregation policy as a medical necessity for inmates who tested positive or had full-blown AIDS (Gido and Gaunay, 1988a). Jail systems like New York City, which estimated seroprevalence rates of 33 percent on Rikers Island, quickly dismissed the notion of supporting a large quarantine inmate population. By 1988, there was a "trend away from blanket segregation of asymptomatic seropositives" (Hammet, 1988: 93) and case-by-case separation based on such assessments as security risk and illness.

Mandatory testing or mass screening in correctional settings was clearly the most debated issue in this phase of the epidemic. Proponents, such as corrections officers' unions, argued that mass screening was the best way to identify at-risk inmates, for the safety of both staff and inmates. Opponents, however, indicated that the testing was not yet perfected and would support the practice of segregation. A subculture of outcasts would create violent environments. While politicians and legislators also took the lead in calling for mass screening and mandatory testing, the National Association of State Corrections

Administrators and the National Commission on Correctional Health Care opposed the policy (Blumberg, 1990). Again, as the hysteria subsided with dissemination of information and education, only a few systems conducted mass screening. Most moved on to anonymous testing, high-risk testing, or no testing (Hogan, 1997).

New York's very strict public health law made it illegal to disclose HIV/AIDS status. In other states and correctional systems, it was claimed that facility staff had the "right to know" in order to protect themselves. Based on the facts that the virus was not transmitted through casual contact, that the period of incubation was not yet pinned down, that universal precautions were the recommended course of action, and that new drugs such as AZT were becoming available even to inmates, most correctional systems developed policies to ensure that the antibody status of infected inmates was protected information (Blumberg, 1990: 203).

Although it may be argued that education and training of inmate populations and staff as the primary tools for addressing HIV/AIDS in correctional settings replaced the hysteria of this era, it is clear that inmates, along with drug abusers, prostitutes, and gay men, were socially marginalized and classified as misfits both in prison and society (Hogan, 1997). As it became clear that the greater percentage of HIV-status inmates are people of color, the interventions of advocacy groups, both medical and civil rights, would come up against the reality of the war on drugs, correctional system overcrowding, new medical tuberculosis and hepatitis crises, and bureaucratic inertia.

THE WAR ON DRUGS AND FEMALE OFFENDERS WITH HIV/AIDS

The war on drugs and its passage of mandatory minimum sentencing laws at the federal and state levels produced systemwide overcrowding and the largest increase in incarcerated women in U.S. history, from 13,400 in 1980 to 84,000 by 1998. In this time period, the number of female offenders serving time for drug offenses almost doubled (Chen, 2000).

Although the first decade of the HIV/AIDS epidemic in correctional facilities barely acknowledged the plight of HIV-infected women (Gido, 1992), the health care needs of women imprisoned in the decade 1988 to 1998 revealed trends linking poverty, race, and victimization with drug use and sexual behaviors (New York State Department of

Health, 1998). Ross and Lawrence (2002) compared mortality rates among women offenders in New York and the five other largest correctional jurisdictions in the country to general population women, ages fifteen to fifty-four. They found that mortality rates for young women in the community have remained stable, but rates for the women in these penal systems exceeded those of the general population.

Because women make up a much lower percentage of federal and state correctional populations (6.4 percent) (DeGroot et al., 1999), correctional health, educational, and vocational programming for incarcerated women has been inferior to similar programming for imprisoned men. As the numbers of women with drug histories have overcrowded U.S. jails and prisons and have challenged already deficient correctional health care systems (Ross and Lawrence, 2002), troubling statistics began to emerge. For example, Chen (2000) found that 3.5 percent of female inmates in state prisons were infected with HIV, compared to 2.2 percent of male inmates. In northeastern U.S. prisons, 13 percent of women inmates were HIV-infected compared to 7.2 percent of men (DeGroot et al., 1999). In addition, HIV-infected women have high rates of cervical cytologic abnormalities, sexually transmitted diseases, and certain gynecologic infections (DeGroot et al., 1999).

In 1991, New York's major metropolitan-area women's health care providers, advocates, and patients provided testimony on the significant health care problems of poor and incarcerated women, noting their nearly complete marginalization by the medical community. As Ross and Lawrence emphasize (2002):

> There has been a traditional reluctance to invest in the services and support mechanisms necessary to adequately address the primary care needs of women prisoners that is only now being addressed in large prison systems . . . the systematic denial to women of parity of services readily and routinely available to incarcerated men is the most widespread and invidious impediment to adequate health care for women offenders. (83–84)

ADVOCACY AND CRISES

With the dissemination of the third edition of the SCOC mortalities report (Gido and Gaunay, 1988b), several constituency groups picked up on the finding that "the available evidence already shows that New York State prisoners diagnosed with AIDS live only half as long as people diagnosed with AIDS of similar backgrounds who are not incarcerated" (Joint Subcommittee on AIDS and the Association of the Bar of the City of New York, 1989). The report and testimony at two days of public hearings from New York State inmate advocacy groups, such as Prisoner Legal Services of New York, the Correctional Association of New York, the American Civil Liberties Union National Prison Project, the National Gay and Lesbian Task Force, and the Fortune Society, were the first public indicators that interest groups were applying pressure on the New York State Department of Correctional Services for its failure to address HIV/AIDS issues. The hearings coincided with the appointment by the DOCS of a full-time medical director in 1989 who announced in September of that year the department's plan for building secure units in the state's hospitals and providing 150 nursing home beds for prisoners with AIDS. This appointment did significantly improve continuity of care and coordination of support services and in-service training in the detection, diagnosis, and management of HIV in the state prison system (Ross and Lawrence, 2002: 83).

As New York State inmate AIDS mortalities climbed steadily through 1994 (Lawrence, 2001), the incidence of tuberculosis related to the epidemic spread of HIV infection also increased—from 15.4 per 100,000 in 1976 through 1978 to 105.5 per 100,000 in 1986. Constituting a significant health risk as a communicable disease, tuberculosis occurred in 56 percent of HIV-positive inmates in 1986 (Braun et al., 1989).

As if the infusion of tuberculosis into the overcrowded New York prison system was not enough, an outbreak of multi-drug-resistant tuberculosis (MDR-TB) in 1990–1991 resulted in the deaths of thirty-six inmates and one correctional officer. Thirty-eight of the thirty-nine inmates diagnosed with MRD-TB were co-infected with HIV (Braithwaite et al., 1999). Following this incident, New York State instituted mandatory, annual TB screening for all staff and inmates.

CONCLUSION

Since 1995, the AIDS mortality rate in New York State prisons has declined from 36.4 per 10,000 inmates in 1990–1995 to 6.1 per 10,000 inmates in 1998 (Correctional HIV Consortium, 1998). This decline in AIDS-related deaths corresponds to the U.S. general population mortalities decline for this period and is attributable to advances in antiviral therapy now widely available to inmates across the system (Centers for Disease Control, 1999). In spite of these advances, New York State and national human rights and health advocates continue to call for more proactive policies for inmates with HIV/AIDS. A report issued by the Correctional Association of New York reviewed services at twenty-two New York correctional facilities. The report noted uneven clinical management; a vagueness among staff physicians about critical HIV/AIDS issues; wide variations in HIV testing, support services, and education; and an absence of prevention measures (Haggerty, 2000).

The AIDS in Prison Project (2001) emphasizes that the vast majority of prisoners with HIV/AIDS survive their prison terms and return to their homes, which are most likely to be in poor, inner-city communities of color, already hard hit by the AIDS epidemic. The AIDS in Prison Project calls for patient education and linkages to community HIV-prevention and disease management. The National Institute of Justice and Centers for Disease Control and Prevention research report has similarly found fewer collaborations between correctional and public health agencies in the areas of discharge planning and transitional services for individuals leaving prison (Hammett, 1998). With the hepatitis C virus and sexually transmitted diseases contributing to the complexity of correctional health care, advocates are also calling for treatment advocacy to challenge the poor care and medical neglect of women prisoners with HIV and hepatitis C (Bartnof, 1999).

One final issue that has resisted change has been prevention programming that provides access to condoms, clean needles and syringes, and dental dams. Four city jail systems and two state correctional departments have made condoms available in their facilities since 1993, without any reported adverse effects (HIV in Prison, 2000). Because of the large number of inmates who engage in consensual same-sex sexual behaviors, allowing inmates to purchase condoms provides sound policy in a world where it is lacking.

8

Consensual Sexual Behavior

Mary Koscheski, Christopher Hensley, Jeremy Wright, and Richard Tewksbury

Cass (1979) defined *homosexuality* as "the feeling of sexual desire for members of the same sex, or the experience of having sex with persons of the same sex, or a combination of both feeling and the experience" (219). The renowned sex researcher Alfred Kinsey and his colleagues (1948) pointed out that it is much more difficult to define what a *homosexual* is:

> People do not represent two discrete populations, heterosexual and homosexual. The world is not to be divided into sheep and goats. Not all things are black nor all things white. It is a fundamental taxonomy that nature rarely deals with discrete categories. Only the human mind invents categories and tries to force facts into separate pigeon holes. The living world is a continuum in each and every one of its aspects. The sooner we learn this concerning human sexual behavior the sooner we shall reach a sound understanding of the realities of sex. (639)

To help determine who was considered homosexual, Kinsey and his colleagues designed a continuum from one extreme being exclusively heterosexual (a score of 0) to the opposite extreme being exclusively homosexual (a score of 6). Kinsey et al. (1953, 1948) found that at least 29 percent of Americans—20 percent of all women and 37 percent of all men—had experienced an orgasm between adolescence and old age during a homosexual act. These individuals were represented by plots 1 through 6 on the Kinsey scale. Plots 4, 5, or 6 represented those individuals whom Kinsey alluded to as more or less exclusively homosexual. Ten percent of the U.S. population—13 percent of all males and 7 percent of all females—fell within this category. Two-and-a-half percent of

111

Americans were classified as exclusively homosexual—4 percent of all males and 1 percent of all females (a plot of 6 only).

It is important to point out that Kinsey's numbers did not accurately reveal the actual number of homosexuals. The numbers only reflected the overt or physical aspect of homosexuality (i.e., the experience of having sex with members of the same sex). The covert or mental and/or emotional aspects of homosexuality (desire, the erotic feeling, attraction for members of the same sex, or fantasy) were ignored. Those individuals who experienced homosexual feelings but neglected to act on them were not included in his numbers. Kinsey's estimates of homosexuals would have perhaps been even higher if he had asked his subjects about both their sexual desire (mental) and experience (physical), rather than experience alone.

Over forty years following Kinsey's studies, many sex researchers proceeded to concentrate on physical sexual acts alone to determine the number of homosexuals. Although some studies have found the number of exclusively homosexual Americans to be approximately the same as Kinsey—between 2 and 3 percent—(Laumann et al., 1994; Michael et al., 1994), the *Janus Report on Sexual Behavior* (Janus and Janus, 1993) disclosed that 9 percent of men and 5 percent of women were involved in a continuing homosexual relationship.

Not all individuals who engage in homosexual activity consider themselves homosexuals. In many circumstances, individuals' sexual behavior contrasts with their sexual identity. The fact that an individual engages in sexual relations with a person of one gender or the other does not make that individual heterosexual or homosexual. The social science and human service arenas have recognized the difference between one's behavior and identity. The HIV/AIDS epidemic led public health officials to acknowledge the distinction between sexual actions and identities. HIV prevention/intervention programs are no longer only aimed at gay men, but rather men who have sex with men.

SITUATIONAL HOMOSEXUALITY

Research focusing on one's behavior versus identity is not completely a contemporary idea. For decades, situational homosexuality has been recognized (Sagarin, 1976). Men who staunchly maintain an identity as heterosexual have long been known to engage in sexual activities with one another. These men do so as a result of being immersed in single-sex environments, such as remote work sites, the military, boarding schools, and correctional institutions. Sexual activities with other men that constitute situational homosexuality are responses to the lack of mixed-sex interactions. In other words, the men are deprived of the opposite sex. Many researchers feel that most situational homosexual men will return to heterosexual sexual activities once they are presented with a two-sex environment.

Although a significant amount of the population has either in the past or present engaged in same-sex sexual activities, the definitions and popular perceptions of homosexuality continue to focus on "deviance." There is a possibility that a major emphasis of the social sciences' studies of deviance may actually be reinforcing negative stereotypes and definitions of same-sex sexual relations. This is a common concern when studying same-sex sexual activities in controlled environments such as prisons. Therefore, there is a minute amount of literature available dealing with consensual sex in prisons.

It is essential to fully comprehend the conditions that lead to situational homosexuality. Ibrahim (1974), the most notable early researcher to address the issue of prison sexuality, argued that most often the environmental influences, not inmates' actual social identities, are responsible for same-sex sexual activities in prison. Six factors regarding the social structure of prisons that produced and promoted homosexual behavior within prison walls were presented:

1. First, the environment within a prison is a unisex community. Inmates are sometimes induced to accomplish their sexual gratification with other inmates due to a lack of the opposite sex.

2. Second, inmate and prison officials often tolerate deviant sexual behavior, even though it is typically officially restricted. There are three reasons for these tolerant attitudes: (1) Deviant behavior enables stronger inmates to intimidate weaker ones, which in turn creates status roles; (2) the behavior is viewed as a necessary means of control by prison officials (i.e., inmates release tension); and (3) the fear of provoking negative public sentiment keeps authorities from addressing such issues.

3. Another factor, insufficient work opportunities in prisons, leads to deviant sexual activity. When inmates are left idle for long periods of time due to the lack of jobs, the likeliness of them to engage in such behavior is increased. When inmates are kept busy, and working, there is less of a chance for them to engage in deviant sexual behavior

(Ibrahim, 1974). It should be noted that as many as 90 percent of inmates in correctional institutions are unemployed while incarcerated (Flanagan and Maguire, 1993).

4. Overcrowding is yet another factor in promoting prison homosexuality. Many prisons have inmates crowded into cells with others, which results in a lack of privacy. In these overcrowded environments, inmates are able to watch one another use the bathroom, change clothes, and take showers. It is virtually impossible for prison officials to control situations in this type of environment. Younger, more naive inmates are often exploited by older, more experienced inmates due to these overcrowded conditions.

5. Another factor in regard to deviant sexual behavior within prisons is the lack of a practical classification system. Prisoners are often placed into cells with offenders convicted of all types of offenses. The lack of a concrete and reliable system of classifying inmates allows homosexuals and sex offenders to work and room within the general population. An environment such as this invites sexual deviants to continue their sexual practices within the prison walls (Ibrahim, 1974). It is important to point out that in present prison systems, classification systems for inmates do exist.

6. The last and most realistic factor in the formation of deviant sexual behavior is the complete detachment from the world outside the prison walls. Some inmates are prohibited from having or viewing any pornographic magazines or hand-drawn illustrations that depict nudity or sex. Due to this isolation, inmates can begin to disregard the societal norms and engage in deviant sexual behavior with other inmates for sexual gratification (Ibrahim, 1974). Although it has been argued that conjugal visits would lower the amount of same-sex sexual activity in prisons (Hopper, 1969, 1989), only five states currently allow conjugal visits in their correctional facilities (Hensley, Rutland, and Gray-Ray, 2000b).

Consensual sex research in correctional facilities is also very important in regard to the study of HIV and other sexually transmitted diseases. Due to the threat of transmitting HIV and other sexually transmitted diseases through unprotected sexual activity, Saum et al. (1995) have stressed the demand for research on the topic. Prison officials can in all actuality prevent or at least delay the spread of sexually transmitted diseases by educating inmates on the severities of unprotected sex. Two of the most common activities reported by inmates to have changed due to the threat of HIV/AIDS are more protected sex when available or less sex altogether (Saum et al., 1995). Presently, only six correctional systems in the United States allow the distribution of condoms within their facilities: Mississippi, Vermont, New York City, San Francisco, Philadelphia, and Washington, D.C. (Blumberg and Laster, 1999). The seeming contradiction of supplying condoms to inmates who are not permitted sex has kept prison officials from meeting the obvious need in correctional facilities (Saum et al., 1995).

CONSENSUAL SEX IN MALE PRISONS

The study of sexual behavior in male prisons, unfortunately, has been largely neglected by researchers. The few studies that do exist address the topic of coerced sexual aggression rather than consensual sex. The sparse research on the topic is perhaps a result of the ideology that consensual sex produces a minute amount of violence. Rape demands significantly more attention because it has traditionally been viewed as much more of a threat to institutional security (Saum et al., 1995). To date, six studies have been conducted on consensual homosexual behavior in male correctional facilities within the United States (Hensley, Tewksbury, and Wright, 2001; Hensley, 2001; Nacci and Kane, 1983; Saum et al., 1995; Tewksbury, 1989b; Wooden and Parker, 1982).

Pioneer Sex Studies of Male Prisons, 1982–1989

Wooden and Parker (1982) completed perhaps the most comprehensive study of sexual behavior of men in prison. They discovered that 65 percent of a random sample of 200 inmates in a California prison took part in one or more homosexual acts while incarcerated. However, more than 78 percent identified themselves as heterosexual, 11 percent defined themselves as bisexual, and 10.5 percent considered themselves heterosexual. Of the respondents who acknowledged engaging in consensual same-sex sexual behavior while incarcerated, 52 percent reported receiving oral sex, while 20 percent performed oral sex on another inmate. In addition, 38 percent had performed anal sex on another inmate and 20 percent had been anally penetrated. Unfortunately, Wooden and Parker's sample was over-represented by "effeminate homosexuals" and "vulnerable heterosexual youngsters" (9). In other words, the California Department of Corrections used this particular prison as a place to house many known homosexuals, a common practice of the 1980s.

Following a violent outbreak in the early 1980s at the United States Penitentiary in Lewisburg, Pennsylvania, Nacci and Kane (1983) launched a two-part research project investigating homosexual activity and sexual aggression. Lewisburg, a predominantly nonviolent institution, encountered eight inmate murders and numerous inmate-on-inmate assaults over a twenty-six-month period. Five of the eight murders were determined to be sexually motivated.

In response to the unexplained increase in violence, 330 face-to-face interviews were conducted, and surveys were distributed to a random sample of male inmates in seventeen federal prison facilities. The findings revealed that 12 percent of the inmates in lower-security institutions had participated in homosexual activity while incarcerated in their current institution. In penitentiaries that housed more dangerous offenders who were serving longer sentences, the percentages were much higher (30 percent). As a method of receiving more detail about the nature of the homosexual acts, inmates who admitted to same-sex activity were asked to specify their role in the activity. The majority of inmates were "inserters" not "insertees." As one would expect, the masculine role (inserter) was identified with being heterosexual, whereas the feminine role (insertee) was associated with being a homosexual or bisexual.

Tewksbury (1989b) conducted a study that explored "sexual activities, fantasies, and orientations of prison inmates" (34). Out of a sample of 150 inmates in an Ohio prison, Tewksbury discovered that three-fourths (75 percent) of the sampled inmates viewed themselves to be exclusively heterosexual. Almost 20 percent of the entire sample reported being involved in homosexual activity during the prior year, with 8.5 percent of these inmates engaged in sex once a week or more. Interestingly, 7.4 percent of the respondents admitted to being involved in a continuing same-sex relationship.

Contemporary Sex Studies of Male Prisons, 1995–2001

In 1995, Saum and colleagues undertook a study to investigate homosexual behavior in male prisons. One hundred and one inmates were interviewed in a medium-security prison in Delaware. The results revealed that 2 percent had engaged in sexual activity with another inmate the previous year. However, this finding greatly contradicted the respondents' opinions of the frequency of consensual homosexual activity within their institution. For example, almost 70 percent of the sample reported that consensual sex in prison occurred every day.

It is important to note that 11 percent of the male inmates declared that they had had a sexual relationship with a female while incarcerated. The sexual contact with the opposite sex could likely account for the low percentage of inmates that admitted to engaging in homosexual activity. The presence of women in the correctional facility for sexual purposes negates the need for men to turn to other men for their sexual needs. The females involved in the sexual relations were female inmates in classes in the male prison as well as correctional officers and visitors.

Hensley (2001) completed a study that examined the actual number of consensual homosexual acts in male prisons. Face-to-face interviews were administered to 174 male inmates in multiple-security-level prisons in Oklahoma. The interviews revealed that 80 percent of the respondents considered themselves heterosexual, 8 percent homosexual, and 13 percent bisexual. The study also revealed that 8 percent of the inmates had kissed another inmate while incarcerated. Twenty-three percent of the inmates had rubbed their body part against a fellow inmate in a sexual manner or allowed another inmate to rub a body part of theirs against him in a sexual manner. Twenty-four percent had allowed another man to touch their penis or touched another man's penis while incarcerated. Twenty-three percent had performed or received oral sex from another inmate while incarcerated. Twenty percent of the inmates admitted to engaging in anal intercourse with another inmate. Interestingly, 18 percent of the respondents in this study had a male sex partner at the time of the study.

In the most recent study of consensual sexual activity within male prisons, Hensley, Tewksbury, and Wright (2001) administered questionnaires to 142 male inmates in a southern maximum-security correctional facility. The questionnaires were designed to gain information regarding inmates' homosexual behavior while incarcerated, as well as their sexual orientation prior to and during incarceration. When asked to identify their sexual orientation before prison, 79 percent considered themselves heterosexual, 6 percent homosexual, and 15 percent bisexual. When asked to identify their sexual orientation since incarceration, 69 percent considered themselves to be heterosexual, 7 percent homosexual, and 23 percent bisexual.

As a method of identifying predictor variables of homosexual behavior, a set of logistic regression analyses were performed. The most salient variables in the models predicting homosexual behavior while incarcerated were religion and race. Protestants were less likely than non-Protestants to engage in homosexual behavior (i.e., kissing, touching, performing oral sex, receiving oral sex, and performing anal sex) while in prison. Nonwhite inmates were less likely than white inmates to engage in homosexual behavior (touching, performing oral sex, receiving oral sex, and performing anal sex) while incarcerated. Factors, including age, education, amount of time served, and type of offense had no statistically significant effect on inmates' sexual activity in prison.

As stated above, the topic of consensual same-sex sexual activity within male prisons has received very little academic attention. The majority of research on sexual activity within correctional facilities has focused on sexual coercion rather than consensual homosexual behavior. Due to the nature of correctional facilities themselves, studies regarding male consensual same-sex activity did not appear until the 1980s. Only recently has a small number of researchers delved into the topic. Although there has been limited examination of consensual same-sex sexual behavior in male prisons, a plethora of studies concerning female same-sex sexual behavior in prisons has existed for almost ninety years.

Consensual Sex in Female Prisons

Pioneer Sex Studies of Female Prisons, 1913–1931

The first sex study conducted on incarcerated females scrutinized the "unnatural relationship" between black and white females in reform schools and institutions for delinquent girls. Otis (1913) argued that same-race homosexual behavior between females was a difficult issue to address. This behavior between white and black females was seen as a "perversion not commonly noted" (113). Girls often entered into these relationships for fun and entertainment. For many, however, it became a serious enthrallment that evolved into a same-sex sexual relationship. The white girls that became involved with blacks in same-sex sexual relationships were termed "nigger-lovers" (114). Any girl, whether black or white, who changed partners frequently was considered fickle.

Otis (1913) stated, "The difference in color, in this case, takes the place of difference in sex, and ardent love-affairs arise between white and colored girls in schools where both are housed together" (113). The white girls disclosed that the black girls predominantly assumed the male role in the relationships. It was assumed by "some interested in this phase of the school life" that only mentally defective white girls would indulge in this type of relationship (116). However, the reverse was discovered. Otis (1913) stated that "some of the girls indulging in this love of colored have, perhaps, the most highly developed intellectual ability of any of the girls in school" (116).

Sixteen years later, Ford (1929) described similar black-white sexual relationships within a different female juvenile institution. Homosexual activity was found to be a voluntary act. The term "friend" was applied to one who engaged in homosexual behavior. The relationship between two individuals was classified as husband and wife. But the assumed role (husband or wife) was not always the same in each "friendship." This study suggested that not only were these girls promiscuous but also that they assumed both dominant and submissive roles with respect to the same behavior.

Approximately two years later, Selling (1931) examined the pseudo-family alliances that developed in female juvenile institutions. These alliances evolved as psychological, nonpathological, substitute families because of the emotional disassociation from their own families. Selling (1931) distinguished four stages (friendship, pseudo-family membership, pseudo-homosexuality, and overt homosexuality) of the homosexual relationship in the female juvenile facility.

The first level was friendship. This was a natural relationship between girls who became fond of each other as acquaintances, sharing confidences and spending time together, much like friendships that developed in society outside the institution. The second level consisted of the formation of the pseudo-family, which contained only platonic roles (i.e., mother, daughter, sister, brother). Titles such as "Mammy" or "Mumsy" were given to females who assumed the maternal roles in the families. Often, these girls were only two or three years older than other family members. "Popsy" was the general title given to the father figure of the families.

Relationships of the third level were characterized by pseudo-homosexual behavior. Administrators at the facilities were "concerned with the intimacies that developed between two girls, one of whom was frequently colored and the other white" (Selling, 1931: 247). This level involved playing the conjugal role of husband or wife. Girls within these relationships addressed each other as "my woman," "my man," or "honey." Thus, the term "honies" was implemented by the other girls within the facility for those who were participants in these relationships. Physical contact in these couples included putting one's arm around one's honey, occasional kissing, and some fondling (Selling, 1931). This was viewed as more social than emotional or sexual role behavior due to two facts. First, if honies were given permission to be together, the white girl often denied the relationship or insisted that she did not want such contact or opportunity. No information was supplied by the researcher concerning the response of the black girls in this given situation. Second, girls who did not want to have a honey were often belittled by other girls within their cottage. They felt pressured and, therefore, often corresponded by letter with other girls in mock relationships to alleviate harassment. Many who were engaged at this level disapproved of those girls who participated in overt homosexual alliances (the fourth level). Girls at the fourth level were repudiated by their peers who labeled these relationships as lesbian. The girls at this level were not classified as "honies and certainly do not exist on the family plane" (Selling, 1931: 253).

It is regrettable that not one of these researchers used any type of statistical analyses or methodological techniques to substantiate their findings. In addition, these early researchers did not provide a clear conceptual or functional definition of sexual acts. Most of their findings on the type and amount of female homosexual behavior within the juvenile institutions were derived from their own perceptions and from estimates supplied by the staff.

Sex Studies of Female Prisons, 1962–1969

In 1962, research-based methodology was incorporated by Halleck and Hersko when they gathered data on fifty-seven girls' homosexual behavior within a juvenile institution in Wisconsin. These researchers used a seventy-three-item biographical inventory and an anonymous questionnaire to "attempt to describe the psychological and social determinants of this behavior" (912). They found that a large majority of the girls became involved in some type of homosexual behavior. However, there were different degrees of emotional involvement and sexual intimacy. The results of the study revealed that 69 percent of the females had engaged in "girl stuff." Seventy-one percent reported "mugging" (kissing limited to the facial area), and 11 percent admitted to fondling another girl. Only 5 percent of the girls reported that they had stimulated another girl's genitalia, while 7 percent had permitted another girl to stimulate hers. Interestingly, only 9 percent of the girls reported that they had been involved in girl stuff prior to their incarceration (Halleck and Hersko, 1962).

While many of the girls did not openly show a preference for a male or female role in the girl-stuff relationships, it was discovered that some of the girls openly changed their mannerisms, grooming, and attire to portray a masculine appearance. These girls were termed "butch" as a status among their peers because of strength and dependability. Both competition and rivalry evolved between the girls who wanted to be with the butches as well as between the butches for a new attractive arrival. Nonetheless, these relationships were often short-lived due to jealousy and infidelity (Halleck and Hersko, 1962).

In 1965, Ward and Kassebaum studied adult female inmates' sexual behaviors at the California Institution for Women in Frontera (a medium-security facility). Prison records (jackets) of 832 female inmates at Frontera were made available by the California Department of Corrections for examination by Ward, Kassebaum, and their staff. In-depth, semistructured interviews were also conducted with members of the staff who worked in close contact with the female inmates and with a random sample of forty-five inmates over a sixteen-month period. In addition, questionnaires were answered by staff members and 293 female inmates concerning issues of prison life, homosexual behavior, staff attitudes, and inmate codes.

To alleviate misconceptions, homosexual behavior was defined as "kissing and fondling of the breasts, manual or oral stimulation of the genitalia and stimulation of intercourse between two women" (Ward and Kassebaum, 1965: 80). Prison records identified 19 percent of the population as homosexual. Results from the staff (33 percent of total staff) and inmate (42 percent of total population) surveys disclosed that between 30 and 75 percent of the inmates had sexual affairs while in prison. Interviews with the inmates estimated the number to be between 60 and 75 percent. It was conservatively estimated by Ward and Kassebaum that approximately 50 percent of the women had engaged in "some form of overt sexual experience at least sometime during their sentence" (92).

Ward and Kassebaum's (1965) study presented no data concerning make-believe (pseudo) families at Frontera. Because the major focus of Ward and Kassebaum's study was about sexual practices within a female facility, either the family issue was not addressed, the families were underground, or they truly did not exist. In addition, this study did not consider age, race, ethnic composition, religion, or other characteristics while investigating the inmates' sexual behaviors. Therefore, the question still remained unanswered as to which inmates were involved in same-sex sexual activity within the facility.

Giallombardo's (1966) study in the West Virginia Women's Federal Reformatory not only complemented Ward and Kassebaum's (1965) review of sexual practices (interpersonal homosexual relations) within a female institution, but it also examined the membership and relationship of inmates involved in make-believe families. It was found that these kinship and dyad relationships evolved as a result of the female inmates' social, psychological, or physiological deficiencies. Giallombardo (1966) examined the women's adaptation of the mainstream "cultural expectations of differential sex roles in society within the prison society" (14). She spent nearly a year interviewing inmates and staff as an observer. Data were collected "by participating in the daily life of the group and by personal observation of the inmates as they participated in the formal inmate activities" (191). While private interviews with the inmates were conducted in their rooms, group sessions often occurred in the various cottages. Employee interviews occurred both in staff meetings and in various offices across the facility.

When questioned about the number of inmates involved in homosexuality within the facility, the inmates placed the number between 90 and 95 percent. The staff gauged the figures between 50 and 75 percent, while the associate warden estimated that 80 percent of the female inmates were involved in homosexual behavior within the facility. This resulted in the estimate that approximately 86 percent of the women had had a homosexual experience of some type during their incarceration (Giallombardo, 1966). The study also revealed that "approximately 5 percent of the inmate population" had practiced homosexuality before incarceration (98).

Giallombardo (1966) discovered that the most important relationships within the facility were the homosexual alliances of inmates who were considered "married." The informal prison structure recognized these marriages as being just as legitimate as marriages outside of prison, for there was a representative role of both husband and wife. Reasons given for participation in these partnerships included companionship, security, accouterment, and interdependence. These unions were strictly established on a voluntary basis. Even though these relationships were conclusive between the two women, the alliance could not be totally self-sufficient. Interactions with other inmates evolved into kinship networks. While these families formed for protection and members shared information, they also supplied members with access to institutional goods and services that would not be readily available to the individual inmate or couple.

These pseudo-families or kinship networks also served as a substitute family for the women while they were incarcerated. Same-sex alliances and age limited the role that one adopted within a family. Older, established married couples often assumed the role of the parents within these families. Other roles within these kinships were adapted to the personality and behaviors of individual inmates (brother, sister, aunt, uncle). This prison family performed all the functions normally attributed to the biological family (economic, protective, affectionate, recreational, and social) with the exception of reproduction. Even though an inmate's role could change within a given family, the kinship ties usually lasted throughout the inmate's sentence. Sexual relationships within the family were limited to the parents (never between daddy/children, mommy/children, or sister/sister, brother/sister, or brother/brother, uncle/niece, etc.). Homosexual activities between members of a kinship were considered a misconduct and classified as incestuous behavior by the inmates at the Federal Reformatory for Women at Alderson (Giallombardo, 1966).

In contrast to previous subject matter, Mitchell (1969) conducted her research in two adult women's prisons (one treatment oriented and one custody oriented) to address the correlation between pre-prison and prison homosexuality. Homosexual behavior was reported by 37 percent of the women in the treatment-oriented facility in contrast to only 21 percent in the custody-oriented facility. Rates of prior homosexual behavior reported by the women in the treatment-oriented facility (31 percent) were higher than the custody-oriented facility (21 percent). The formation or inclusion in make-believe families by inmates was not addressed in Mitchell's study.

Sex Studies of Female Prisons, 1972–1982

Another variation into the study of homosexual behavior of female inmates was conducted by Tittle (1972) in a small coed narcotic treatment center for inmates. Respondents were asked both about their participation in homosexual activities and their estimates of the number of inmates that had participated in homosexual behavior since being incarcerated at the center. Tittle (1972) found that 14 percent of the women reported homosexual involvement. An additional 5 percent indicated that they had been involved while at the institution but were not currently involved. Comparatively to Giallombardo's (1966) study, 21 percent of the females described their homosexual relationships as voluntary, involving love, affection, and companionship.

Heffernan (1972) conducted both structured interviews and surveys of 100 female inmates in the Women's Reformatory of the District of Columbia in Occoquan, Virginia. Interviews were also conducted with the correctional staff and administrators. The study focused on the solidarity of the various inmate subcultures within the social organization of the facility. Heffernan was given access to all inmate records—criminal history, medical, financial, and demographic—as well as administrative records and reports. This study included, but was not limited to, involvement of inmates in make-believe families and estimates of inmates who "played." The term "played" was used by the inmates to distinguish those females who were involved in conjugal roles from those who were not. It was difficult to ascertain reliable data concerning homosexual behavior and the number of "marriages" within the institution.

Due to negative institutional policies against homosexual behavior, many inmates were reserved discussing these issues. At the same time, these inmates estimated that 71 percent of the population were involved in sexual relationships, but only 50 to 60 percent of the inmates were involved in a marriage. Staff members interviewed for the study considered only those inmates in marriages when asked about rates of homosexual behavior and approximated that 37 percent of the inmates were involved. Roughly 13 percent of the prison population had an outside history of homosexual behavior according to their records and interview material. It was assumed that this behavior continued during incarceration.

The make-believe families at Occoquan were viewed by inmates as a critical element of social order within the facility. Memberships within these families supplied the inmate with a sense of stability and support during their incarceration. Overall, results indicated that 60 percent of the respondents favored and accepted the formation of the families. Half of the seventy-two women who discussed the families were either a current member or had been a member in a family during their incarceration. While the members of these families offered both affection and advice, it appeared the family unit was also the "basic economic unit in the inmate system of exchange" (91). It was discovered that the familial kinships were not limited to individual buildings or dormitories as in Giallombardo's (1966) study but extended throughout the institution. With members active throughout the facility, the family had access to more goods, services, and information (new inmate arrivals, staff changes, schedule changes, access to contraband or scarce commodities, gossip, and news from outside the facility). The interviewees also revealed that within a family, all four stages of Selling's (1931) homosexuality continuum were observed. The homosexual relationship was available "for anyone who is willing or capable of sustaining it—this is a part of the life, part of the institution" (Heffernan, 1972: 101).

Nelson (1974), expanding on the aforementioned studies by Ward and Kassebaum (1965), Giallombardo (1966), and Heffernan (1972), conducted a study of female homosexual behavior both in a New Jersey and a Pennsylvania female correctional facility. The basis of Nelson's inquiry was whether racial diversity had an impact on pre-prison homosexual behavior, incarcerated homosexual behavior, conjugal roles, and membership in make-believe families. One hundred and nineteen female inmates from both facilities voluntarily filled out questionnaires. But due to a time lapse of several months between the questionnaire and the semistructured interviews, many of the volunteers had either been released or paroled. Only thirty-four of the original 119 volunteers were interviewed.

Based on questionnaire responses, Nelson (1974) found that 44 percent of the 119 respondents reported having had sexual relations with another woman prior to incarceration. Of these women, 57 percent of the respondents were black, 37 percent were white, and 6 percent were other races. The questionnaires further disclosed that 55 percent of all the black female inmates and 37 percent of all the white inmates at the prison considered themselves to be homosexual during their incarceration. Psychological security and sexual satisfaction were the important factors listed for participation in voluntary homosexual alliances. Concerning homosexual behavior within the facility, the questionnaires and interviews revealed that homosexual behavior was considered the norm in both prisons. Specifically, "53 percent of the inmates believed that 'most' other inmates held hands; 48 percent of the inmates believed 'most' other inmates kiss women; 53 percent of the inmates believed that 'most' other women hug other inmates; and 49 percent of the inmates believe 'about half' of the other women have sexual relations with other inmates" (143).

Nelson (1974) also found that black women were more likely to play the male role in the homosexual dyad. She felt that the socialization of black women to be aggressive, dominant, primary care-givers, self-sufficient, and strong predisposed them to acquire the role of husband. Of the seven interracial couples interviewed, six consisted of black studs or butches and white femmes. Pertaining to marriages, the majority of the respondents affirmed that marriages were not only present, but mock ceremonies were performed for the couples.

Responses from both the questionnaires and interviews revealed that the make-believe family network was prevalent at both facilities. Due to the total institutional nature of these facilities (demographic isolation, long distance from natural families, limited telephone privileges, and highly censored mail), make-believe families were formed. Inmates at the New Jersey facility often belonged to more than one family and had a different role in each family. In addition, sexual relationships occurred within these family structures.

Two years later, one of the most exhaustive studies of homosexual behavior in correctional institutions was undertaken by Propper (1976). In a comparative study of four female juvenile institutions and three coed juvenile institutions, self-report data from the 396 female respondents revealed that 14 percent of the females were "going with" or married to another girl. Additionally, 10 percent of the females reported passionately kissing another girl, 10 percent wrote love letters to another girl, and 7 percent reported sexual behavior beyond just hugging and kissing (Propper 1976, 1978, 1981, 1982). The "percentage reporting at least one of these homosexual experiences varied from 6 percent to 29 percent depending upon the institution, with an overall average of 17 percent" (Propper, 1978: 269). In addition, Propper found that the rates for preincarceration homosexual behavior ranged from 3 to 32 percent at all seven institutions, making the overall rate 9 percent. In addition, 71 percent of the females who had preincarceration homosexual experiences disclosed having homosexual experiences during incarceration (Propper, 1978).

Based on her original data, Propper (1981) constructed a social-psychological model of the causes of prison homosexuality. The multi-causal model proposed that prison homosexuality was affected by countless cultural, personality, and biological variables prior to incarceration. She stated that "previous homosexuality was included . . . because this study found that it had strong and direct effects upon prison homosexuality" (184). Propper concluded that dominance and self-esteem issues were also associated with participants of homosexual behavior while incarcerated. If the homosexual experience was found to be satisfying both physically and emotionally, individuals would be more inclined to repeat the experience.

When examining make-believe families, Propper (1982) extended her original thesis (1976) on incarcerated female homosexuality to determine if there was a link between those who participated in make-believe families and homosexual behavior. Propper (1982) found that 49 percent of the 382 respondents reported membership in a make-believe family. She found that (1) participation rates were equal in both the coed facilities and in the female institutions; (2) both male and female inmates were included in the families in the coed facilities; (3) homosexual marriages were rare; (4) the families consisted of basically asexual relationships (mother/daughter, sister/sister); and (5) membership in the make-believe families was not associated with the potentiality of homosexual behavior. Affiliation with these families was not for sexual gratification. Rather, it was for a sense of security, companionship, affection, attention, status, prestige, and acceptance.

In contrast, Hopper's (1980) study of 176 female inmates in the Florida Correctional Institution in Lowell found that two separate make-believe families existed. The conventional family foundation still revolved around security, companionship, and affection without the presence of homosexual behavior. However, a second, smaller family unit had evolved that centered not only on the traditional initiatives but hosted homosexual relationships within its framework. Hopper proposed that membership into this second type of family provided an outlet of new sexual partners for females who were predisposed to homosexual behavior.

The predominate roles within these families were mother and sister. While only 27 percent of the "mothers" reported homosexual behavior, 43 percent of the "daughters/sisters" reported such behavior. Hopper (1980) discovered that "a greater proportion of younger inmates (age group twenty-one to twenty-five) engaged in homosexual activities than the total in any of the remaining groups" (64). Race was not a determinant, for no statistically significant differences were found between black/white involvement. It was also revealed that the majority of the women's first homosexual experiences occurred before incarceration (75 percent of these eighty-four women reported pre-prison homosexual experience). Notably, only 5 percent of these women reported their sexual orientation as homosexual.

Contemporary Sex Studies
of Female Prisons, 1998–2002

It would be eighteen years later before another major publication appeared concerning incarcerated female same-sex sexual behavior. In 1998, after a three-year study in the Central California Women's Facility (CCWF), Owen reported her findings concerning friendships, make-believe families, and homosexual behavior within this facility. The study was considered by Owen (1998) to be a quasi-ethnography because observation and evaluation of an inmate's life within the facility was limited. Face-to-face interviews were conducted with 294 female inmates as well as staff members at the facility. From these interviews, it was confirmed that a complex system of interpersonal relationships based on emotional, practical, material, sexual, and familial overtones existed among the inmates. Most of the relationships were temporary, whereas others lasted the duration of the inmate's sentence. It was also discovered that the prison families and dyads crossed both racial and ethnic boundaries.

Friendships were defined as being equal and reciprocal affairs between the inmates. Friends performed the same functions in prison as they did outside of prison. These were allies that you could rely on, talk to, share confidences with, and know that they were there for you if you needed support. However, most of the respondents argued that you "harden" the longer incarcerated, causing one to become less dependent on friends (Owen, 1998).

The make-believe family structure at CCWF resembled the basic family structures discovered in previous institutions. An older woman assumed the role of mother with younger inmates taking the role of the "kids." The more aggressive, dominant woman assumed the role of dad or brother. These designations were flexible and could change over time. Many entered into the prison family because they had either no family or a disruptive family on the outside. The family members had reciprocal social and material responsibilities. The older inmates, in terms of both their actual age and time being served, often assisted new arrivals by becoming mentors. They offered advice, guidance, and protection to them (Owen, 1998).

Concerning homosexual behavior within the prison, most of the staff and inmates claimed that everybody was involved. However, conservative estimates ranged from 30 to 60 percent of the inmate population actually engaging in homosexual behavior. Many of the women interviewed denied any such behavior, while others disclosed that they had been lesbian on the streets and were active participants within the facility. The social construction of the couples and families in Owen's (1998) study paralleled the findings of Halleck and Hersko (1962), Giallombardo (1966), and Ward and Kassebaum (1965).

In 2000, Greer conducted a study in a Midwestern state female correctional facility. Of the 238 women who were incarcerated, only thirty-five agreed to participate in semistructured interviews that addressed the subject of friendships, sexual relationships between the inmates, and the lack of kinship networks. The demographic data of the respondents disclosed variables of age, race, type of crime, and length of time served. A table was supplied with percentages of their responses of involvement within same-sex sexual relationships while incarcerated. Yet no associations between the responses and the specific demographics were supplied.

The results of the study disclosed that ten of the thirty-five women had been involved in a sexual relationship with another women while incarcerated. Five of the thirty-five respondents reported that they were currently involved with a woman in a sexual relationship. The reasons given by the respondents for being involved in this type of relationship included game playing, economic manipulation, loneliness, the need for companionship, and genuine affection.

Many (twenty-one of the thirty-five) of the respondents described themselves as loners. These women observed their peers as manipulative and self-serving. Mistrust was cited as the main reason for no established friendships. Others hesitated in establishing alliances because of the frequent discharges and transfers of inmates from one facility to another. There was not enough time to establish a trustful relationship with another inmate.

Greer also discovered that the kinship network (make-believe families) did not exist at this facility. Respondents indicated that these families were not part of the prison culture within their facility. The families were usually formed as a proxy for the family on the outside and as a means of obtaining information. Because correctional facilities of today are no longer considered total institutions that disallow exposure to the outside world, not only has communication with family on the outside become more prevalent, but access to media coverage of local and world events (television and newspapers) is an everyday occurrence.

Both Owen (1998) and Greer (2000) reported that at least one-third of the women in their respective studies were sexually active with other female inmates. Although the subcultures and behaviors of incarcerated women have changed, the female inmates continued to be same-sex sexually active during incarceration. This was evident in the most recent study of female consensual prison sex conducted by Hensley, Tewksbury, and Koscheski (2002). The purpose of their study was to address not only same-sex sexual behavior within a female correctional facility but to ascertain from several demographic and incarcerated-related variables which female inmates were more likely to participate in five same-sex sexual behaviors (kissing, touching, receiving oral sex, performing oral sex, and a fifth variable constructed as a composite of the first four to measure the rate of homosexual behavior) during incarceration.

A series of logistic regression analyses were performed to test if the predictor variables had an effect on the dependent variables. The most salient variables in the models that predicted consensual same-sex sexual activity while incarcerated were age and amount of time served. Both variables were statistically significant predictors of all five dependent variables. Age showed the greatest influence on female inmates' same-sex sexual behavior. Women under the age of thirty-four were more likely to have engaged in all five types of behavior. The length of time that a woman had served in prison was also a statistically significant predictor of all five dependent variables. Women who had served longer periods of time incarcerated were more likely than women who had served shorter periods of time to have engaged in same-sex sexual activities with another inmate. Race, however, was a statistically significant predictor of only two forms of same-sex sexual behavior (touching another inmate in a sexual way and receiving oral sex). Nonwhite women were more likely to admit to touching another woman in a sexual manner and to receiving oral sex from another female inmate. The only other statistically significant variable in the equation was religion. Women who reported a non-Protestant religious affiliation were more likely to have performed oral sex on another inmate than those who reported a Protestant religious affiliation. Factors including education, type of offense, and security level had no statistically significant effects on female inmates' sexual activity in prison.

As one can discern from the sparse research since the early twentieth century on the sexual behavior of incarcerated females, it is evident that this behavior has continued to be a major component within the prison setting. From the pioneer studies that addressed the issue of the unnatural alliances between "colored" and white females in juvenile correctional facilities and building upon the evidence that homosexual behavior and make-believe families did exist within both juvenile and adult female correctional facilities, only a few contemporary researchers have continued to address studies concerning these issues.

CONCLUSION

Research on consensual sex in prison provides correctional administrators and staff with more knowledge of their institutions. All forms of consensual sex are illegal and forbidden in prison. According to Saum et al. (1995), sex is forbidden "so that correctional officers can fulfill their objective of a safe and secure environment" (414). Correctional administrators and staff must be aware of the amount of consensual sex occurring in their institutions so that they may provide additional safety and security measures to their inmate populations as well as society. Tewksbury and West (2000) stated, "It should be of institutional concern to understand sexual expression among inmates who are safe and discreet, and to control unsafe and unwanted sexual expression among inmates who use sex as a weapon" (375).

However, as we have already seen, correctional facilities are anything but safe and secure. For example, the most recent data on nonconsensual same-sex sexual behavior estimates that approximately 20 percent of all male inmates are sexually coerced. In addition, much of the consensual sex that occurs within U.S. prisons can be described as pseudo-consensual. Punks, for example, must offer their sexual services in return for protection. Is this consensual same-sex sexual behavior? Or is it just another form of nonconsensual same-sex sexual activity?

Thus, given what we know about prison sexuality and its relationship to violence, researchers must continue to strive to recommend policy changes within prisons. As we shall see in the next chapter, we must consider decriminalizing and destigmatizing the main alternative method of sexual release within all of our correctional facilities, masturbation.

9

MASTURBATION

Deanna McGaughey and Richard Tewksbury

In 1992, Otis Rodgers filed a complaint against the Ohio Department of Rehabilitation and Correction stating that the department's policy against conjugal visitation and masturbation violated his human rights. In particular, he argued that during his nine years of incarceration, he had to endure embarrassment and degradation because of nocturnal emissions as a result of the department's policy prohibiting sexual activity. In response to the complaint, the court issued summary judgment stating that the department's policy was immune from attack. On appeal, Rodgers clarified his argument by stating that the policy constituted domestic war crimes and psychological genocide because it violated his right to relieve himself of an excessive buildup of bodily fluid (semen) in a hygienic manner. The trial court again disagreed (*Rodgers v. Ohio Department of Rehabilitation and Correction,* 1993).

In an affidavit submitted to the court hearing Rodgers's case, David Turner, the institutional inspector for the Ohio Department of Rehabilitation and Correction, identified two main reasons for the department's prohibition. First, sexual acts are not conducive to an orderly prison because of the close living arrangements of the inmates. Second, there is an increased risk of contracting or spreading sexually transmitted diseases including HIV (*Rodgers v. Ohio Department of Rehabilitation and Correction,* 1993).

The Rodgers case is significant for a number of reasons. In particular, it highlights some of the issues involved regarding masturbation from both the inmates' perspective as well as the institution's perspective. From the inmates' perspective, masturbation is perceived as a means for relieving sexual tension. Furthermore, the consequence of being deprived of the ability to relieve oneself may lead to psychological and physical trauma. From the institution's perspective, as suggested in Turner's affidavit, the positive consequences of masturbation do not outweigh the negative ones. In this context, masturbation and other sexual activities are perceived as negatively affecting the maintenance of order and control within the prison as well as contributing to the spread of disease.

As our preceding paragraph suggests, sexual behavior in general and masturbation in particular are related to two very important concerns within prison: social control and health maintenance/promotion. However, there have been only a few prison studies that have focused on masturbation within a constellation of sexual practices that inform prison sexuality, and there have been even fewer studies on sex in prison that have focused exclusively on masturbation.

Masturbation is a sexual practice that is part of a larger group of behaviors that together form sexuality. Therefore, any effort to understand masturbation must be framed within a discussion of sexuality. In the next section, we will contextualize masturbation in prison by describing several models for understanding sexuality and discussing how these models influence the study of prison sexuality. Following our discussion of prison sexuality, we will discuss the current state of knowledge regarding masturbation in prison, highlighting the theoretical and methodological issues involved in understanding prison masturbation.

SEXUALITY

Sexuality covers many domains of social life (Connell and Dowsett, 1993) and is not simply physical acts divorced from the social context (Foucault, 1978). Given that sexuality is not simply an act but is saturated with meaning (Dean, 1996), some sexual behaviors are considered more meaningful than others depending on whether the behavior is considered "real" sex (Grosz and Probyn, 1995).

The most common models for understanding sexuality are the androcentric and feminist models. The androcentric model approaches sexuality from a male perspective in that sex is defined by two of three factors: preparation for penetration (foreplay), penetration, and orgasm (Maines, 1999). If two of the three of these factors are not met, then the sexual behavior is not considered real sex. Otherwise an act is considered petty sex and subordinate to those sexual practices (Grosz and

Probyn, 1995) that are perceived as approximating more fully the (androcentric) sexual ideal (foreplay, penetration, and orgasm) (Maines, 1999). The feminist model is critical of the androcentric model. The feminist model of sexuality criticizes the male bias of androcentric models of sexuality by concentrating on the social construction of sexuality and individual desire (Jackson, 1996).

PRISON SEXUALITY

Research on prison sexuality has been sparse (Donaldson, 1993a; Tewksbury and West, 2000). The research that has been conducted has drawn on androcentric and feminist models of sexuality. Most of the existing research on prison sexuality demonstrates a clear masculine bias, typically because men are perceived as more sexual than women (Tewksbury and West, 2000). Additionally, most of the existing research focuses on rape and sexual coercion, as well as the social construction of sexual identities and sexual experiences within prison walls (Alarid, 2000b; Saum et al., 1995; Tewksbury and West, 2000; Ward and Kassebaum, 1965).

The structure of the prison environment makes prison sexuality a unique focus for research. When inmates enter prison society, they lose many of their basic human rights. In the United States, one of the most important of these rights is that of privacy. In U.S. culture, privacy signifies that which we protect from the state and that which will be destroyed if "contaminated" by the public (Boling, 2000). Privacy is considered to be very sacred and is conceptualized as a special relation to oneself (Morris, 2000). Privacy is compromised within the prison system because the prison is, according to Goffman (1961), a "total institution."

A total institution completely encompasses the inmate's life. Features of the total institution include hierarchy, routine, rituals of degradation and initiation, and segregation. Total institutions involve "batch" living, which involves running inmates' lives collectively and at intimate levels (Goffman, 1961). Sexual behavior, which is generally considered in mainstream society to be private, becomes a public/social issue within the context of institutionalization.

Prison is an unnatural environment because it deprives the individual of fundamental rights, possessions, experiences, and relationships (Kassebaum, 1972). Sex is prohibited in prison so that order can be maintained (Saum et al., 1995). Because of these conditions, prisons inherently create conflict because they are dominating institutions (Sparks, Bottoms, and Hay, 1996).

MASTURBATION

For several reasons, masturbation is a unique aspect of the prison experience to study. For one, it is the most common form of sex in prison (Tewksbury, 1989b). However, as suggested by the Rodgers case, masturbation has a problematic status as sexual behavior in prison. For example, as we have seen, masturbation is linked as a sexual problem to administrative issues such as social control and health maintenance/promotion. In the following section, we will describe the existing literature on masturbation in society and prison and discuss some of the possible reasons for its problematic status both within and out of prison.

Masturbation in Society

One of the first researchers to study masturbation in society was Alfred Kinsey. His groundbreaking studies on both males and females of the late 1940s enlightened the public about attitudes and behaviors regarding sexuality. It was not only an avenue for those involved in the study to discuss and answer questions about different aspects of their sexuality, but it was also an opportunity for society to realize that their ideas, beliefs, and activities were shared by others. Kinsey brought to light the influence of age, education, rural versus urban background, and religion on masturbation. Kinsey and his associates found that 92 percent of male and 62 percent of females studied had masturbated at some point in their lives (Kinsey et al., 1953).

Over two decades passed before another major study of sexuality was conducted. *The Hite Report* (Hite, 1976) dealt only with the subject of female sexuality. The data revealed that out of the 1,844 women surveyed, approximately 82 percent masturbated. The results of the next significant sexual research project, *The Janus Report* (Janus and Janus, 1993), revealed that 55 percent of males and 38 percent of females were regular masturbators (daily to monthly masturbation), and 66 percent of men and 67 percent of women viewed masturbation as a natural part of life.

In 1994, a study of 647 never-married female undergraduate students in a Midwestern residential state university was conducted by Davidson and Moore. The study revealed that 16.3 percent of respondents had engaged in masturbation. Also in 1994, *Sex in America* was published (Michael et al.). This study, conducted through the National Opinion Research Center at the University of Chicago, drew on a random sampling of more than 3,400 respondents to assess a wide range of sexual information including sexual histories and beliefs. The researchers also found that masturbation is not rare. Sixty percent of males and 40 percent of females in the survey were found to have masturbated at least once in the prior year. Given these statistics, masturbation is "normal" in normal society. Therefore, why is masturbation an infraction of policy and procedure within the correctional institution? It is possible that the stigma even in mainstream society has infiltrated the prison system.

Masturbation in Prison

As with the general male population, rates of masturbation in men's prison are quite high (Kassebaum, 1972; Tewksbury, 1989b). In their classic study on sexual behavior and sexual exploitation in prison, Wooden and Parker (1982) found that all 200 of their respondents masturbated. Typically, masturbation took place in late afternoon and evening hours when inmates were sent back to their rooms. The prison administration had no prohibitions on masturbation as long as the practice was not done in a threatening manner and did not interfere with prison functioning (Wooden and Parker, 1982). Tewksbury's (1989b) study also found that male prisoners continued to be sexually active when entering prison and that masturbation was the most common means of sex for the inmates. And more recently, Hensley, Tewksbury, and Wright (2001) found that 99 percent of their sample of incarcerated men masturbated, and more than 22 percent masturbated more than once a day. Education was the most significant variable in determining the frequency of masturbation, with those with more education being more frequent masturbators. Therefore, men, regardless of prohibitions set forth by the administration, continue to be sexually active while in prison (Tewksbury, 1989b).

While a couple of studies have addressed masturbation in men's prisons, only one study has been published that addresses these same issues in women's prisons. Hensley, Tewksbury, and Koscheski (2002) found that almost 67 percent of females in a southern correctional facility had masturbated while incarcerated. Inmates who engaged in homosexual behavior while incarcerated were more likely to masturbate and to be frequent masturbators than inmates who did not engage in homosexual behavior in prison. In other words, inmates who were sexually active while incarcerated were more likely to masturbate while in prison. White inmates and inmates in higher security levels were also more likely to report engaging in frequent masturbation. As with men's prisons, we can expect masturbation to be a common method of sexual activity in women's prisons. It is ironic that although masturbation in prison and in mainstream society is common, it continues to be stigmatized.

The next section will highlight how masturbation has historically and socially been conceptualized and how these various conceptualizations contribute to researching masturbation in prison.

THE "M" WORD

Masturbation has a rather insidious reputation. As noted several times in this chapter, masturbation is extraordinarily common, yet highly stigmatized. The 1994 firing of U.S. surgeon general Joycelyn Elders, who advocated masturbation as a means for controlling sexually transmitted diseases, HIV-infection, and unwanted pregnancy, is illustrative of the stigmatization that continues to accompany masturbation (Rosselini, 1997).

There are two themes common to the problematic status of masturbation in society. The first theme is the association of masturbation with physical and psychological problems; the second theme is the perception of masturbation as subordinate to so-called real sex.

Until the twentieth century, for both men and women, masturbation had been perceived as causing physical and mental problems. For men, masturbation was perceived as causing problems because the body was to be drained of essential seminal fluid and because nervous energy was believed to cause brain damage (MacDonald, 1967; Money and Prakasam, 1991). For women, masturbation has been linked with a host of physical and mental "female problems." In particular, masturbation has been perceived as interfering with women's natural maternal qualities including the abilities to conceive and nurture children (Maines, 1999). Havelock Ellis (1942), an influential sexologist, for example, believed that masturbation led to "marital aversion." In other words, Ellis believed masturbation offered women a sexual substitute to marriage, which would cause women to avoid, or be uninterested in, marriage. This avoidance of marriage was believed to interfere with women's maternal qualities, which would result in psychological and physical health consequences. So, although the specific problems for men and women have been perceived as different, in general, both men and women have been perceived as suffering from the practice.

Later in the twentieth century, masturbation was demedicalized, or stripped of its medical meanings (Conrad, 1992), yet it continued to have a problematic status. In the late twentieth and early twenty-first centuries, we have seen the remedicalization of masturbation and other sexual behaviors (Parker, Barbosa, and Aggleton, 2000), particularly when it is associated with the spread of HIV infection. In mainstream society, masturbation has been advocated as an alternative safer sex practice to decrease the spread of HIV (Rosellini, 1997). In prison, though, as the Rodgers case suggests, masturbation is associated with the spread of disease. In both cases, masturbation has been remedicalized in that it is perceived as influencing the direction of the spread of disease. Therefore, masturbation has become resituated under the purview of medicine, health, and welfare.

The second theme is that masturbation is not regarded as real sex (Soble, 1996, 1997). As Soble (1996) notes:

> [Masturbation] is unpaired and flagrantly nonprocreative sex in which pleasure is relished for its own sake. As we have learned from pundits, masturbation mocks the categories of our sexual discourse: it is sex with someone I care about, to whose satisfaction and welfare I am devoted; it is incestuous; if I am married, it is sex with someone not my spouse and hence adulterous; it is homosexual; it is often pederastic; it is sex we occasionally fall into inadvertently ("if you shake it more than twice, you're playing with it"). . . . No wonder, then, that we advertise our marriages and brag about our affairs, but keep our masturbatory fantasies to ourselves. The masturbatory closet remains shut. (60)

The subordinate status that masturbation is ascribed is an effect of its nonconformity to the androcentric model that we discussed earlier. As Soble (1996) suggests in the previous quote, the practice lies outside of the typical frame of reference (heterosexuality) used to clarify and understand sexuality.

In sum, masturbation is a problematic concept because it is not defined as real sex and because of its association with health and social problems. Next, we will describe some of the methodological issues associated with researching masturbation in prison.

METHODOLOGICAL ISSUES

Studying prison sexuality is important for several reasons: (1) Understanding the prison as an institution requires an understanding of all aspects of prison life, including sexuality; (2) sexuality is a basic and fundamental human need; (3) the deprivation of sexuality in prison can create maintenance problems for the inmate population and prison administration; (4) there are health and social problems (such as rape and the spread of HIV) that are associated with prison sexuality; and (5) most inmates currently incarcerated will re-enter society, so a comprehensive understanding of the prison experience on post-prison behavior is imperative (Tewksbury and West, 2000). Prison masturbation in particular should be studied because it is the most common form of prison sex and because of its connection to administrative issues such as social control and health promotion/maintenance. This section will discuss some methodological issues to consider when studying prison sexuality in general and masturbation in particular.

Masturbation, which is generally considered a very private sexual behavior, is a sensitive topic. In the prison setting, in addition to being a sensitive topic, masturbation can also be illegal. These two issues raise important methodological issues with respect to reporting, establishing rapport, and definitional ambiguity. Given that sexual behavior in prison is controlled or prohibited (Tewksbury, 1989b), reporting presents a major methodological concern. Respondents may be reluctant to report, and there may be issues of validity because of fears of repercussions from the administration and other inmates (Saum et al., 1995). Considering this, establishing rapport with inmate respondents is essential.

Rapport is paramount when studying marginalized groups, particularly when their behavior is illegal, because these groups tend to be suspicious of "outsiders" (Miller and Tewksbury, 2001; Tewksbury and Gagne, 2001). In the prison context, researchers epitomize outsiders as they are typically located in mainstream society and in powerful institutions such as the government and the academy. In establishing rapport, Berk and Adams (1970) suggested being honest with respondents about the nature and goal of the research and explaining and demonstrating a commitment to the goals of the research.

A second methodological issue pertains to definitional ambiguity. As we noted earlier, masturbation is difficult to conceptualize (Soble, 1996, 1997). The definitions of masturbation change historically, culturally, and in given social situations (Muehlenhard, 2000; Soble, 1996,

1997). Given definitional ambiguities, it is imperative that researchers define their sexual terminology for their respondents and their readers. In a recent study of sex in prison that assessed the nature and frequency of sex among inmates in a Delaware prison therapeutic community, Saum et al., (1995) responded to definitional ambiguity by explicitly defining the sexual terminology they were using and measuring. In response to the sensitivity of the issues the researchers were addressing, they did not ask their respondents about their current sexual activities but instead inquired into the activities the inmates had seen, heard about, and participated in when housed in the general population. In this way, the inmates avoided stigmatization by inmates in the general population.

In sum, the methodological concerns and issues when studying sexuality and masturbation in prison include reporting, establishing rapport, and definitional ambiguity. Responding to these issues requires honesty, explicit definitions of the sexual terminology used, and sensitivity to the fact that what is being measured can be considered deviant and/or illegal with respect to the prison context.

CONCLUSION

Although masturbation is an important issue in prison, there has been little research that has focused both on masturbation within the range of other sexual practices in prison and masturbation in its own right. Masturbation should be researched because of its relation to issues of overall importance to the prison environment. These concerns are social control and health maintenance. As previously stated, masturbation in prison is almost always a rule infraction. However, it provides inmates an alternative outlet to release pent-up frustrations and stresses. It may also possibly reduce the amount of consensual and coerced homosexual behavior behind bars.

We must recommend to prison administrators that masturbation is a natural part of life. In addition, masturbation in prison, unlike consensual and coerced sex, can prevent the spread of sexually transmitted diseases such as HIV/AIDS for both male and female inmates. Therefore, it is important for correctional administrators and policymakers to reconsider the definition of masturbation as a violation of institutional rules. Most important, the justification and rationale for instructing inmates that autoerotic activities are wrong needs to be revisited and reconsidered. To do so, it is important that policymakers first understand the motivations, dynamics, frequencies, and characteristics of practitioners of masturbation in prison. In addition, as we shall see in the next chapter, conjugal visitation programs could also decrease the amount of consensual and coerced same-sex sexual activity within correctional facilities.

10

Conjugal Visitation Programs: The Logical Conclusion

Christopher Hensley,
Sandra Rutland, and Phyllis Gray-Ray

Conjugal visitation programs allow inmates and their spouses personal time together on prison grounds during which they may engage in sexual intercourse (Hensley, Rutland, and Gray-Ray, 2000a, 2000b; Hensley et al., 2000; Hopper, 1962, 1969, 1989; Kent, 1975). Conjugal visitation programs in recent years have become one of the most debated topics within the correctional arena. Public pressure and the "lock 'em up and throw away the key" attitude of society and politicians have called for several states to drop their conjugal visitation programs. Currently, only five states (Mississippi, New York, California, Washington, and New Mexico) allow private conjugal visitations for inmates and their spouses (Hensley, Rutland, and Gray-Ray, 2000a, 2000b).

Conjugal visitation programs also exist outside of the United States. These programs have been used in Latin American and European countries for a significant period of time (Goetting, 1982a). Such prison systems outside the United States have been complimented for their strategies, which are directed at promoting stability in the families of incarcerated individuals (Goetting, 1982a). For example, in Mexico as well as various other Latin American countries, conjugal visits are part of correctional policy (Goetting, 1982a; Hayner, 1972). As Hayner stated:

> The practice of conjugal visits in Mexican prisons is a realistic method of meeting the sex problem. Not only does it combat homosexuality; it often changes the entire behavior of a convict. It should be remembered that Mexico has a very strong family tradition. Even

more than in the United States the family is regarded as a fundamental institution. Anything that tends to destroy the family meets with opposition; anything that strengthens it is supported. It is believed the conjugal visit keeps couples together. When the manager of a Mexican hotel gave his assistant cook her free day on Thursday so that she could visit her husband in the local bastille on that day, he was acting in harmony with Mexican mores. (quoted in Balogh, 1964: 52)

HISTORY OF CONJUGAL VISITATION PROGRAMS IN THE UNITED STATES

Mississippi was the first state to allow inmates to participate in conjugal visits. However, no formal penitentiary records exist indicating the actual onset of conjugal visitations at the Mississippi State Penitentiary in Parchman. Nevertheless, this privilege is almost as old as the institution itself. Informal conjugal visitations have probably been allowed among inmates since the institution opened at its present location in the Mississippi Delta in 1900 (Hopper 1969, 1989).

The practice of conjugal visitations was first allowed for black inmates only (Braswell and Cabana, 1975; Hopper, 1969, 1989). During the early 1900s, authorities apparently viewed conjugal visits as a valuable tool in the management of what they deemed an insatiable sexual appetite by black inmates. A second belief was that black males possessed superhuman strength. Given this context, the conjugal visitation program was introduced to control aggression against correctional staff and inmates (Hensley, Rutland, and Gray-Ray, 2000a). Unfortunately, black inmates were not afforded facilities to engage in conjugal visits. Many inmates used their sleeping quarters while others slipped into storage shelters or tool sheds to engage in sexual activity (Hopper, 1969, 1989).

During the 1930s, the privilege continued to be restricted to black inmates. Also during this time period, prostitutes were allowed to visit Parchman. They would arrive "every Sunday afternoon on a flatbed truck driven by a pimp as lordly as any who ride city streets in pink Cadillacs" (Hopper, 1989: 103). According to a song written at that time, inmates paid up to fifty cents for the services of the prostitutes, which was a large sum of money following the days of the Great Depression (Hopper, 1969, 1989). The practice of allowing prostitutes on prison grounds continued for two additional decades (Hensley, Rutland, and Gray-Ray, 2000a, 2000b; Hensley et al., 2000; Hopper, 1989).

Around 1940, makeshift facilities, known as "red houses," were constructed by inmates for the purpose of conjugal visits for all incarcerated males at Parchman regardless of race. The name "red houses" actually came from the red paint used on the outside of the buildings rather than as a reference to the "red light district." These red houses were an attempt to make the conjugal visitation program more respectable (Hensley, Rutland, and Gray-Ray, 2000a; Hopper, 1969, 1989).

By the late 1950s, every unit with the exception of the maximum-security unit and prison hospital had facilities for conjugal visits. However, prostitutes were no longer allowed to visit the prison grounds. Spouses, common-law wives, and female friends were allowed to visit the inmates for the purpose of maintaining family ties and sexual satisfaction. The day of the visit often had a family atmosphere, as many inmates and their families would have picnics in the prison yard. Because of the family atmosphere during visiting days and policy changes regarding the conjugal visitation program, these "private" visits became dominated by legally married male inmates (Hensley, Rutland, and Gray-Ray, 2000a, 2000b; Hensley et al., 2000; Hopper, 1969, 1989).

Official recognition of the program was not established until 1965 (Hopper, 1969, 1989). The First Offender's Unit and the first brick red house were also established that same year (Goetting, 1982b; Hopper, 1969, 1989). In 1971, a federal district court order (*Gates v. Collier*) mandated many changes at Parchman. Among other things, outdated inmate housing units had to be revamped. The red houses were also improved at the same time as the other buildings (Hensley, Rutland, and Gray-Ray, 2000a; Hopper, 1969, 1989).

Along with facility improvements, other significant advancements were generated toward the conjugal visitation program. In 1972, the prison administration officially began to manage and support the program. Still, no records were kept as to which inmates had such visits, nor did an inmate have to make a request to partake in the program (Hopper 1969, 1989). Another advancement was made in 1972 that allowed female inmates to participate in conjugal visitations at Parchman (Hopper, 1969, 1989). In 1974, the conjugal visitation program was expanded to include a three-day family visit. The program addition allowed the inmate's family to spend up to three days and two nights in apartments located on prison grounds that were built for these purposes (Hopper, 1969, 1989). Thus, the typical inmate at that time could get a conjugal visit every two weeks and a three-day family visit every other month (Hensley, Rutland, and Gray-Ray, 2000a, 2000b; Hensley et al., 2000; Hopper, 1969, 1989).

In 1987, the Central Mississippi Correctional Facility for Women was constructed in Rankin County. All female prisoners were moved to this facility. Married female inmates in Mississippi were afforded the same program privileges as the married male inmates, including conjugal visits (Hensley, Rutland, and Gray-Ray, 2000a, 2000b; Hensley et al., 2000; Hopper, 1989).

In 1999, there were approximately 5,300 inmates housed in the Mississippi State Penitentiary and the Central Mississippi Correctional Facility. Because of strict eligibility requirements, approximately 350 inmates were allowed to participate in conjugal visits (Hensley, Rutland, and Gray-Ray, 2000b; Hensley et al., 2000). In addition, condoms were provided to participants in these prisons to keep pregnancy and sexually transmitted diseases (such as HIV/AIDS) to a minimum (Lillis, 1993).

EXISTING CONJUGAL
VISITATION PROGRAMS IN THE UNITED STATES

Mississippi

There are three requirements that inmates must meet prior to participation in conjugal visits in Mississippi. First, inmates must be housed in a minimum- or medium-security unit. Consequently, those individuals housed in the maximum-security unit make up the only division of inmates automatically denied visits. Inmates must also provide proof of marriage, thereby rendering unmarried inmates ineligible for such visits. Furthermore, conjugal visits must be earned through good behavior (Hensley, Rutland, and Gray-Ray, 2000a, 2000b; Hensley et al., 2000). Inmates receiving conjugal visits in red houses can get a conjugal visit every two weeks and a three-day family visit every other month. Records are kept by each respective correctional institution in Mississippi that allows conjugal visits.

At-risk inmates, such as those who have sexually transmitted diseases including HIV/AIDS, may be denied eligibility. The conjugal visits policy states that "in the event that a spouse of an HIV-infected inmate is also HIV-positive, the spouse may petition the Commissioner of Corrections for continuation of conjugal visits. If the spouse is HIV-negative, but desires conjugal visits and states in writing that they will practice safe sex, the spouse may petition for an exception" (Lillis, 1993: 3).

California

On July 1, 1968, the state of California launched its conjugal visitation program, the Family Visiting Program, at the Tehachapi Institution (Goetting, 1982b; Kent, 1975). The program was measured as "an unqualified success" because of its ability to maintain family ties (Goetting, 1982b: 56), and it was decided to expand the program to other institutions throughout the state in 1971. Today, thirty-two of California's thirty-three male and female state prisons have the program (Hensley, Rutland, and Gray-Ray, 2000b; Hensley et al., 2000). The emphasis of the program is to promote family stability rather than sexual release. These visits often include children, siblings, and parents of the inmates in addition to the inmate's spouse. The visits (lasting from forty-eight to seventy-two hours) take place in modular homes on correctional facility grounds. Common-law wives are not eligible for these types of visits. Those inmates who are unmarried are only allowed family visits from immediate family members (Goetting, 1982b).

There are several requirements for participation in the Family Visiting Program. Participants must be in the general population and be engaged in work and training programs. New arrivals, maximum-security inmates, and sex offenders are not allowed such visits. The spouses of those inmates eligible for conjugal visits must provide condoms and other forms of birth control. Inmates with HIV/AIDS are not allowed to participate in conjugal visits. However, they may receive regular visits from their families (Lillis, 1993).

New York

The New York State Department of Corrections began the Family Reunion Program in 1976 at seven institutions to strengthen and preserve families. Immediate family members, including the inmate's spouse, are allowed these visits. The visits take place in mobile homes separate from general population facilities at the male and female prisons. The department provides these facilities with pillows, blankets, sheets, towels, and soap (Goetting, 1982b).

There are strict eligibility criteria for those inmates who participate in the Family Reunion Program of New York. An individual must have been in the general population for at least ninety days, must be suitably adapting to prison life, have a clean record, and be housed in minimum or medium security. Inmates who engage in continuous disruptions while incarcerated are not eligible for participation. Those convicted of sex offenses, heinous crimes, or mentally ill inmates are not allowed these visits (Goetting, 1982b). The number of visits for any individual depends on the amount of applicants and the available space (Goetting, 1982b; Hensley, Rutland, and Gray-Ray, 2000b; Hensley et al., 2000).

If the incarcerated individual is HIV-infected and they wish to participate in the program, they must first disclose this information to their spouse. Condoms are provided by the correctional system to prevent the spread of sexually transmitted diseases. Other birth control devices are provided by the spouse of the inmate (Lillis, 1993).

Washington

The Extended Family Visiting Program began in Washington in 1980 at the Purdy Treatment Center for Women (Goetting, 1982b). Today, the program is available at eleven of the twelve main prisons in the state of Washington (Hensley, Rutland, and Gray-Ray, 2000b; Hensley et al., 2000). Family visiting takes place within mobile homes on prison grounds. There are several qualifications for admittance into the program. The prisoner must not have been found guilty of major disturbances or escape attempts within the prior twelve months. The inmate must also currently be involved in schooling or employment programs. Inmates in maximum security, on death row, housed in disciplinary or administrative units, or charged with a felony and awaiting prosecution are not eligible to participate. To prevent pregnancy and the spread of sexually transmitted diseases, the Washington Department of Corrections provides contraceptives and counseling to inmates and their spouses (Lillis, 1993).

New Mexico

The Extended Family Visitation Program in New Mexico was established in 1983 and currently operates in four state prisons. The visitation program serves as a means of promoting family stability and enhancing the rehabilitative process. Because it is considered a privilege, the program attempts to promote positive behavior among prisoners (Hensley, Rutland, and Gray-Ray, 2000b; Hensley et al., 2000). Visits occur within mobile homes on prison grounds.

Strict criteria must be met before an inmate becomes eligible for the Extended Family Visitation Program. The criteria include a careful review of the inmate's record to establish his or her inclination toward violence. If the reason for incarceration is due to a violent act (such as rape or murder), extensive psychiatric evaluations are necessary and the final decision regarding participation resides with the warden of each facility. A clearance is also required from the medical department prior to the initial visit (Hensley, Rutland, and Gray-Ray, 2000b; Hensley et al., 2000; Sandlin, 1993). In addition, inmates are required to pay a fee for the visits (Lillis, 1993).

There is a forty-five-day and an eighty-day waiting period between visits for minimum-restricted custody and medium-custody prisoners, respectively. Inmates may also be asked to submit to a urinalysis test once the conjugal visit is complete to determine whether substance abuse occurred during the visit. If the results are positive, future conjugal visitation privileges may be denied (Hensley, Rutland, and Gray-Ray, 2000b; Hensley et al., 2000; Sandlin, 1993). Inmates are provided condoms during visits. According to correctional policy, "inmates with HIV infection shall be required to attend a counseling session with the spouse before conjugal visits can be approved" (Lillis, 1993: 3).

THE IMPACT OF CONJUGAL VISITS ON INMATES

Since the first famous *Sex in Prison* study on conjugal visits at Parchman in 1969, advocates of conjugal visits argue that these programs increase family stability and reduce homosexual behavior, violence, and sexual assaults in prison (Burstein, 1977; Hopper, 1969, 1989). However, Bennett (1989), in his study of wardens and superintendents with and without private family visiting programs, found that slightly more than half of the administrators did not believe that homosexual behavior and sexual assaults could be reduced by conjugal visitation programs. In contrast, many inmates—particularly those participating in the program—feel that it does increase family stability and reduce homosexual behavior and violence (Burstein, 1977; Hopper, 1989). Burstein (1977) found that 90 percent of all inmate participants of the conjugal visiting program and 85 percent of the nonparticipants in Soledad Prison (California) agreed that the program was an important method of behavior control. In addition, Howser, Grossman, and MacDonald (1983) found that those inmates who participated in family

reunion programs in New York had improved disciplinary records compared to nonparticipants. They also found that these inmates had a
lower likelihood of recidivism upon release from the correctional facility.

Holt and Miller (1972) also argued that parole success was greater
for those inmates who had the opportunity to participate in family visiting. They found that inmates who received three or more family visits
were six times less likely to return than those who did not. In addition,
Carlson and Cervera (1991) and MacDonald and Kelly (1980) found
that inmates in New York who participated in the Family Reunion
Program were less likely to be reincarcerated. Thus, conjugal visits
were seen as a way to maintain family ties and keep the prisoner cognizant of the external culture.

Family Stability

Correctional systems in the United States that allow conjugal visitation
programs stress the preservation of family (Goetting, 1982b). Conjugal
visits tend to maintain the nuclear family and, at the same time, lessen
the emotional stress of the inmate's spouse (*Clarion Ledger,* 1994).
During the 1969 study conducted at Parchman, inmates appreciated the
emotional satisfaction of visiting privately with their spouse more than
the sexual release (Hopper, 1969). As Lawrence Wilson (1969), former
deputy director of the California Department of Corrections, stated,
"California wants family visiting aimed at preserving the family relationship and helping families grow stronger. The fact that husbands and
wives engage in sexual intercourse is incidental to our main objectives:
the preservation and strengthening of the family" (261).

Studies support the idea that conjugal visitation programs strengthen or at least keep inmate marriages together (Burstein, 1977; Hensley,
Rutland, and Gray-Ray, 2000b; Rutland, 1995). In two separate studies
(1963 and 1984) of inmates' ratings of the functions of conjugal visits
in Mississippi, Hopper (1989) found that the majority of inmates felt
that conjugal visits kept marriages together. In 1994, Hensley, Rutland,
and Gray-Ray studied the effects of conjugal visits on family stability in
Mississippi. Questionnaires were administered to 256 inmates at the
Central Mississippi Correctional Facility and the Mississippi State
Penitentiary (Parchman). They found that participation in the conjugal
visitation program had a positive effect on the inmate's relationship
with their spouse (Hensley, Rutland, and Gray-Ray, 2000b; Hensley et
al., 2000). As one camp sergeant stated in Hopper's (1969) study:

Most problems the inmates have are concerned with worrying about their families. And most people who come to the penitentiary are concerned about how the inmate is getting along, how his health is, and so on. The best thing I can do is allow them to see each other and judge for themselves. A common thing in prison is for a married man to worry about his wife, whether or not she still loves him, and is faithful to him. One visit in private with her is better than a hundred letters. (42–43)

Violent Behavior

If violent behavior is to be repressed in prison, it is argued that some type of control mechanism must be implemented. As seen by a few prison officials, conjugal visitation programs may serve as a behavior-controlling mechanism. Unfortunately, no research has adequately addressed this issue. Yet it is assumed that such programs enhance equilibrium within the correctional system by functioning as a reward for compliance with the institution's rules and regulations (Goetting, 1982b). As found in Balogh's (1964) sample of prison wardens, conjugal visitations could act as a stimulus for the inmates to comply with the policies of the prison. In this way, conjugal visits could serve as a device for the control of inmates' behavior (Goetting, 1982b). "Otherwise, the lid will blow off the joint. It's happened in Attica. It's happened in Michigan and at other prisons around the country" (*Clarion Ledger*, 1994: 13A).

In a study of the effects of conjugal visits on violent behavior in Mississippi prisons, Hensley, Rutland, and Gray-Ray (2000b) and Hensley et al. (2000) asked inmates, "Do conjugal visitations reduce tension and violence in prison?" Results indicated that 80 percent of nonparticipants perceived that conjugal visits did reduce tension and violence. Additionally, 90 percent of all participants in the conjugal visitation program felt that the visits did reduce tension "within the walls." This finding was consistent with earlier research on the topic (Burstein, 1977).

Hensley, Rutland, and Gray-Ray (2000b) and Hensley et al. (2000) also studied the effects of conjugal visitations on violent behavior, including sexual assaults, in prison. They found that those who engaged in conjugal visitations were less likely to display violent behavior while incarcerated as compared to those who did not participate in such a program. When the researchers examined the differences between males and females on this item, they found that conjugal visits decreased the amount of violent behavior in prison for males only. As Sheldon (1972) so eloquently stated:

Conjugal visitation could be instituted in many prison settings without disruption of proper procedures and with a lessening of tension and frustration. Complete isolation of men and women from all sexual activities of a heterosexual nature is completely unrealistic and results in homosexual behavior or in other displacement of the sexual drive in hostile, aggressive and sometimes dangerous behavior toward other inmates and prison personnel. (20)

Homosexual Behavior

Although there have been studies on same-sex sexual activity in prison, there are no reliable statistics on the amount that occurs (Hensley, 2001; Nacci and Kane, 1983; Saum et al., 1995; Tewksbury, 1989b; Wooden and Parker, 1982). Wooden and Parker (1982) found that 65 percent of a random sample of 200 California male inmates had engaged in homosexual activity. Nacci and Kane (1983) found that of 211 male federal prison inmates, almost 30 percent had reported engaging in homosexual activities. Of the 150 Ohio male inmates in Tewksbury's study (1989b), over 19 percent reported having had engaged in homosexual behavior while incarcerated. Saum et al. (1995) studied a male Delaware prison and found only 2 percent of a sample of 101 inmates had engaged in homosexual behavior. Finally, Hensley (2001) found that approximately one-fourth of his sample of 174 Oklahoma male inmates had engaged in homosexual activity while behind bars.

Advocates of conjugal visitation programs have argued that much of this behavior could be reduced, especially for participants in the program. In 1974, Stanley Telega, the vice president of the Fortune Society (a national rehabilitative organization for ex-convicts), stated:

Most homosexual acts in prison are done by inmates whose former and primary orientation was heterosexual. However, due to the imposed unisexual atmosphere, homosexual desires and acts developed. . . . Conjugal visits would help . . . maintain a heterosexual orientation for those who are concerned about homosexuality. It would also help to alleviate general tensions because sexual tensions turn into fights among the men, in order to find some release. (Telega, 1974: 4)

It has also been argued that most inmates who engage in consensual homosexual activity do so because of loneliness or as a sexual outlet (Gordon and McConnell, 1999). Thus, one can assume that conjugal visits may meet these particular needs for inmates who participate in the program. Inmates, especially those participating in conjugal visitation programs, believe that homosexual activity can be reduced by these programs (Burstein, 1977; Hopper, 1989).

In their study of conjugal visits in Mississippi, Hensley, Rutland, and Gray-Ray (2000b) and Hensley et al. (2000) asked prisoners if conjugal visits reduced same-sex activities while in prison. The findings revealed that 59 percent of the nonparticipants of the program felt that conjugal visits did reduce homosexual behavior. Seventy-four percent of participants in the program felt that conjugal visits did reduce homosexual behavior in prison. However, when the researchers examined this issue using statistical analysis, they found that participation in conjugal visitations did not have a statistically significant effect on homosexual behavior in prison (Hensley, Rutland, and Gray-Ray, 2000b; Hensley et al., 2000). It is important to reiterate, however, that consensual same-sex sexual behavior is less of a threat to institutional safety and security, inmate psychological well-being, and if afforded condoms in prison, less of a health issue to correctional staff, inmates, and their families.

PROBLEMS ASSOCIATED WITH CONJUGAL VISITS

Conjugal visitation programs have been criticized on several grounds. First, opponents of the programs argue that conjugal visits generate negative attitudes on the part of those inmates who are not allowed to participate. Yet in Hopper's (1969, 1989) studies, he found less than 15 percent of the nonparticipating inmates had concerns about letting married inmates have conjugal visits with their spouses. In addition, Hensley, Rutland, and Gray-Ray (2000a) found that no difference existed between participants and nonparticipants' attitudes toward the conjugal visitation program in Mississippi.

Second, critics of these programs argue that prison systems with conjugal visits will have more problems dealing with drugs and contraband. Bennett (1989) found that the administrators he surveyed saw drug smuggling as a danger. However, the administrators felt that the drug supply could be reduced with more constant supervision and precautionary measures.

Another argument against conjugal visits involves negative public opinion. Critics argue that there is a "social condemnation of prison sex" in the United States (Goetting, 1982b: 68). A staff member at a correctional institution once stated, "If we are going to place them in individual cells with clean sheets every night, feed them family style, work them short hours under ideal conditions, provide hours of recre-

ation every day and frequent conjugal visits with their respective spouses, I can see no particular reason for containing them at all" (Balogh,
1964: 57). However, Hopper (1989) found that the Mississippi public
was generally in favor of allowing conjugal visits for married inmates.
In a Mississippi public opinion poll in 1985, Hopper found that 52.8
percent of males and 71.7 percent of females had either medium or high
levels of support for the program. However, most Mississippians do not
favor allowing conjugal visits for single inmates (Hopper, 1989).

Many inmates have claimed that denying conjugal visitation programs violates the marital right to privacy, the equal protection clause,
the practice of religion, and constitutes cruel and unusual punishment
(Medellin, 1992; Mushlin, 1993; Palmer, 1999). However, despite the
apparent benefits of conjugal visitation programs, the U.S. courts have
held that inmates do not have a constitutional right to conjugal visits
(*Lyons v. Gilligan*, 1974; *Payne v. District of Columbia*, 1953; *Rodgers
v. Ohio Department of Rehabilitation and Correction*, 1993; *Stuart v.
Heard*, 1973; *Tarlton v. Clark*, 1970).

One of the most disturbing problems associated with conjugal visitation programs is the spread of HIV/AIDS (Bates, 1989; Goldstein,
1990; Olivero et al., 1992). This issue potentially puts correctional systems at risk of lawsuits. According to Lillis (1993), "Too strict or not
strict enough HIV/AIDS policy, testing, matters of privacy, and dis-
crimination could all be conceivably touchy issues" (2). But in states
that allow conjugal visits, most policy is shaped by these concerns. All
five states that allow conjugal visitations have some type of policy in
place regarding HIV and other sexually transmitted diseases.

As can be seen, most of these problems can be resolved. If correctional administrators use standard precautionary measures in their facilities, many concerns associated with conjugal visitation programs can
be alleviated. Problematic inmates can be screened through a better
classification system. According to Wright (1997), "Conjugal visitation
can be an asset to the criminal justice system if used wisely and responsibly" (n.p.).

FUTURE RESEARCH

Future research is desperately needed in the area of conjugal visits.
Most studies of conjugal visitation programs on family stability, violence, and homosexual behavior are outdated. Research should continue
to see if conjugal visits really do increase family stability and reduce

violent behavior and homosexual behavior in prison. Research should also include a comparison between those inmates who are married prior to incarceration and those who are married after they are incarcerated to see if there are differences between the two groups in terms of the reduction of certain behaviors in prison. Additionally, future research should focus on the impact of conjugal visits on recidivism. In other words, does participation in conjugal visits have an impact on the recidivism rates of those inmates who participate in comparison to those who do not participate in such programs? Other topics of research should focus on whether conjugal visits have a positive parole outcome for participants, if participants have a higher likelihood of being employed after release, if the program is an "effective management tool for correctional officers and administrators" (Gordon and McConnell, 1999: 121), and if conjugal visits could reduce the spread of HIV in prisons.

CONCLUSION

Given what we do know about prison sexuality, researchers and inmate advocates must continue to strive to recommend policy changes within the walls of confinement. For instance, correctional administrators should consider adopting or readopting conjugal visitation programs. The few studies that have been conducted on conjugal visits have shown that they maintain family stability and decrease violent behavior including sexual assaults in prison. Conjugal and family visitation programs are easy to implement within correctional facilities especially if correctional administrators make the effort to address the positive consequences to the general public.

Second, administrators must wake up to the grim reality that inmates are contracting sexually transmitted diseases including HIV/AIDS. The Canadian prison system, for example, has gone as far as to advocate that consensual sex between inmates be taken off the list of institutional infractions in order to prevent the spread of HIV/AIDS (Correctional Service of Canada, 1994). In addition to this recommendation, correctional administrators must provide preventative measures including bleach, dental dams, clean needles, and—most important—condoms.

In addition to these recommendations, researchers must continue to undertake projects within women's correctional facilities. Researchers who study human sexuality have addressed the distinction between male and female attitudes and behaviors, though very little is known about the incidence and prevalence of consensual and coerced sexual activity or female inmates' attitudes toward homosexuality and sexuality in general.

It should be duly noted that prison sex researchers have made important contributions to the study of this issue. For example, Hopper's (1969, 1989) research on conjugal visits had an impact on the Mississippi Department of Correction's decision to allow married female inmates to have the same privilege as their male counterparts. In addition, the conjugal visitation policy shifted from a racist issue in the early 1900s to a more humanitarian concern in later decades. Prison sex researchers have also offered prevention and intervention programs and training for reducing the amount of sexual assaults in correctional facilities. Again, very few state department of corrections have positively responded to these efforts.

Prison sex researchers have opened the eyes of many people into an unseen world of violence, neglect, and abuse. Because inmates typically return to society, we must continue to make every effort to stop prisoner rape, fight the spread of HIV/AIDS, and implement more conjugal visitation programs in U.S. prisons to increase their chances for positive reintegration into society and our chances of maintaining a feeling of safety and security. Therefore, we all must work together to provide a safe and secure environment for our inmates.

In conclusion, academicians who study prison sex have undertaken great challenges since the early twentieth century. Not only do professional colleagues view their work with skepticism and distaste, but so do correctional administrators and society. However, research of this nature is not only important for correctional administrators but also sex research in general. Sex researchers must continue to delve into these "forbidden topics." According to Tewksbury and West (2000), "Refusal or reluctance to acknowledge that sex in prison exists is one thing, but refusal or reluctance even to devote research attention to the issue is detrimental to the study of corrections, to the discipline, and to society as a whole" (377).

REFERENCES

Adams, K. (1992). Adjusting to prison life. In M. Tonry (ed.), *Crime and Justice: A Review of Research*. Chicago: University of Chicago Press.

AIDS in Prison Project. (2001). Facts sheet: New York State. Online. Available at: http://www.aidsinfonyc.org/aip/facts.html.

Alarid, L. F. (2000a). Sexual assault and coercion among incarcerated women prisoners: Excerpts from prison letters. *The Prison Journal, 80*(4):391–406.

Alarid, L. F. (2000b). Sexual orientation perspectives of incarcerated bisexual and gay men: The county jail protective custody experience. *The Prison Journal, 80*(1):80–95.

Allen, H. E. (1995). The American dream and crime in the twenty-first century. *Justice Quarterly, 12*(3):427–445.

Allen, H. E., and C. E. Simonsen. (2000). *Corrections in America: An Introduction*. 9th ed. Upper Saddle River, N.J.: Prentice Hall.

Allison, J. A., and L. S. Wrightsman. (1993). *Rape: The Misunderstood Crime*. Newbury Park, Calif.: Sage Publications.

American Psychiatric Association. (2000). *Diagnostic and Statistical Manual of Mental Disorders*. Revised 4th ed. Washington, D.C.: American Psychiatric Association.

American Psychiatric Association. (1994). *Diagnostic and Statistical Manual of Mental Disorders*. 4th ed. Washington, D.C.: American Psychiatric Association.

American Psychiatric Association. (1987). *Diagnostic and Statistical Manual of Mental Disorders*. Revised 3rd ed. Washington, D.C.: American Psychiatric Association.

American Psychiatric Association. (1980). *Diagnostic and Statistical Manual of Mental Disorders*. 3rd ed. Washington, D.C.: American Psychiatric Association.

American Psychiatric Association. (1968). *Diagnostic and Statistical Manual of Mental Disorders.* 2nd ed. Washington, D.C.: American Psychiatric Association.

American Psychiatric Association. (1952). *Diagnostic and Statistical Manual of Mental Disorders.* 1st ed. Washington, D.C.: American Psychiatric Association.

Amir, M. (1971). *Patterns of Forcible Rape.* Chicago: University of Chicago Press.

Amnesty International. (2001). *Broken Bodies, Shattered Minds: Torture and Ill-Treatment of Women.* London: Amnesty International.

Amnesty International. (1999). *Not Part of My Sentence: Violations of the Human Rights of Women in Custody.* New York: Amnesty International.

Anderson, C. L. (1981). Males as sexual assault victims: Multiple levels of trauma. *Journal of Homosexuality, 7*(2/3):145–162.

Bailey, S. (2001). High court to rule on extradition process as Canadians face U.S. trials. Online. Available at: http://www.canoe.ca/CNEWSLaw0104/05_gem.cp.html.

Balogh, J. (1964). Conjugal visitations in prisons: A sociological perspective. *Federal Probation, 28–29*:52–58.

Bartnof, H. S. (1999). Selected highlights from the 1999 national conference on women and HIV/AIDS. Online. Available at: http://www.hivandhepatitis.com/conferences/women.html.

Basu, R. (1988). Focus: AIDS behind bars. *The Communicator, 5-7*:10–12.

Bates, T. M. (1989). Rethinking conjugal visitation in light of the "AIDS" crisis. *New England Journal of Criminal and Civil Confinement, 15*(1):121–145.

Beck, A. J. (2000). *Prisoners in 1999.* Washington, D.C.: U.S. Department of Justice.

Beck, A. J., and P. M. Harrison. (2001). *Bureau of Justice Statistics Bulletin: Prisoners in 2000.* Washington, D.C.: U.S. Department of Justice.

Beck, A. J., and J. C. Karberg. (2001). *Bureau of Justice Statistics Bulletin: Prison and Jail Inmates at Midyear 2000.* Washington, D.C.: U.S. Department of Justice.

Beers, M. H., and R. Berkow. (1999). *The Merck Manual of Diagnosis and Therapy.* Whitehouse Station, N.J.: Merck Research Laboratories.

Bennett, L. A. (1989). Correctional administrators' attitudes toward private family visiting. *The Prison Journal, 69*(1):110–114.

Berk, R., and J. Adams. (1970). Establishing rapport with deviant groups. *Social Problems, 18*(1):102–117.

Beyzarov, E. P. (2000). New alliance, new approval put PTSD in the spotlight. *Drug Topics, 144*(7):16–17.

Bienen, L., and H. Field. (1980). *Jurors and Rape: A Study in Psychology and Law.* Lexington, Mass.: Lexington Books.

Bland, R., S. Newman, R. Dyck, and H. Orn. (1990). Prevalence of psychiatric disorders in suicide attempts in a prison population. *Canadian Journal of Psychiatry, 35*:407–413.

Blumberg, M. (1990). *AIDS: The Impact on the Criminal Justice System.* Columbus, Ohio: Merrill Publishing Company.

Blumberg, M. (1989). Issues and controversies with respect to the management of AIDS in corrections. *The Prison Journal, 69*(1):1–14.

Blumberg, M., and J. D. Laster. (1999). The impact of HIV/AIDS on corrections. In K. Haas and G. Alpert (eds.), *The Dilemmas of Corrections: Contemporary Perspectives*. Prospect Heights, Ill.: Waveland Press, Inc.

Boling, P. (2000). Comments on Morris's "privacy, privation, perversity: Toward new representations of the personal." *Signs: Journal of Women in Culture and in Society, 25*(2):353–359.

Bondesson, U. (1989). *Prisoners in Prison Societies*. New Brunswick, N.J.: Transaction.

Book Essentials Publications. (1987). *Webster's General Dictionary*. Larchmont, N.Y.: Book Essentials Publications.

Bottoms, A. E. (1999). Interpersonal violence and social order in prisons. In M. Tonry and J. Petersilia (eds.), *Prisons*. Chicago: University of Chicago Press.

Boudreaux, E., et al. (1998). Criminal victimization, post-traumatic stress disorder, and comorbid psychopathology among a community sample of women. *Journal of Traumatic Stress, 11*(4):665–678.

Bowker, L. (1980). *Prison Victimization*. New York: Elsevier North Holland.

Braithwaite, R., et al. (1999). Tuberculosis and other infectious diseases in correctional facilities. Online. Available at: http://www.mrc.ac.za/UHDbulletin/sep99/tuberculosis.htm.

Braswell, M., and D. A. Cabana. (1975). Conjugal visitation and furlough programs for offenders in Mississippi. *New England Journal of Prison Law, 2*(1):67–72.

Braun, M., et al. (1989). Increasing incidence of tuberculosis in a prison inmate population. *Journal of American Medical Association, 261*(3):393–397.

Brown, S. E., F. A. Esbensen, and G. Geis. (1998). *Criminology: Explaining Crime and Its Context*. 3rd ed. Cincinnati: Anderson Publishing Company.

Buffum, P. (1972). *Homosexuality in Prisons*. Washington, D.C.: U.S. Department of Justice.

Burgess, A. W. (1985). Rape trauma syndrome: A nursing diagnosis. *Occupational Health Nursing, 33*(8):405–406.

Burgess, A. W., and L. L. Holmstrom. (1975). Sexual assault: Signs and symptoms. *Journal of Emergency Nursing, 1*(2):1115.

Burgess, A. W., and L. Holmstrom. (1974a). Crisis and counseling requests of rape victims. *Nursing Research, 23*:196–202.

Burgess, A. W., and L. Holmstrom. (1974b). Rape syndrome. *American Journal of Psychiatry, 131*(9):981–986.

Burgess, A. W., and L. Holmstrom. (1974c). Rape: The victim goes on trial. In I. Drapkin and E. Viano (eds.), *Victimology*. Lexington, Mass.: Lexington Books.

Burstein, J. (1977). *Conjugal Visits in Prison: Psychological and Social Consequences*. Lexington, Mass.: Heath.

Burt, M. (1980). Cultural myths and supports for rape. *Journal of Personality and Social Psychology, 38*(2):217–230.

Burton, D., et al. (1999). *Women in Prison: Sexual Misconduct by Correctional Staff*. Washington, D.C.: U.S. General Accounting Office.

Calderwood, D. (1987). The male rape victim. *Medical Aspects of Human Sexuality, 21*(5):53–55.

Calhoun, A. J. (1996). Correctional worker risk for perpetrating sexual abuse of female inmates. Ph.D. dissertation, University of Hawaii.

Camp, C. G., and G. M. Camp. (2001). *The Corrections Yearbook, 2000*. Middletown, Conn.: Criminal Justice Institute.

Camp, C. G., and G. M. Camp. (1998). *The Corrections Yearbook, 1998*. Middletown, Conn.: Criminal Justice Institute.

Camp, G. M., and C. G. Camp. (1988). *Managing Strategies for Combating Prison Gang Violence*. South Salem, N.Y:. Criminal Justice Institute.

Campbell, R., and C. Johnson. (1997). Police officers' perceptions of rape: Is there consistency between state law and beliefs? *Journal of Interpersonal Violence, 12*(2):255–274.

Carlson, B. E., and N. J. Cervera. (1991). Inmates and their families: Conjugal visits, family contact, and family functioning. *Criminal Justice and Behavior, 18*(3):318–331.

Carroll, L. (1977). Humanitarian reform and biracial sexual assault in a maximum security prison. *Urban Life, 5*(4):417–437.

Cass, V. (1979). Homosexual identity formation: A theoretical model. *Journal of Homosexuality, 4*(3):219–235.

Centers for Disease Control. (1999). Decrease in AIDS-related mortality in a state correctional system: New York 1995–1998. *MMWR Weekly, 47*(51):1115–1117.

Champion, D. J. (2001). *Corrections in the United States: A Contemporary Perspective*. 3rd ed. Paramus, N.J.: Prentice Hall.

Chelala, C. (1999). More mentally ill people reported in US prisons. *British Medical Journal, 319*(7204):210.

Chen, H. H. (2000). Number of women behind bars skyrockets. Online. Available at: http://www.apbnews.com/cjsystem/justicenews/2000/02/01/prisoners0201_01.html.

Chonco, N. R. (1989). Sexual assaults among male inmates: A descriptive study. *The Prison Journal, 69*(1):72–82.

Clarion Ledger. (1994, September 11). Prison room for conjugal visits no honeymoon suite. 13A.

Clemmer, D. (1940). *The Prison Community*. New York: Rinehart.

CNN. (2000, April 24). Segment on prison sex research during CNN Headline News.

Connell, R., and G. Dowsett. (1993). The unclean notion of the generative parts: Frameworks in Western thought on sexuality. In R. Connell and G. Dowsett (eds.), *Rethinking Sex: Social Theory and Sexuality Research*. Philadelphia: Temple University Press.

Conrad, P. (1992). Medicalization and social control. *Annual Review of Sociology, 18*:209–232.

Cooksey, M. (1999). Custody and security. In P. Carlson and J. S. Garrett (eds.), *Prison and Jail Administration: Practice and Theory*. Gaithersburg, Md.: Aspen Publishers, Inc.

Correctional HIV Consortium (1998). Estimated annual costs for the treatment of an HIV+ inmate. Online. Available at: http://www.silcom.com/^chc/costs.html.

Correctional Service of Canada. (1994). *HIV/AIDS in Prisons: Final Report of the Expert Committee on AIDS in Prisons*. Ontario: Correctional Service of Canada.

Corrections Compendium. (1995, July). Breaking the silence on prison rape and AIDS, 20:14.

Cotton, D. J., and A. N. Groth. (1984). Sexual assault in correctional institutions: Prevention and intervention. In I. Stuart and J. Greer (eds.), *Victims of Sexual Aggression: Treatment of Children Women, and Men*. New York: Van Nostrand Reinhold Company.

Cotton, D. J., and A. N. Groth. (1982). Inmate rape: Prevention and intervention. *Journal of Prison and Jail Health, 2*(1):47–57.

Crouch, B., and J. Marquart. (1980). On becoming a prison guard. In B. Crouch (ed.), *The Keepers: Prison Guards and Contemporary Corrections*. Englewood Cliffs, N.J.: Prentice Hall.

Cusac, A. M. (2000). The judge gave me ten years. He didn't sentence me to death. (Inmates with HIV or AIDS, U.S.). *The Progressive, 64*(7):22–26.

Danto, B. (1981). *Crisis Behind Bars—The Suicidal Inmate: A Book for Police and Correctional Officers*. Warren, Mich.: Dale Corporation.

Davidson, J., and N. Moore. (1994). Masturbation and premarital sexual intercourse among college women: Making choices for sexual fulfilment. *Journal of Sex and Marital Therapy, 20*(3):179–199.

Davis, A. J. (1971). Sexual assaults in the Philadelphia prison system and sheriff's vans. In L. Radzinowicz and M. E. Wolfgang (eds.), *The Criminal in Confinement*. New York: Basic Books, Inc.

Davis, A. J. (1968). Sexual assaults in the Philadelphia prison system and sheriff's vans. *Trans-Action*:8–16.

Dean, C. (1996). *Sexuality and Modern Western Culture*. New York: Twayne Publishing.

DeGroot, A. S. (2001). HIV among incarcerated women: An epidemic behind the walls. *Corrections Today, 63*(1):77–81, 97.

DeGroot, et al. (1999). Women in prison: The impact of HIV. *HEPP News, 2*(6):2–4.

DeGroot, A. S., T. Hammett, and R. G. Scheib. (1996). Access to HIV services in prison and jails: A public health concern. *AIDS Reader*, May–June.

Deitz, S., and L. Byrnes. (1981). Attribution of responsibility for sexual assault: The influence of observer empathy and defendant occupation and attractiveness. *Journal of Psychology, 108*:17–29.

Dennis, S. (1999). Sex, lies, and no videotape. *American Jails, 13*(4):41–44.

DeNoon, D. J. (1999, September). Prevention opportunities missed in jails, prisons. *Tuberculosis and Airborne Disease Weekly*.

Ditton, P. M. (1999). *Mental Health Treatment and Treatment of Inmates and Probationers*. Washington, D.C.: U.S. Department of Justice.

Donaldson, S. (1997). *Prisoner Rape Education Program: Manual/Overview for Jail/Prison Administrators and Staff*. 2nd ed. Brandon, Vt.: Safer Society Press.

Donaldson, S. (1995). *Rape of Incarcerated Americans: A Preliminary Statistical Look*. A newsletter of Stop Prisoner Rape, Inc.

Donaldson, S. (1993a). A million jockers, punks, and queens: Sex among male prisoners and its implications for concepts of sexual orientation. Online. Available at: http://www.igc.apc.org/spr/docs/prison-sex-lecture.html.

Donaldson, S. (1993b). *Prisoner Rape Education Program: Overview for Jail/Prison Administrators and Staff*. Brandon, Vt.: Safer Society Press.

Dooley, E. (1990). Unnatural deaths in prison. *British Journal of Criminology*, 30:299–334.

Dubler, N. N. (1998). The collision of confinement and care: End-of-life care in prisons and jails. *Journal of Law, Medicine and Ethics*, 26(2):149–156.

Dumond, R. W. (2000). Inmate sexual assault: The plague which persists. *The Prison Journal*, 80(4):407–414.

Dumond, R. W. (1992). The sexual assault of male inmates in incarcerated settings. *International Journal of the Sociology of Law*, 20(2):135–157.

Eigenberg, H. M. (2000a). Correctional officers and their perceptions of homosexuality, rape, and prostitution in male prisons. *The Prison Journal*, 80(4):415–433.

Eigenberg, H. M. (2000b). Correctional officers' definitions of rape in male prisons. *Journal of Criminal Justice Review*, 28(5):435–449.

Eigenberg, H. M. (1994). Male rape in prisons: Examining the relationship between correctional officers' attitudes toward male rape and their willingness to respond to acts of rape. In M. Braswell, R. Montgomery, and L. Lombardo (eds.), *Prison Violence in America*. 2nd ed. Cincinnati: Anderson.

Eigenberg, H. M. (1992). Homosexuality in male prisons: Demonstrating the need for a social constructionist approach. *Criminal Justice Review*, 17(2):219–234.

Eigenberg, H. M. (1990). The national crime survey and rape: The case of the missing question. *Justice Quarterly*, 7(4):92–113.

Eigenberg, H. M. (1989). Male rape: An empirical examination of correctional officers' attitudes toward male rape in prison. *The Prison Journal*, 68(2):39–56.

Einat, T., and H. Einat. (2000). Inmate argot as an expression of prison subculture: The Israeli case. *The Prison Journal*, 80(3):309–325.

Eisikovits, Z., and M. Baizerman. (1982). "Doin' time": Violent youth in a juvenile facility and an adult prison. *Journal of Offender Counseling Services and Rehabilitation*, 6(3):5–19.

Ellis, H. (1942). *Studies in the Psychology of Sex*. New York: Random House.

Engle, L. (1999). It's a crime! HIV behind bars. Online. Available at: http://www.thebody.com/bp/jan99/crime.html.

Fagan, T. J., D. Wennerstrom, and J. Miller. (1996). Sexual assault of male inmates: Prevention, identification, and intervention. *Journal of Correctional Health Care*, *3*(1):49–66.

Federal Bureau of Prisons. (1997). *Sexual Abuse/Assault Prevention and Intervention Programs*. Washington, D.C.: U.S. Department of Justice.

Feldman-Summers, S., and C. Palmer. (1980). Rape as viewed by judges, prosecutors, and police officers. *Criminal Justice and Behavior*, *7*:19–40.

Field, H. (1978). Attitudes toward rape: A comparative analysis of police, rapists, crisis counselors, and citizens. *Journal of Personality and Social Psychology*, *36*:156–179.

Fishman, J. F. (1968). *Crucibles of Crime: The Shocking Story of the American Jail*. Montclair, N.J.: Patterson Smith.

Fishman, J. F. (1951). *Sex in Prison*. London: John Lane, the Bodley Head.

Fishman, J. F. (1934). *Sex in Prison: Revealing Sex Conditions in America's Prisons*. New York: National Library Press.

Flanagan, L. (1997). Prison is a luxury we can no longer afford. *Corrections Management Quarterly*, *1*(1):60–63.

Flanagan, T., and K. Maguire (1993). A full employment policy for prison in the United States: Some arguments, estimates, and implications. *Journal of Criminal Justice*, *21*(2):117–130.

Fleisher, M. (1989). *Warehousing Violence*. Newbury Park, Calif.: Sage Publications.

Fleisher, M., and R. Rison. (1999). Gang management in corrections. In P. Carlson and J. S. Garrett (eds.), *Prison and Jail Administration: Practice and Theory*. Gaithersburg, Md.: Aspen Publishers, Inc.

Foa, E. B., J. R. T. Davidson, and A. Frances. (1999). Treatment of post-traumatic stress disorder. The expert consensus guidelines series. *The Journal of Clinical Psychiatry*, *60*:Supplement 16.

Foa, E. B., and B. O. Rothbaum. (1997). *Treating the Trauma of Rape: Cognitive-Behavioral Therapy for PTSD*. New York: Guilford Publications, Inc.

Fong, R., R. Vogel, and S. Buentello. (1992). Prison gang dynamics: A look inside the Texas Department of Corrections. In P. Benekos and A. Merlo (eds.), *Corrections: Dilemmas and Directions*. Cincinnati: Anderson Publishing Company.

Ford, C. (1929). Homosexual practices of institutionalized females. *Journal of Abnormal and Social Psychology*, *23*:442–449.

Foucault, M. (1978). *History of Sexuality: An Introduction*. Vol. 1. New York: Pantheon Books.

Fruend, K. (1991). Caring for the victim of sexual assault. *American Journal of Preventative Medicine*, *7*(6):459–460.

Fulero, S,. and C. Delara. (1976). Rape victims and attributed responsibility: A defensive attribution approach. *Victimology*, *1*(4):551–563.

Gager, N., and D. Schurr. (1976). *Sexual Assault: Confronting Rape in America*. New York: Grosset and Dunlap.

Gardner, G. (2000). *Prison Population Exploding.* Washington, D.C.: Worldwatch Institute.

Gaunay, W., and R. Gido. (1986). *Acquired Immune Deficiency Syndrome: A Demographic Profile of New York State Inmate Mortalities, 1981–1985.* Albany: New York State Commission of Correction.

Georgia Department of Corrections. (1996). *Georgia Department of Corrections Standard Operating Procedure.* Atlanta: Georgia Department of Corrections.

Georgia Department of Corrections. (1994). *Georgia Department of Corrections Standard Operating Procedure.* Atlanta: Georgia Department of Corrections.

Giallombardo, R. (1966). *Society of Women: A Study of a Woman's Prison.* New York: Wiley.

Gido, R. L. (1992). Invisible women: The status of incarcerated women with HIV/AIDS. *The Justice Professional, 7*(1):25–33.

Gido, R. L. (1989). A demographic and epidemiological study of New York State inmate AIDS mortalities, 1981–1987. *The Prison Journal, 69*(1):27–32.

Gido, R. L., and W. Gaunay. (1988a, April 6). Field visit to California State Prison at Vacaville.

Gido, R. L., and W. Gaunay. (1988b). *Acquired Immune Deficiency Syndrome: A Demographic Profile of New York State Inmate Mortalities, 1986–1987.* 3rd ed. Albany: New York State Commission of Correction.

Gido, R. L., and W. Gaunay. (1987). *Acquired Immune Deficiency Syndrome: A Demographic Profile of New York State Inmate Mortalities, 1981–1986.* 2nd ed. Albany: New York State Commission of Correction.

Gilmore, T. (1985, November). Developmental challenges in monitoring and oversight roles. Prepared for the Building Capacity of State Community Corrections Oversight Agencies Seminar, Boulder, Colo.

Goering, C. (2001, April 17). An ugly portrait of rape in prison. *New York Times.* 18A.

Goetting, A. (1982a). Conjugal association in prison: A world view. *Criminal Justice Abstracts, 14*(3):406–416.

Goetting, A. (1982b). Conjugal association in prison: Issues and perspectives. *Crime and Delinquency, 28*(January):52–71.

Goffman, E. (1961). *Asylums: Essays on the Social Situation of Mental Patients and Other Inmates.* Garden City, N.J.: Anchor.

Goldstein, S. (1990). Prisoners with AIDS: Constitutionality and statutory rights implicated in family visitation programs. *Boston College Law and Review, 31*(4):967–1025.

Gordon, J., and E. McConnell. (1999). Are conjugal and familial visitations effective rehabilitative concepts? *The Prison Journal, 79*(1):119–135.

Greer, K. R. (2000). The changing nature of interpersonal relationships in a women's prison. *The Prison Journal, 80*(4):442–468.

Grosz, E., and E. Probyn. (1995). Introduction. In E. Grosz and E. Probyn (eds.), *Sexy Bodies: The Strange Carnalities of Feminism.* New York: Routledge.

Groth, A. N. (1979). *Men Who Rape: The Psychology of the Offender.* New York: Plenum Publishing Company.

Groth, A. N., and A. W. Burgess. (1980). Male rape: Offenders and victims. *American Journal of Psychiatry, 137*(7):806–819.

Groth, A. N., A. W. Burgess, and L. L. Holmstrom. (1977). Rape: Power, rage and sexuality. *American Journal of Psychiatry, 134*(11):1239–1243.

Guenther, A., and M. Guenther. (1974). Screws vs. thugs. *Society, 11*(5):42–50.

Haggerty, M. F. (2000). Incarcerated populations and HIV. Online. Available at: http://www.thebody.com/cria/summer00/prison.html.

Halleck, S. L., and M. Hersko. (1962). Homosexual behavior in a correctional institution for adolescent girls. *American Journal of Orthopsychiatry, 32*:911–917.

Hammet, T. M. (1998). *Public Health/Corrections Collaborations: Prevention and Treatment of HIV/AIDS, STDS, and TB.* Washington, D.C.: National Institute of Justice and Centers for Disease Control and Prevention.

Hammet, T. M. (1988). *AIDS in Correctional Facilities: Issues and Options.* 3rd ed. Washington, D.C.: U.S. Department of Justice.

Hammet, T. M. (1987). *AIDS in Correctional Facilities: Issues and Options.* 2nd ed. Washington, D.C.: U.S. Department of Justice.

Hammet, T. M. (1986). *AIDS in Correctional Facilities: Issues and Options.* Washington, D.C.: U.S. Department of Justice.

Hammet, T. M., P. Harmon, and L. M. Maruschak. (1999). *1996–1997 Update: HIV/AIDS, STDS, and TB in Correctional Facilities.* Washington, D.C.: National Institute of Justice.

Harlow, C. (1999). *Prior Abuse Reported by Inmates and Probationers.* Washington, D.C.: U.S. Department of Justice.

Harrington, S. P. M. (1999). New Bedlams: Jails—not psychiatric hospitals— now care for the indigent mentally ill. *The Humanist, 59*(3):9.

Hassine, V. (1999). *Life Without Parole: Living in Prison Today.* 2nd ed. Los Angeles: Roxbury Publishing Company.

Haycock, J. (1991). Capital crimes: Suicides in jail. *Death Studies, 15*(5):417–433.

Hayner, N. (1972). Attitudes toward conjugal visits for prisoners. *Federal Probation, 36*:43–49.

Heffernan, E. (1972). *Making It in Prison: The Square, the Cool, and the Life.* New York: John Wiley and Sons, Inc.

Hensley, C. (2001). Consensual homosexual activity in male prisons. *Corrections Compendium, 26*(1):1–4.

Hensley, C. (2000). What we have learned from studying prison sex. *Humanity and Society, 24*(4):348–360.

Hensley, C., S. Rutland, and P. Gray-Ray. (2000a). Inmate attitudes toward the conjugal visitation program in Mississippi prisons: An exploratory study. *American Journal of Criminal Justice, 25*(1):137–145.

Hensley, C., S. Rutland, and P. Gray-Ray. (2000b). The effects of conjugal visits on Mississippi inmates. *Corrections Compendium, 25*(4):1–3, 20–21.

Hensley, C., et al. (2000). Conjugal visitations in Mississippi. *The Researcher, 16*(4):1–15.

Hensley, C., R. Tewksbury, and M. Koscheski. (2002). The characteristics and motivations behind female prison sex. Forthcoming in *Women and Criminal Justice*.

Hensley, C., R. Tewksbury, and J. Wright. (2001). Exploring the dynamics of masturbation and consensual same-sex sexual activity within a male maximum security prison. *Journal of Men's Studies, 10*(1):59–71.

Herman, J. L. (1992). Complex PTSD: A syndrome in survivors of prolonged and repeated trauma. *Journal of Traumatic Stress, 5*(3):377–389.

Herrick, E. (1991). Prison literacy connection. *Corrections Compendium, 16*(12):1, 5–9.

Hite, S. (1976). *The Hite Report: A Nationwide Study on Female Sexuality*. New York: Macmillan Publishing.

HIV in prison: A special report. (2000). Online. Available at: http://www.aids.infonyc.org/hivplus/issue6/report/picture.html.

Hobbs, W., et al. (1998). *Preventing Inappropriate Staff/Inmate Relationships*. Alexandria: Virginia Department of Corrections.

Hogan, N. L. (1997). The social construction of target populations and the transmission of prison-based AIDS policy: A descriptive case study. *Journal of Homosexuality, 32*(3/4):77–113.

Holt, N., and D. Miller. (1972). *Explorations in Inmate-Family Relationships*. Sacramento, Calif.: Department of Corrections.

Hopper, C. (1980). A study of homosexuality and surrogate families in an institution for women. Master's thesis, University of South Florida, Tampa.

Hopper, C. B. (1989). The evolution of conjugal visiting in Mississippi. *The Prison Journal, 69*(1):103–109.

Hopper, C. B. (1969). *Sex in Prison*. Baton Rouge:: Louisiana State University Press.

Hopper, C. B. (1962). The conjugal visit at Mississippi state penitentiary. *Journal of Criminal Law, Criminology, and Police Science, 53*(3):340–343.

Howser, J., J. Grossman, and D. MacDonald. (1983). Impact of family reunion programs on institutional discipline. *Journal of Offender Counseling, Services, and Rehabilitation, 8*:27–36.

Huffman, G. B. (2000). Postexposure HIV prophylaxis after sexual assault. *American Family Physician, 60*(17):2123.

Human Rights Watch. (1996). *All Too Familiar: Sexual Abuse of Women in U.S. State Prisons*. New York: Human Rights Watch.

Ibrahim, A. (1974). Deviant sexual behavior in men's prisons. *Crime and Delinquency, 20*(1):38–44.

Jackson, S. (1996). Heterosexuality and feminist theory. In D. Richardson (ed.), *Theorizing Heterosexuality: Telling It Straight*. Buckingham, UK: Open University Press.

Jacobs, S. (1995). AIDS in correctional facilities: Current status of legal issues critical to policy development. *Journal of Criminal Justice, 23*(3):209–221.

Janus, S., and C. Janus. (1993). *The Janus Report on Sexual Behavior*. New York: John Wiley and Sons, Inc.

Jenkins, M., and F. Dambrot. (1987). The attribution of date rape: Observer's attitudes and sexual experiences and the dating situation. *Journal of Applied Social Psychology, 17*(10):875–895.

Joint Subcommittee on AIDS in the Criminal Justice System of the Committee on Corrections and the Committee on Criminal Justice Operations and Budget of the Association of the Bar of the City of New York. (1989). *AIDS and the Criminal Justice System: A Final Report and Recommendations.* New York: Joint Subcommittee on AIDS.

Joint United Nations Programme on HIV/AIDS (UNAIDS). (1996, April). HIV/AIDS in prisons.

Jones, R., and T. Schmid. (1989). Inmates' conceptions of prison sexual assault. *The Prison Journal, 69*(1):53–61.

Kanekar, S., and A. Nazareth. (1988). Attributed rape victim's fault as a function of her attractiveness, physical hurt, and emotional disturbance. *Social Behavior, 3*:37–40.

Karmen, A. (1990). *Crime Victims: An Introduction to Victimology.* Monterey, Calif.: Brooks/Cole.

Karpman, B. (1948). Sex life in prison. *Journal of Criminal Law and Criminology, 38*:475–486.

Kassebaum, G. (1972). Sex in prison: Violence, homosexuality, and intimidation are everyday occurrences. *Sexual Behavior, 2*(1):39–45.

Katz, J. (ed.). (1976). *Gay American History.* New York: Thomas Crowell.

Kaufman, A., et al. (1980). Male rape victims: Noninstitutionalized assault. *American Journal of Psychiatry, 137*:221–223.

Kent, N. E. (1975). The legal and sociological dimensions of conjugal visitation in prisons. *New England Journal on Prison Law, 2*:47–65.

Kinsey, A., et al. (1953). *Sexual Behavior in the Human Female.* Philadelphia: W. B. Saunders Company.

Kinsey, A., W. Pomeroy, and C. Martin. (1948). *Sexual Behavior in the Human Male.* Philadelphia: W. B. Saunders Company.

Kirkham, G. L. (1971). Homosexuality in prison. In J. M. Henslin (ed.), *Studies in the Sociology of Sex.* New York: Appleton-Century-Crofts.

Klotter, J. C. (1994). *Criminal Law.* 4th ed. Cincinnati: Anderson Publishing Company.

Knowles, G. J. (1999). Male prison rape: A search for causation and prevention. *The Howard Journal, 38*(3):267–282.

Koss, M., C. Gidycz, and N. Wisniewski. (1987). The scope of rape: Incidence and prevalence of sexual aggression and victimization in a national sample of higher education students. *Journal of Consulting and Clinical Psychology, 55*:162–170.

Laumann, E., et al. (1994). *The Social Organization of Sexuality: Sexual Practices in the United States.* Chicago: University of Chicago Press.

Lawrence, B. (2001, April 12). Personal communication.

LeDoux, J., and R. Hazelwood. (1985). Police attitudes and beliefs toward rape. *Journal of Police Science and Administration, 13*:211–220.

Lee, D. (1965). Seduction of the guilty: Homosexuality in American prisons. *Fact Magazine* (November):57–61.

Lehrer, E. (2001). Hell behind bars: The crime that dares not speak its name. *National Review, 53*(2):24–26.

Lennox, M. C., and L. R. Gannon. (1983). Psychological consequences of rape and variables influence recovery: A review. *Women and Therapy, 2*(1):37–49.

Lewin, T. (2001, April 15). Little sympathy or remedy for inmates who are raped. *New York Times.* 1.

Lillis, J. (1993). Family visitation evolves. *Corrections Compendium, 18*(November):1–4.

LIS, Inc. (1996a). *Sexual Misconduct in Prison: Law, Agency Response, and Prevention.* Longmont, Colo.: U.S. Department of Justice.

LIS, Inc. (1996b). *Special Issues in Corrections: Survey of Mental Health Services in Large Jails and Jail Systems.* Longmont, Colo.: U.S. Department of Justice.

Lockwood, D. (1996, November 21). Personal communication.

Lockwood, D. (1995, August 30). Personal communication.

Lockwood, D. (1992). Living in protection. In H. Toch (ed.), *Living in Prison: The Ecology of Survival.* Washington, D.C.: American Psychological Association.

Lockwood, D. (1982). Reducing prison sexual violence. In J. Robert and H. Toch (eds.), *The Pains of Imprisonment.* Newbury Park, Calif.: Sage Publications.

Lockwood, D. (1980a). *Prison Sexual Violence.* New York: Elsevier Press.

Lockwood, D. (1980b). *Sexual Aggression in Prison.* New York: Elsevier Press.

Lockwood, D. (1978). Sexual aggression among male prisoners. Ph.D. dissertation, State University of New York, Albany.

Lockwood, F. (2000, April 23). Professor plans survey about sex at state prisons. *Lexington Herald Leader.* B1, B5.

Lombardo, L. (1981). *Guards Imprisoned: Correctional Officers at Work.* New York: Elsevier Press.

MacDonald, D. G., and D. Kelly. (1980). *Follow-up Survey of Post-Release Criminal Behavior of Participants in Family Reunion Programs.* New York: New York State Department of Correctional Services.

MacDonald, R. (1967). The frightful consequences of onanism: Notes on the history of a delusion. *Journal of the History of Ideas, 28*(3):423–431.

MacIntyre, C. R., N. Kendig, and L. Kummer. (1999). Unrecognized transmission of tuberculosis in prisons. *European Journal of Epidemiology, 15*(8):705–709.

Maghan, J. (1997). Training cannot do what management cannot do: The evolvement of centralized training in modern correctional services. *Correctional Management Quarterly, 1*(1):40–48.

Mahoney, J. (1988, November). Corrections chief's AIDS remark upsets prison guard union. (Albany) *Times Union.* B-2.

Mailander, J. (1990a, May 6). GCI changes: "Purgatory compared to hell." *Palm Beach Post.* 1A, 10A.

Mailander, J. (1990b, May 1). GCI inmates to get rape protection. *Palm Beach Post.* 1A, 8A.

Maines, R. (1999). *The Technology of Orgasm: "Hysteria," the Vibrator, and Women's Sexual Satisfaction.* Baltimore: Johns Hopkins University Press.

Maitland, A., and R. Sluder. (1998). Victimization and youthful prison inmates: An empirical analysis. *The Prison Journal, 78*(1):55–73.

Maitland, A., and R. Sluder. (1996). Victimization in prisons: A study of factors related to the general well-being of youthful inmates. *Federal Probation, 60*(2):24–31.

Mariner, J. (2001). *No Escape: Male Rape in U.S. Prisons.* New York: Human Rights Watch.

Marton, F. K. (1988). Defenses: Invincible and vincible. *Clinical Social Work Journal, 16*(2):143–155.

Maruschak, L. M. (1999). *HIV in Prisons 1997.* Washington, D.C.: National Institute of Justice.

Maruschak, L. M., and A. J. Beck. (2001). *Bureau of Justice Statistics Special Report: Medical Problems of Inmates, 1997.* Washington, D.C.: U.S. Department of Justice.

Masci, D. (1999). Prison building boom. Online. Available at: http://www.wysiwg://129/http://webspirs4.silverplatter.com:8100/c11824.

Massachusetts Department of Correction. (2001a). *103 DOC 520: Inmate Sexual Assault Response Plan.* Milford: Massachusetts Department of Correction.

Massachusetts Department of Correction. (2001b). *Staff Sexual Misconduct with Inmates.* Milford: Massachusetts Department of Correction.

Massachusetts General Law. (2000). *General Laws of Massachusetts, Part IV. Crimes, Punishments and Proceedings in Criminal Cases. Title 1. Crimes and Punishments. Chapter 265. Crimes Against the Person. Chapter 265: Section 22: Rape.* Boston. Legislature of the Commonwealth of Massachusetts.

Mawn, B. (1999). *Nursing Care of the Sexual Assault Victim.* Lowell: University of Massachusetts.

McCorkle, R. (1993a). Fear of victimization and symptoms of psychopathology among prison inmates. *Journal of Offender Rehabilitation, 19*(1/2):27–41.

McCorkle, R. (1993b). Living on the edge: Fear in a maximum-security prison. *Journal of Offender Rehabilitation, 20*(1/2):73–91.

McCorkle, R., T. Miethe, and D. Terance. (1995). The roots of prison violence: A test of the deprivation, management, and "not-so-total" institution models. *Crime and Delinquency, 41*(3):317–331.

McDonald, D. C. (1999). Medical care in prisons. In M. Tonry and J. Petersilia (eds.), *Prisons.* Chicago: University of Chicago Press.

Medellin, R. L. (1992). *Anderson v. State of California*: Do death row inmates have a fundamental right to procreate through conjugal visits and/or artificial insemination? *Criminal Justice Journal, 14*(2):425–450.

Mezey, G., and M. King. (1989). The effects of sexual assault on men: A survey of 22 victims. *Psychological Medicine, 19*(1):205–209.

Michael, R., et al. (1994). *Sex in America: A Definitive Survey.* Boston: Little, Brown and Company.

Michigan Department of Corrections. (2000). New tracking system to monitor employee misconduct allegations: Piloting at women's facilities first. Online. Available at: http://www.state.mi.us/mdoc/FYI/10-14-99/Tracking.html.

Miller, J. M., and R. Tewksbury. (2001). *Extreme Measures: Innovative Approaches to Social Science Research*. Needham Heights, Mass.: Allyn and Bacon.

Mitchell, A. (1969). Informal inmate social structure in prisons for women: A comparative study. Ph.D. dissertation, University of Washington, Pullman.

Money, J., and S. Prakasam. (1991). Semen-conservation doctrine from ancient Ayurvedic to modern sexological theory. *American Journal of Psychotherapy, 45*(1):9–13.

Morris, D. (2000). Privacy, privation, perversity: Toward new representations of the personal. *Signs: Journal of Women in Culture and in Society, 25*(2):323–351.

Morse, A. (2001). Brutality behind bars: Savage prison gang rapes turn many run-of-the-mill prisoners into violent felons in waiting. *World, 3*(February):21–22.

Moss, A. (2000, December 18). Personal communication.

Moss, C. S., R. E. Hosford, and W. R. Anderson. (1979). Sexual assault in prison. *Psychological Reports, 4*:823–828.

Mott, F. W. (1919). *War Neuroses and Shell Shock*. London: Oxford Medical Publications.

Muehlenhard, C. (2000). Categories and sexuality. *Journal of Sex Research, 37*(2):101–107.

Mushlin, M. (1993). *Rights of Prisoners*. 2nd ed. Colorado Springs, Colo.: Shepard's/McGraw-Hill.

Nacci, P. L. (1978). A federal study: Sexual assault in prisons. *American Journal of Corrections, 40*(1):30–31.

Nacci, P., and T. Kane. (1984a). Inmate sexual aggression: Some evolving propositions and empirical findings, and mitigating counter-forces. *Journal of Offender Counseling, Services, and Rehabilitation, 9*(1/2):1–20.

Nacci, P. L., and T. Kane. (1984b). Sex and sexual aggression in federal prisons: Inmate involvement and employee impact. *Federal Probation, 48*(1):46–53.

Nacci, P. L., and T. Kane. (1983). The incidence of sex and sexual aggression in federal prisons. *Federal Probation, 47*(4):31–36.

Nacci, P. L., and T. R. Kane. (1982). *Sex and Sexual Aggression in Federal Prisons*. Washington, D.C.: U.S. Federal Prison System.

National Commission on Correctional Health Care. (1997). *Standards for Health Services in Prisons—1997*. Chicago: National Commission on Correctional Health Care.

National Institute of Corrections. (2000). *Training Curriculum for Investigating Allegations of Staff Sexual Misconduct with Inmates*. Longmont, Colo.: U.S. Department of Justice.

Nelson, C. (1974). A study of homosexuality among women inmates at two state prisons. Ph.D. dissertation, Temple University.

New York State Commission of Correction. (1988). *Special Needs Management of AIDS in the Department of Correctional Services*. Albany: New York State Commission of Correction.

New York State Commission of Correction. (1984). *State Correctional Facility Health Services: A Systemwide Perspective*. Albany, NY: New York State Commission of Correction.

New York State Department of Health. (1998). HIV quarterly update. Online. Available at: http://www.health.state.ny.us/nysdoh/aids/dec.1998/table4d.htm.

New York Times. (2001, April 23). Rape in prison. 16.

Nice, R. (1966). The problem of homosexuality in corrections. *American Journal of Corrections* (May–June):30–32.

Olivero, J. M., et al. (1992). Comparative view of AIDS in prisons: Mexico and the United States. *International Journal of Criminal Justice Review, 2*:105–118.

Otis, M. (1913). A perversion not commonly noted. *Journal of Abnormal Psychology, 8*:113–116.

Owen, B. (1998). *"In the Mix": Struggles and Survival in a Women's Prison*. Albany: State University of New York Press.

Palmer, J. W. (1999). *Constitutional Rights of Prisoners*. 6th ed. Cincinnati: Anderson Publishing Company.

Paparozzi, M., and C. Lowenkamp. (2000). To be or not to be—a profession—that is the question for corrections. *Corrections Management Quarterly, 4*(2):9–16.

Parker, R., R. M. Barbosa, and P. Aggleton. (2000). Introduction: Framing the sexual subject. In R. Parker, R. M. Barbosa, and P. Aggleton (eds.), *Framing the Sexual Subject: The Politics of Gender, Sexuality, and Power*. Berkeley: University of California Press.

Pensacola News Journal. (2001, January 7). White man too thin for prison, judge rules. 2A.

Peretti, P., and M. Hooker. (1976). Social role self-perceptions of state prison guards. *Criminal Justice Behavior, 3*(2):187–195.

Perkins, C., J. Stephan, and A. Beck. (1995). *Jail and Jail Inmates: 1993–1994*. Washington, D.C.: U.S. Department of Justice.

Petersilia, J. (1999). Parole and prisoner re-entry in the United States. In M. Tonry and J. Petersilia (eds.), *Prisons*. Chicago: University of Chicago Press.

Phelps, M. J. (1999). Officers having sex with inmates. *Corrections Technology and Management, 3*(1):12–20.

Philliber, S. (1987). The brother's keeper: A review of the literature on correctional officers. *Justice Quarterly, 4*(1):9–37.

Pitts, T. (2001). Sexual aggression in prisons and jails: Awareness, prevention, and intervention. In J. Mariner (ed.), *No Escape: Male Rape in U.S. Prisons*. New York: Human Rights Watch.

Poole, E., and R. Regoli. (1980). Role stress, custody orientation, and disciplinary actions: A study of prison guards. *Criminology, 18*(2):215–226.

Powelson, M., and J. F. Fletcher. (2000). Sexually transmitted diseases, drug use, and risky behavior among Miami-Dade county jail detainees. *Corrections Today*, *62*(16):108.

Propper, A. M. (1982). Make-believe families and homosexuality among imprisoned girls. *Criminology, 20*(1):127–138.

Propper, A. M. (1981). *Prison Homosexuality: Myth and Reality.* Lexington, Mass.: Lexington Books.

Propper. A. M. (1978). Lesbianism in female and coed correctional institutions. *Journal of Homosexuality, 3*(3):265–274.

Propper, A. M. (1976). Importation and deprivation perspectives on homosexuality in correctional institutions: An empirical test of their relative efficacy. Ph.D. dissertation, University of Michigan, Ann Arbor.

Reid, S. (1991). *Crime and Criminology.* 6th ed. Chicago: Holt, Rinehart, and Winston, Inc.

Reindollar, R. W. (1999). Hepatitis C and the correctional population. *American Journal of Medicine*, *107*(6B):1005–1035.

Rideau, W. (1992). The sexual jungle. In W. Rideau and R. Wikberg (eds.), *Life Sentences: Rage and Survival Behind Bars*. New York: Time Books.

Ross, D. (1991). A model for psychodynamic psychotherapy with the rape victim. *Psychotherapy, 26*(1):85–95.

Ross, D. L. (1997). Emerging trends in correctional civil liability cases: A content analysis of federal court decisions of title 42 United States code section 1983: 1970–1994. *Journal of Criminal Justice*, *25*(6):501–515.

Ross, P., and J. Lawrence. (2002). Health care for women offenders: Challenge for the new century. In R. L. Gido and T. Alleman (eds.), *Turnstile Justice: Issues in American Corrections*. Upper Saddle River, N.J.: Prentice Hall.

Rosselini, L. (1997, November 3). Joycelyn Elders is master of her domain. *U.S. News and World Report, 123*:65.

Rothbaum, B. O. (2000). *Reclaiming Your Life After Rape: A Cognitive-Behavioral Therapy for PTSD*. San Diego: Academic Press, Inc.

Ruch, L. O., S. M. Chandler, and R. A. Harter. (1980). Life change and rape impact. *Journal of Health and Social Behavior, 21*(3):248–260.

Ruch, L. O., and J. J. Leon. (1983). Sexual assault trauma and trauma change. *Women and Health*, *8*(4):5–21.

Russell, D. (1984). *Sexual Exploitation: Rape, Child Sexual Abuse, and Workplace Harassment*. Newbury Park, Calif.: Sage Publications.

Rutland, S. (1995). Examining the effects of conjugal visitations within the Mississippi department of corrections: Family stability, violence, and homosexuality. Master's thesis, Mississippi State University, Starkville.

Ryan, T. A. (1990). Effects of literacy training on reintegration of offenders. Paper presented at Freedom to Read: An International Conference on Literacy in Corrections, Ottawa, Ontario.

Sagarin, E. (1976). Prison homosexuality and its effect on post-prison behavior. *Psychiatry, 39*(3):245–257.

Sandlin, K. (1993). New Mexico's family visitation program. *Corrections Compendium, 18*(November):5–6.

Saum, C., et al. (1995). Sex in prison: Exploring the myths and realities. *The Prison Journal*, 75(4):413–430.

Scalia, J. (1997). *Prisoner Petitions in the Federal Courts, 1980–96.* Washington, D.C.: U.S. Department of Justice.

Scacco, A. (1975). *Rape in Prison.* Springfield, Ill.: Charles C. Thomas.

Scacco, A. M. (1982). *Male Rape: A Casebook of Sexual Aggression.* New York: AMS Press, Inc.

Schiraldi, V., J. Ziedenberg, and J. Irwin. (1999). *America's One Million Nonviolent Prisoners.* Washington, D.C.: Justice Policy Institute.

Scully, D. (1990). *Understanding Sexual Violence.* Boston: Unwin Hyman.

Selling, L. (1931). The pseudo-family. *American Journal of Sociology,* 37:247–253.

Sennott, C. M. (1994, May 17). Poll finds wide concern about prison rape. *Boston Globe.* 22.

Sheldon, R. (1972). Rehabilitation programs in prison. *Psychiatric Opinion,* 9(5):20–21.

Silberman, M. (1994). Resource mobilization and the reduction of prison violence. Paper presented at the American Sociological Association, Los Angeles.

Smith, B. (1998). *Testimony of Brenda V. Smith, Senior Counsel Director, Women in Prison Project Before the Maryland Senate on SB 156 Sexual Offenses—Custodial Employees and Persons in Custody.* Washington, D.C.: National Women's Law Center.

Smith, N. E., and M. E. Batiuk. (1989). Sexual victimization and inmate social interaction. *The Prison Journal,* 69(2):29–38.

Smith, W. R. (2000). Rethinking corrections. *Corrections Today,* 62(6):100–103.

Soble, A. (1997). Masturbation. In A. Soble (ed.), *The Philosophy of Sex: Contemporary Readings.* 3rd ed. Lanham, Md.: Rowman and Littlefield Publishers.

Soble, A. (1996). *Sexual Investigations.* New York: New York University Press.

Sparks, R., A. Bottoms, and W. Hay. (1996). *Prisons and the Problem of Order.* Oxford: Clarendon Press.

St. Petersburg Times. (2001, January 27). Judge regrets remark about inmate safety. 3B.

Stanko, E. (1993). Ordinary fear: Women, violence, and personal safety. In P. Bart and E. Moran (eds.), *Violence Against Women: The Bloody Footprints.* Newbury Park, Calif.: Sage Publications.

Stanko, E. (1985). *Intimate Intrusions: Women's Experience of Male Violence.* New York: Routledge and Kegan Paul.

Stinchcomb, J. B. (1995). Breaking with tradition: Linking correctional training and professionalism. *American Jails,* 9(4):29–32.

Stinchcomb, J. B., and S. W. McCampbell. (1999). Transitioning staff to the 21st century: Moving from inmate instructors and court orders to the interactive Internet and cyberspace. *American Jails,* 12(2):9–20.

Stop Prison Rape. (1997). U.S. court of appeals upholds victory in the lower court! Online. Available at: http://www.spr.org/docs/farmer/farmer.html.

Struckman-Johnson, C. J. (1991). Male victims of acquaintance rape. In A. Parrot and L. Bechhover (eds.), *Acquaintance Rape: The Hidden Crime.* New York: Wiley and Sons, Inc.

Struckman-Johnson, C. J., and D. L. Struckman-Johnson. (2000a). Sexual coercion rates in seven Midwestern prison facilities for men. *The Prison Journal, 80*(4):379–390.

Struckman-Johnson, C. J., and D. L. Struckman-Johnson. (2000b, March). Sexual coercion rates in ten prison facilities in the Midwest. Paper presented at the annual meeting of the Academy of Criminal Justice Sciences, New Orleans, La.

Struckman-Johnson, C. J., and D. L. Struckman-Johnson. (1999, November). Pressured and forced sexual contact reported by women in three Midwestern prisons. Paper presented at the annual meeting of the Society for the Study of Sexuality and the American Association of Sex Educators, Counselors, and Therapists, St. Louis, Mo.

Struckman-Johnson, C. J., et al. (1996). Sexual coercion reported by men and women in prison. *The Journal of Sex Research, 33*(1):67–76.

Struckman-Johnson, C. J., et al. (1995, May). A survey of inmate and staff perspectives on prisoner sexual assault. Paper presented at the annual meeting of the Midwestern Psychological Association, Chicago.

Sykes, G. M. (1958). *The Society of Captives: A Study of a Maximum Security Prison.* Princeton, N.J.: Princeton University Press.

Sylvester, S., J. Reed, and D. Nelson. (1977). *Prison Homicides.* New York: Spectrum Publications.

Symonds, M. (1980). The "second injury" to victims. *Evaluation and Change,* November:36–38.

Telega, S. (1974). *The Fortune News* (April):4.

Tewksbury, R. (1989a). Fear of sexual assault in prison inmates. *The Prison Journal, 69*(1):62–71.

Tewksbury, R. (1989b). Measures of sexual behavior in an Ohio prison. *Sociology and Social Research, 74*(1):34–39.

Tewksbury, R., and P. Gagne. (2001). Assumed and presumed identities: Problems of self-presentation in field research. In J. M. Miller and R. Tewksbury (eds.), *Extreme Measures: Innovative Approaches to Social Science Research.* Needham Heights, Mass.: Allyn and Bacon.

Tewksbury, R., and A West. (2000). Research on sex in prison during the late 1980s and early 1990s. *The Prison Journal, 80*(4):368–378.

Tittle, C. (1972). *Society of Subordinates: Inmate Organization in a Narcotic Hospital.* Bloomington: Indiana University Press.

Toch, H. (1992a). *Living in Prison: The Ecology of Survival.* Revised ed. Washington, D.C.: American Psychological Association.

Toch, H. (1992b). *Mosaic of Despair: Human Breakdowns in Prison.* Revised ed. Washington, D.C.: American Psychological Association.

Toch, H. (1985). Warehouses of people. *Annals of the American Academy of Political and Social Science, 478*(March):58–72.

Toch, H. (1977). *Living in Prison.* New York: Free Press.

Toch, H., and T. A. Kupers. (1999). *Prison Madness: The Mental Health Crisis Behind Bars and What We Must Do About It.* San Francisco: Jossey-Bass.

Toller, W., and B. Tsagaris. (1996). Managing institutional gangs: A practical approach combining security and human services. *Corrections Today, 58*(6):110–111, 115.

Tonry, M., and J. Petersilia. (2000). *Prisons Research at the Beginning of the 21st Century.* Washington, D.C.: U.S. Department of Justice.

Topham, J. (1999). Complete guide to inmate transport. *Corrections Technology and Management, 3*(6):44–48.

Torrey, E. F. (1997). *Out of the Shadows: Confronting America's Mental Illness Crisis.* New York: John Wiley and Sons.

Turner, S. (1992). Surviving sexual assault and sexual torture. In G. C. Mezey and M. B. King (eds.), *Male Victims of Sexual Assault.* New York: Oxford University Press.

USA Today. (2000, April 24). USA Today states. 15A.

U.S. Department of Justice. (2001a). *Prison and Jail Inmates at Midyear 2000.* Washington, D.C.: U.S. Department of Justice.

U.S. Department of Justice. (2001b). *Sourcebook of Criminal Justice Statistics, 2000.* Washington, D.C.: U.S. Department of Justice.

U.S. Department of Justice. (1997). *Census of State and Federal Correctional Facilities, 1995.* Washington, D.C.: U.S. Department of Justice.

U.S. Department of Justice. (1995). Program Statement #5324.02. Online. Available at: http://www.igc.apc.org/spr/docs/bop.html.

Vedder, C., and P. King. (1967). *Problems of Homosexuality in Corrections.* Springfield, Ill.: Charles C. Thomas.

Walmsley, R. (1999). World prison populations: An attempt at a complete list. In D. van Zyl Smit and F. Dunkel (eds.), *Imprisonment Today and Tomorrow.* 2nd ed. Boston: Kluwer Law International.

Ward, D., and G. Kassebaum. (1965). *Women's Prison: Sex and Social Structure.* Chicago: Aldine.

Ward, D., and G. Kassebaum. (1964). Homosexuality: A mode of adaption in a prison for women. *Social Problems, 12*(2):59–117.

Washington Post. (2001, April 23). Cruel and usual. A14.

Weis, K., and S. Borges. (1973). Victimology and case of the legitimate victim. In L. Schultz (ed.), *Rape Victimology.* Springfield, Ill.: Charles C. Thomas.

Weiss, C., and D. Friar. (1974). *Terror in the Prisons.* New York: Bobbs-Merrill Company, Inc.

Whatley, M., and R. Riggio. (1993). Gender differences in attributions of blame for male rape victims. *Journal of Interpersonal Violence, 8*(4):502–511.

White, B., and D. Mosher. (1986). Experimental validation of a model for predicting the reporting of rape. *Sexual Coercion and Assault, 1*:43–55.

Widney-Brown, A. (1998). Nowhere to hide: Retaliation against women in Michigan state prisons. *Human Rights Watch, 10*(2):2–27.

Widom, R., and T. M. Hammett. (1996). *HIV/AIDS and STDs in Juvenile Facilities.* Washington, D.C.: U.S. Department of Justice.

Wiggs, J. W. (1989). Prison rape and suicide. *The Journal of the American Medical Association, 262*(24):3403.

Wilson, L. E. (1969). Conjugal visiting and family participation in California. *Proceedings of the American Correctional Association.*

Wooden, W., and J. Parker (1982). *Men Behind Bars: Sexual Exploitation in Prison.* New York: Plenum Press.

Wright, K. (1997). Conjugal visitation: A U.S. perspective. Unpublished manuscript.

Zimbardo, P. G., C. Haney, and W. Banks. (1973, April 8). A priandellian prison. *New York Times Magazine.* 38–40.

Cases Cited

Farmer v. Brennan, 511 U.S. 825 (1994).

Gates v. Collier, 349 F. Supp. 881 (N.D. Miss., 1971).

Lamarca v. Turner, 662 F. Supp. 647 (S.D. Fla., 1987).

Lyons v. Gilligan, 382 F. Supp. 198 (N.D. Ohio, 1974).

Mathie v. Fries, 935 F. Supp. 1284 (E.D. N.Y., 1996).

Payne v. District of Columbia, 102 U.S. App. D.C. 345; 253 F.2d 867 (D.C. Cir., 1953).

Redmond v. Baxley, 475 F. Supp.1980.

Rodgers, v. Ohio Department of Rehabilitation and Correction (1993). 91 Ohio App. 3d 565; 632 N.E.2d 1355; 1993 Ohio App. LEXIS 5397.

Smith v. Wade, 461 U.S. 30 (1983).

Stuart v. Heard, 359 F. Supp. 921 (S.D. Tex., 1973).

Tarlton v. Clark, Civil No. 13972 (D. Ga., 1970).

THE CONTRIBUTORS

Tammy Castle holds a bachelor's degree in psychology and a master's degree in sociology with an emphasis in criminology from Morehead State University. She is currently a doctoral student in criminology at Indiana University of Pennsylvania. Her research and publications center on serial murder and argot roles in correctional facilities.

Doris A. Dumond has been providing human services in a variety of settings for many years, including homeless shelters, in-patient and deinstitutionalized psychiatric programs, drug treatment facilities, and high schools. She has been a volunteer with the Massachusetts Office for Children and was recently appointed by the governor to serve on the Citizen's Advisory Committee for the New Hampshire Department of Corrections. She recently completed a master's degree in criminal justice and two graduate certificates in domestic violence and leadership and policy development from the University of Massachusetts at Lowell.

Robert W. Dumond is a licensed and certified clinical mental health counselor who has served in a number of criminal justice venues since 1970. He has held a faculty appointment with Franklin Pierce College, Division of Continuing Education and Graduate and Professional Studies since 1984. He has written and presented extensively on the issue of prison sexual assault and developed the first curriculum for Rape Training Awareness in the Massachusetts Department of Corrections. Although he became disabled in 1995, he continues to study in this area and is involved in prison ministries, provides volun-

177

teer consultation with the New Hampshire Department of Corrections, and also serves as a governor's appointee to the Citizen's Advisory Committee for the New Hampshire Department of Corrections.

Helen M. Eigenberg is professor and department head in the School of Social and Community Services at the University of Tennessee at Chattanooga. Her research interests are in the areas of violence against women and corrections. She has studied male rape and consensual sex in prisons for more than a decade and has published several articles in the field. She worked for the federal prison system for five years in a medium-security male facility, and this work experience helped fuel her interest in male rape in prisons.

Rosemary L. Gido is associate professor in the Department of Criminology at the Indiana University of Pennsylvania. As the former director of research in the Office of Program and Policy Analysis at the New York State Commission of Correction, she directed the first national prison-based study of HIV/AIDS in the New York State prison system. Dr. Gido has been a teacher at the college or university level for thirty years, and her current research interest is a criminological analysis of the Molly Maguires. She also serves as the editor of *The Prison Journal*.

Phyllis Gray-Ray is research coordinator of the Institute for Disability Studies at the University of Southern Mississippi in Jackson. She received her doctorate from Iowa Sate University. Her research interests include criminological theory, juvenile delinquency, and race relations. Her recent works have appeared in *Journal of Research in Crime and Delinquency, Corrections Compendium*, and the *American Journal of Criminal Justice*.

Christopher Hensley is director of the Institute for Correctional Research and Training and assistant professor of sociology in the Department of Sociology, Social Work, and Criminology at Morehead State University. He received his doctorate from Mississippi State University. His most recent publications appear in the *American Journal of Criminal Justice, International Journal of Offender Therapy and Comparative Criminology, Humanity and Society,* and *Corrections Compendium*. His research interest includes prison sex, inmate attitudes, and program evaluation.

Mary Koscheski holds a bachelor's degree in social work from Northeastern State University and a master's degree in sociology with an emphasis in criminology from Morehead State University. Her research and publications center on issues of homosexual behavior in female correctional facilities.

Julie Kunselman is assistant professor in the Division of Criminal Justice and Legal Studies at the University of West Florida. She holds a doctorate in urban affairs from the University of Louisville. Her current research interests are criminal careers and recidivism, program evaluation and policy analysis in criminal justice, and police management and administration.

Deanna McGaughey is a doctoral student in the Department of Justice Administration at the University of Louisville. She holds a bachelor's degree in justice administration and a master's degree in sociology from Ohio University. Her research and publications center on issues of sex and gender identity, embodiment, and poststructural understandings of human experience.

Sandra Rutland is a U.S. probation officer in Biloxi, Mississippi. She received her master's degree from Mississippi State University. Her research interests include conjugal visitation programs and probation Her most recent publications appear in the *American Journal of Criminal Justice* and *Corrections Compendium.*

Richard Tewksbury is professor in the Department of Justice Administration at the University of Louisville. He holds a doctorate in sociology from Ohio State University. His research interests include correctional institution culture and programming, men's studies, and issues of sex and gender identity.

Jeremy Wright holds a bachelor's degree in sociology with an emphasis in criminology and a master's degree in sociology with an emphasis in criminology from Morehead State University. His research interests include serial murder and consensual homosexual behavior in male correctional facilities.

INDEX

ABOUT THE BOOK

Sex in prison remains a taboo topic, largely ignored by scientists and society alike. This comprehensive volume explores prison sex, presenting original research on consensual and nonconsensual intercourse, as well as the effects of conjugal visitation policies, HIV/AIDS management, and the treatment of sexually assaulted inmates. The contributors also shed light on the sexual hierarchies that form in prisons. The data, interview excerpts, and policy recommendations found throughout the work provide an evocative illustration of U.S. prison systems and their profound effect on society.

Christopher Hensley is director of the Institute for Correctional Research and Training and assistant professor of sociology at Morehead State University.